THE SEIZURE OF

TINIAN

HISTORICAL DIVISION

HEADQUARTERS

U. S. MARINE CORPS

Major Carl W. Hoffman, USMC

1951

Other Marine Corps Monographs
in This Series

COVER PICTURE: H-plus 4 minutes; the first wave LVT's are leaving Beach White 1, second wave is approaching. Across this 60-yard beach, the entire 24th Regiment landed on Jig-Day.

Foreword

TINIAN is a small island. In 1944 it was held by only 9,000 Japanese. Yet it was so well defended by nature against an amphibious operation that it might have proved a formidable and costly barrier to the final conquest of the Marianas. It had only one beach area suitable—by previous standards—for a major amphibious landing and that beach was heavily mined and skillfully defended.

The enemy, although long alerted to our intentions to attack Tinian, was tactically surprised when we avoided his prepared defenses and landed on two small beaches totalling in width only about 220 yards. Before he could recover from the shock, he was out-numbered and out-equipped on his own island. His subsequent effort to throw us into the water resulted in complete failure. We then pushed the length of the island in nine days, while suffering casualties light in comparison with those of most other island conquests.

As a participant in the operation, I naturally take pride in this achievement, as well as in Admiral Raymond A. Spruance's evaluation: "In my opinion, the Tinian operation was probably the most brilliantly conceived and executed amphibious operation in World War II."

C. B. CATES
GENERAL, U. S. MARINE CORPS
COMMANDANT OF THE MARINE CORPS

Preface

TINIAN is the eighth in a series of operational monographs being prepared by the Historical Division, Headquarters, United States Marine Corps, a series designed to present for military students and other interested readers accurate narratives of the Marine Corps' World War II operations.

After monographs of all the operations of the Marines in the Pacific are completed, it is planned to integrate them into the operational history of the Marine Corps in World War II.

Sketches or maps have been inserted to portray daily progress lines. Those sketches relating to actions described on two or more pages of the monograph fold out beyond the margins of the text to aid the reader in following the narrative.

Grateful acknowledgement is hereby made to the scores of Marine, Navy and Army officers and persons now outside the services who read and commented upon the preliminary draft of this monograph and who contributed a wealth of information not otherwise available. Appreciation is likewise expressed for the willing assistance provided by the following: the Office of Naval Records and History, Navy Department; and the Office of the Chief of Military History, Department of the Army.

Maps and sketches were prepared by the Reproduction Department, Marine Corps Schools, Quantico, Virginia. All photographs are official Marine Corps, Navy, or Air Force.

J. C. McQUEEN
BRIGADIER GENERAL, U. S. MARINE CORPS
DIRECTOR OF MARINE CORPS HISTORY

Contents

CHAPTER I

Plans and Preparations

STRATEGIC SITUATION

THE FIRST six months of 1944 produced a pattern of rapid-fire events that identified for both opponents the eventual victor in the Pacific. The war's center of conflict had begun to gravitate toward the larger land masses—toward China, the Philippines, and the home islands of Japan itself. This gravitation had been paced by victories of U. S. Central Pacific forces in the Marshalls; successful carrier raids against Truk, the Marianas, and the Western Carolines; island seizures by South and Southwest Pacific forces of the Admiralties, Emirau and Hollandia; and finally, the long leap to Saipan and the ensuing decisive Battle of the Philippine Sea.[1] United States forces had gathered an irresistible, crushing momentum. The Saipan operation (15 June–9 July), signalling the beginning of the end, had pierced like a knife into Japan's outer defense. Seizure of Guam and Tinian in the Marianas and Peleliu in the Palaus [2] would twist that inserted blade, cutting vital arteries of the Japanese empire.

The necklace of islands stretching 1,350 miles southward from Tokyo had provided Japan at best a shield to intrusion, at least a screen to observation. Penetrations of U. S. forces by mid-1944 had revealed the islands neither a shield nor an effective screen, but rather a series of stepping stones by which U. S. carrier and amphibious power could move rapidly against the heart of the Empire.

Islands of the southern Marianas—Saipan, Tinian, Rota and Guam—had constituted vital parts of the Japanese outer ring of defense. Now, with Saipan neatly cut out, U. S. attention focused on the other three. Of these, only Tinian and Guam would be attacked. After capture of these two islands, Rota, lying between them, could conveniently be subjected to almost continuous air and sea attacks that would void the island's effectiveness. Admiral Nimitz therefore classified Rota as a "neutralized enemy base." [3] Islands of the northern Marianas were not considered worthwhile military objectives because of their small size and mountainous terrain. (See Map 1.)

---

[1] See Maj C. W. Hoffman, *Saipan: The Beginning of the End*, MarCorps Historical Monograph (U. S. Government Printing Office, 1950).

[2] See Maj F. O. Hough, *The Assault on Peleliu*, MarCorps Historical Monograph (U. S. Government Printing Office, 1950).

[3] GRANITE II, 3Jun44, CINCPOA Campaign Plan for the Central Pacific. This placed Rota in the same category with Truk, Ponape, Woleai, Pagan and Yap.

1

Historical Background [4]

Tinian, like the other 14 islands of the Marianas, was discovered and claimed for Spain by Magellan in 1521. For over three and one-half centuries (1521–1899), the islands remained under Spanish domination, with only Tinian changing hands during the period. This shift occurred in the mid-1700's, when England was at war with Spain. Lord George Anson, one of England's foremost admirals, had been sent with a six-ship squadron to attack Spanish possessions in South America and in the Pacific. Following several successful raids along the South American coast, during which time bad weather had claimed three of his six ships and scurvy two-thirds of his personnel, Anson decided to move all survivors aboard his flagship and press into the Pacific with the single vessel.

Going for months without finding land where fresh meat and vegetables could be obtained, Anson saw his crewmen die at an alarming rate. Small wonder that Tinian looked like paradise itself when he sighted it on the morning of 27 August 1742. Desperate to the point of recklessness, Anson anchored his ship and headed an expedition ashore. On the beach he was met by the opposition: a single Spanish sergeant supervising several Chamorros in jerking beef. Fortune had brought Anson to the only cattle range in that part of the world. Tinian furnished beef to the Spanish colony on Guam.

According to the diary of the ship's chaplain:

The Spanish sergeant assured us that there was plenty of very good water; that there was an incredible number of cattle, hogs, and poultry running wild on the island, all of them excellent in their kind; that the woods afforded sweet and sour oranges, limes, lemons, and coconuts in great abundance, besides a fruit peculiar to these islands, which served instead of bread.[5]

Anson and his men were completely taken with the beautiful island they had found. The ship's chaplain took time from the feasting to describe Tinian's terrain; his description in most respects holds true to the present day:

The soil is everywhere dry and healthy, and being withal somewhat sandy, it is thereby the less disposed to a rank and overluxuriant vegetation; and hence the meadows and bottoms of the woods are much neater and smoother than is customary in hot climates . . . These vallies and the gradual swellings of the ground which their different combinations gave rise to were most beautifully diversified by the mutual encroachments of woods and lawns, which coasted each other and traversed the island in large tracts. . . . Hence arose a number of the most entertaining prospects.[6]

Anson's small force remained in control of Tinian for two months. By conquest, the island paradise was a British possession, but Anson had no means of enforcing his claim unless he also conquered Guam, the seat of the Spanish island government. To attempt such a seizure with his single, undermanned ship was out of the question. Regretfully he sailed away and left Tinian to the Spanish.

Spain controlled the Marianas until the Spanish-American War, when the U. S. Cruiser *Charleston*[7] entered the harbor of Guam and seized that island for the United States. A year later, in 1899, Spain sold all her remaining holdings in the Marianas and the Carolines (including the Palaus) to Germany for about $4,500,000.

Germany's domination of the island lasted only until shortly after outbreak of World War I, when Japan seized most of Germany's Pacific territory. After that war, the League of Nations mandated the Carolines, Marshalls and Marianas (excepting only Guam) to Japan.

In defiance of the terms of the Mandate, Japan immediately set about developing some of the islands into fortresses. Her annual reports to the League of Nations at Geneva were

---

[4] Synthesized from the following sources: Tadao Yanaihara, *Pacific Islands Under Japanese Mandate* (New York: Oxford University Press, 1940), 8–28; R. W. Robson, *The Pacific Islands Handbook* (New York: The MacMillan Company, 1945), 150–151; *Encyclopedia Brittanica* (Chicago: University of Chicago, 1944), Volume 17, 4–5; Herbert W. Krieger, Smithsonian Institution War Background Studies Number 16, "Peoples of the Western Pacific, Micronesia and Melanesia" (Baltimore: Lord Baltimore Press, 1943), 7 and 33–36; Willard Price, *Japan's Islands of Mystery* (New York: John Day Company, 1944), 47–49.

[5] Price, *op. cit.*, 47.

[6] *Ibid.*, 48.

[7] The USS prefix has been omitted from the names of all ships throughout this monograph.

2

of airfields. The major Japanese strip at Ushi Point was one in a series of fields used in staging planes to Truk and other points in the Central and South Pacific Areas. Ushi Point Airfield extended in a single hard-surfaced runway for 4,750 feet, over 1,000 feet longer than Aslito Airfield on Saipan.[10]

Three other airstrips, two of which were in use and the other near completion, indicated that the Japanese had not overlooked the potentialities of Tinian as an "anchored aircraft carrier."

Sunharon Harbor on Tinian's western coast provided limited anchorage for a few ships and an emergency seaplane stopping point. But the anchorage was so poor that, in bad weather, Japanese ships often moved to Garapan anchorage off Saipan, which itself offered only mediocre facilities.

In addition to the airfields, Tinian assumed military importance because of her proximity to Saipan. It was possible, from observation posts on Tinian, for Japanese to watch activities of U. S. ships and planes at Saipan and to communicate information to Tokyo.

Tinian's countryside, free of heavy vegetation except in the island's higher portions and in the stair-stepped cliff elevations, offered excellent agricultural possibilities that the Japanese exploited fully. They planted sugar cane on the 90 percent of the island considered arable. With 15,000-odd acres under sugar cultivation, Tinian produced approximately 50 percent more sugar than Saipan. (See Map 3.) Those parts of the island devoted to sugar cane were divided into numerous square or rectangular sections by a pattern of irrigation ditches and by trees or scrub laid out in perfect alignment, apparently to provide windbreaks. Seen from the air, the island had a checkerboard appearance.

The island had but two settlements of any consequence: Tinian Town and Ushi Point Airfield. The latter was merely the living area for personnel working at the airfield. Tinian Town

---

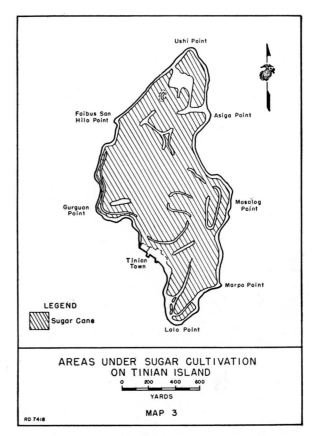

Map 3. **AREAS UNDER SUGAR CULTIVATION ON TINIAN ISLAND.**

was the administrative center of the Tinian Branch Bureau of the South Seas Government, a title more imposing than the town itself. Most of the town lay along the waterfront between two piers that jutted into Sunharon Harbor. Buildings for the most part were light and thin, looking as if they had been thrown together in an afternoon. They stood elbow to elbow as if supporting one another: homes, stores, school, hairdressing parlor, theater, phonograph shop, fish-monger's stall, Shinto temple and Buddhist temple.

Contrasting markedly with the flimsy town were the majestic ruins nearby (which stand to the present day). A prehistoric race has left behind what appear to be the foundations of several substantial buildings. Twelve stone columns, 15 feet high and five feet in diameter, are topped with great stone hemispheres, flat on their upper sides as if to support the floor of an important building, possibly a temple. At the time of the Spanish conquest, the natives

5

WHITE 1 BEFORE naval gunfire, artillery, air and bulldozers altered its appearance.   This 60-yard beach later became the port of entry for most of the V Corps' heavy equipment.

referred to the ruins as the "House of the Ancients," but they were no more certain of the real significance or history of the structures than we are today.   The pillars were made of coral rubble solidified by a mortar made of burnt coral lime and sand.   How the great half-balls weighing several tons each were raised to the tops of the pillars is a mystery.[11]

The road network at Tinian was simple and direct.   Routes followed the straight edges of the cane fields for miles without a curve or change of direction.   All primary roads, hardsurfaced with crushed coral rock, were approximately 18 feet wide.   Numerous narrowgauge (30-inch) railways connected the sugar plantations with Tinian Town, where there was a large multi-tracked terminal.   The railroad had approximately 40 miles of track, on which the 14-ton engines pulled cargo to all parts of

[11] The possibility is that the pedestals were the work of the same unknown people who raised gigantic structures and images at Yap, Ponape and Easter during the centuries when the pyramids in Egypt were under construction.   The construction at Tinian bears no inscriptions to tell its story.

the island except the extreme southern portion, where a sharp rise defied easy grading.

Tinian's climate is generally healthful, with very little seasonal variation in either temperature or relative humidity.   Mean temperature varies between 76° in January and February to 80° in June.   Only occasionally in June does the thermometer climb as high as 95°.   The humidity (78% in winter, 84% in summer), however, makes most days seem uncomfortably warm.

While the temperature and humidity vary but little between winter and summer, all other seasonal phenomena have marked differences.   The dry winter monsoon (November through March) is characterized by fair weather, interrupted only occasionally by storms of short duration.   The wet summer monsoon (April to November), on the other hand, brings more showers, greater frequency of typhoons and thunderstorms, and higher cloud cover.   During the wettest months (July to October), Tinian is deluged with nearly a foot of rainfall per month.   During other months the average varies from two and one-half to six inches.

WHITE 2 accommodated two battalions, each landing with a single company in the assault. The 25th Marines crossed this 160-yard beach on Jig-Day, followed by two light artillery battalions and the 23d Marines.

Since rainfall provided them all the water they required for drinking, washing and bathing, Japanese at Tinian exerted little effort to the development of other sources. Collected and stored in cisterns adjoining practically all of the island's buildings, water was never in short supply. Using the same means on a much larger scale, Marpo Wells, an interesting land feature north of Marpo Point, stored thousands of gallons of rain water. There, a circle of hills and rock walls funneled rain water into a natural depression that could easily be tapped. The whole, well-irrigated valley was covered with huge breadfruit trees, banana plants, and other lush vegetation. A number of ancient pillars there indicated that the area had long been a favorite one. The Japanese had dug 26 artesian wells in Tinian Town, but the potability of the water from these was questionable.

A Japanese census report for 1 January 1944 showed nearly 18,000 civilians on Tinian. Among all these, the native Tinian islanders, the Chamorros, numbered but 26, others having been moved to less desirable Marianas islands by the encroaching Japanese. Here, then, was worse treatment than that which the Chamorros received at Saipan, where the Japanese forced the natives to move from coastal areas to less desirable inland locations but did not make them leave the island. This and other similarly unsavory Japanese practices encouraged the Chamorros at Saipan and Tinian to espouse, when possible, the U. S. cause.

JAPANESE ORGANIZATION AND DEFENSE[12]

Tinian's defense forces totalled slightly over 9,000, divided almost equally between Army and

[12] Unless otherwise indicated, this section is derived from the following sources: NTLF G–2 Report,

7

BETWEEN THE WHITE BEACHES stretched nearly 1,000 yards of low, jagged coral ledges.

Navy.[13] (For detailed order of battle see Appendix V.) The main organized ground fighting force and backbone of the island's defense was the Japanese Army's 50th Infantry Regiment, commanded by Colonel Kiyochi Ogata.[14] This regiment had been stationed near Mukden, Manchuria, from 1941 until early 1944 when it

was transferred to Tinian, arriving in March 1944. The 50th was the only major unit of the 29th Division not stationed on Guam, 100 miles to the south. Operationally, the Tinian defenders fell under the Northern Marianas Army Group with headquarters at Saipan. On 7 July 1944, when Japanese top-level commanders decided that Saipan was lost, area responsibility for Tinian's defense shifted to the Southern Marianas Army Group at Guam. This was a mere paper change, however; Colonel Ogata was in command at Tinian, and nothing material could get into, or out of, the island because of U. S. blockade.

The regiment was composed of three infantry battalions,[15] one 75mm mountain artillery bat-

7–9, 19–41, 50–51, App. C; TF 56 G–2 Report, 36–40, 57–58, 63, 66, 67.

[13] At Saipan Japanese naval personnel had comprised slightly less and at Guam considerably less than one-third of the total forces.

[14] Had the U. S. move into the Marianas been delayed a few months, the 50th Infantry Regiment might have been gone from Tinian. Lieutenant General Hideyoshi Obata, commanding general of the 31st Army and administrative commander for the Marianas-Bonins-Marshalls-Carolines, had ordered the 50th Regiment to move to, and defend, Rota beginning on 15 June. As part of the same shift, the 47th Independent Mixed Brigade was to move from Saipan to Tinian and assume the defense there. Task Force 58's move into the Marianas on 11 June disrupted these transfer plans.

[15] Each infantry battalion had three companies (each with three rifle platoons and a heavy machine gun platoon), one battalion gun platoon armed with two 70mm guns, and a headquarters company.

FLIMSY TINIAN TOWN fronted Sunharon Harbor, along the only beach that would accommodate landing boats. The commander of the Japanese defense force considered it the logical landing point, until General Holland Smith demonstrated otherwise. This photograph was taken during TF 58's raids on 22–23 February 1944. Mt. Tapotchau on Saipan appears in the distance.

talion (three four-gun batteries, distributed one to each infantry battalion), one engineer, one supply, one signal, and one medical company, one antitank platoon (six 37mm guns), and three attached units: a tank company (12 light tanks), a detachment from 29th Division Field Hospital, and one vehicle platoon. By chance rather than design, the 1st Battalion, 135th Infantry, also participated in Tinian's defense. Regularly stationed at Saipan, this unit had been engaged in an amphibious exercise at Tinian when interrupted by the U. S. move into the Marianas on 11 June. This circumstance afforded Colonel Ogata an additional 900-man fighting force.

Of the Japanese Navy units at Tinian the principal one was the 56th *Keibitai* (Naval Guard Force), commanded by Captain Goichi Oya. This organization included about 1,400 troops and 600 laborers. The 56th *Keibitai*

manned the bulk of the "fixed artillery" (discussed later) and most of the antiaircraft weapons, including 24 25mm antiaircraft guns, six 7cm antiaircraft guns and three 12cm dual-purpose guns.[16] On one of the 56th *Keibitai's* subordinate units, the Coastal Security Force, rested the tasks of laying beach mines and operating small patrol boats off Tinian's shores.

Naval defenders of Tinian also included several small air detachments. For reasons of rank and command the most significant of these was the Headquarters, 1st Air Fleet, the commandant of which was also the senior officer on the island. He was Vice Admiral Kakuji Kakuda, an unusual Japanese in appearance, habits and spirit. He stood over six feet tall

---

[16] An operation order of 7 July 1944 mentioned five more batteries of indeterminate size or caliber. One prisoner testified that the guard force had "50 to 100 machine guns."

CANEFIELDS covered about 90 per cent of Tinian. A good network of coral-surfaced roads, generally following the cane fields' straight edges, facilitated vehicular movement.

and weighed in excess of 200 pounds; he willingly catered to his almost unquenchable thirst for liquor; he lacked the fortitude to face the odds arrayed against him at Tinian.[17]

Nine days before the U. S. invasion of Tinian the admiral and his headquarters group embarked in twelve rubber boats and paddled toward Aguijan Island in a futile attempt to keep a radio-arranged rendezvous with a Nipponese submarine. Kakuda's mission of supervising and administering the 1st Air Fleet could better be accomplished from some other locale. After his first failure on 15 July he made similar efforts on the next three nights—all to no avail. His failure almost reached the ultimate on 19 July, when U. S. Navy patrol units took the rubber boats under fire.

Following further unsuccessful rubber-boat ventures on the nights of 20 and 21 July, Ka-

kuda resigned himself to a Tinian fate, fled with his party to a dugout on the east coast, and was not heard from again. The Japanese sailor who supplied the facts of the escape efforts presumed that Kakuda committed suicide sometime after the U. S. landings. Available evidence indicates that the admiral made no effort to influence decisions or the course of the battle. All Japanese later questioned about Kakuda's status testified that he was relegated to the background because he was an airman.[18]

As at Saipan and many other places, there was considerable friction between the Japanese Army and Navy on Tinian. Though Captain Oya, commanding the 56th Naval Guard Force, knew that he was under Colonel Ogata's command, he apparently did not pass on the infor-

[17] Maj F. O. Hough, *The Island War* (Philadelphia and New York: J. B. Lippincott, 1947), 254–255. Ltr from LtCol G. L. McCormick to author, 8Jun50.

[18] Kakuda was an airman in name only. Before early 1944, when he was appointed to head the 1st Air Fleet, he had served his entire career as a Navy line officer. United States Pacific Fleet and Pacific Ocean Areas, *Weekly Intelligence*, 11Aug44, Vol. I, No. 5.

TINIAN CHESSBOARD, where Colonel Ogata, with 9,000 stubborn Japanese soldiers and sailors, hoped to stalemate the vastly superior U. S. forces.

mation to his men. When asked who held over-all command of forces at Tinian, Japanese sailors invariably responded, "Captain Oya." Colonel Ogata and Captain Oya each made independent preparations for Tinian's defense; and, under these circumstances, the execution of the plans naturally proceeded without relation of one to the other. A careful perusal of documents and operation orders of the two commanders reveals a scrupulous avoidance of even mentioning the other service. This "every-man-for-himself" attitude served U. S. purposes just as surely as did U. S. ships and planes.

A soldier of the artillery battalion, 50th Infantry Regiment, recorded one side of the ill-feeling in his diary:

9 March—The Navy stays in barracks buildings and has liberty every night with liquor to drink and makes a great row. We, on the other hand, bivouac in the rain and never get out on pass. What a difference in discipline!

12 June—Our AA guns spread black smoke where the enemy planes weren't. Not one hit out of a thousand shots. The Naval Air Group has taken to its heels.

15 June—The naval aviators are robbers. . . . When they ran off to the mountains, they stole Army provisions. . . .

18 June—Admiral Toyoda, CinC Combined Fleet, reported 'We have the enemy just where we want him.' Where is the fleet?

25 June—Sailors have stolen our provisions. . . .

6 July—Did Vice Admiral Kakuda (Commander in Chief 1st Air Fleet) when he heard that the enemy had entered our area [Marianas] go to sleep with joy? [19]

[19] CINCPAC-CINCPOA Item #11,405.

Whatever the failures of coordination between the Army and Navy, however, the fighting tenacity of the individual Japanese was as pronounced at Tinian as it had been everywhere before. Despite the fact that the island had been under almost continuous, ever-increasing bombardment since Vice Admiral Marc A. Mitscher's Task Force 58 entered the Marianas on 11 June, and despite recognition by the defenders that Tinian would be attacked sooner or later, the fighting spirit never wavered or varied.

This stubborn spirit, transcending all other considerations, was reflected in the diary of a soldier of the 2d Battalion, 50th Infantry Regiment:

30 June—We have spent twenty days under unceasing enemy bombardment and air raids, but have suffered only minor losses. Everyone from the Commanding Officer to the lowest private is full of fighting spirit.

10 July—When I thought of the desperate fight of the . . . Saipan Garrison Force, who carried out the final charge on the anniversary of the China Incident, the desire to destroy the enemy once again filled my whole body.

19 July—How exalted are the gallant figures of the Force Commander, the Battalion Commander and their subordinates, who have endured the violent artillery and air bombardment.[20]

In addition to Army and Navy defenders, Tinian boasted three civilian loyalty groups: Civilian Militia, Home Guard Organization, and Youth Organization. These were almost entirely ineffective from a military point of view. Most of the civilian men thought first of their families and fled with them. Small wonder, since they received no weapons except for grenades with which to destroy themselves if necessary. Low-ranking Japanese soldiers interrogated about the civilian organizations were generally unaware that such groups even existed.

Colonel Ogata's plan for the defense was based upon the logical assumption that U. S. forces would land either on the beaches facing Tinian Town or on the east coast between Asiga and Masalog Points. The possibility of a major U. S. landing over the tiny beaches on the northwest coast (White 1 and 2), while not

VICE ADMIRAL KAKUJI KAKUDA, Commandant 1st Air Fleet. Although senior Japanese officer present, he exercised no command during the battle for Tinian.

ignored completely, was never recognized as a plausible course of action. As late as 25 June Ogata issued an operation order, which said:

. . . the enemy on Saipan . . . can be expected to be planning a landing on Tinian. The area of that landing is estimated to be either Tinian Harbor or Asiga (northeast coast) Harbor.[21]

On 28 June Ogata showed that he was convincing himself, by sheer repetition, of the soundness of his earlier estimate. His "Defense Force Battle Plan" stated only two contingencies:

(A) In the event the enemy lands at Tinian Harbor.
(B) In the event the enemy lands at Asiga Bay.[22]

Ogata apparently considered a major landing on the northwest beaches not enough of a U. S. capability to warrant mention in his defense plans. The only concrete indication that the

---

[20] CINCPAC-CINCPOA Item #11,962.

[21] Operational Order A–58 of Tinian Garrison Force, 25Jun44. Representative Translations Made on Tinian by 4th Mar Div.

[22] Defense Force Battle Plan 28Jun44. Representative Translations Made on Tinian by 4th Mar Div.

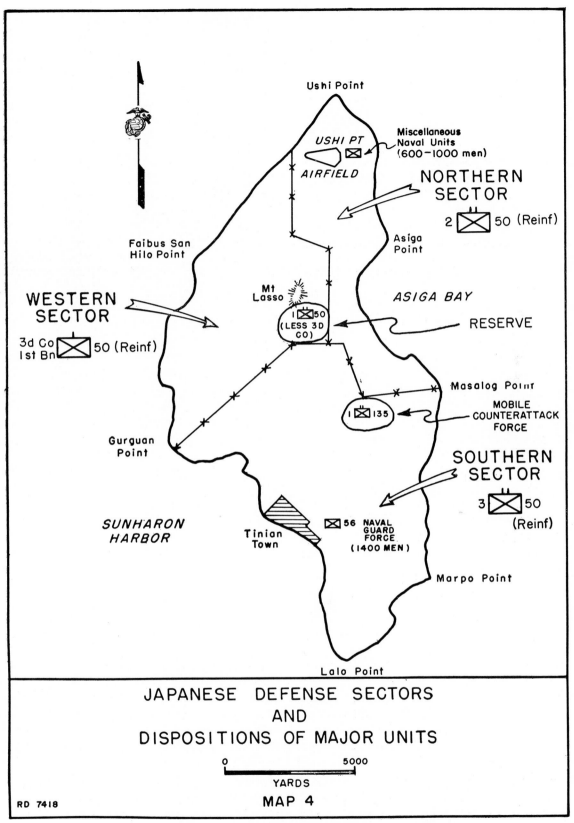

Ushi Point

USHI PT

Miscellaneous
Naval Units
(600-1000 men)

NORTHERN
SECTOR

2 ⊠ 50 (Reinf)

AIRFIELD

Faibus San
Hilo Point

Asiga
Point

ASIGA BAY

Mt
Lasso

WESTERN
SECTOR

1 ⊠ 50
(LESS 3D
CO)

RESERVE

3d Co
1st Bn   ⊠ 50 (Reinf)

Masalog Point

MOBILE
COUNTERATTACK
FORCE

1 ⊠ 135

Gurguan
Point

SOUTHERN
SECTOR

3 ⊠ 50
(Reinf)

SUNHARON
HARBOR

Tinian
Town

⊠ 56 NAVAL
GUARD
FORCE
(1400 MEN)

Marpo Point

Lalo Point

JAPANESE DEFENSE SECTORS
AND
DISPOSITIONS OF MAJOR UNITS

0   5000
YARDS

RD 7418   MAP 4

Map 4. JAPANESE DEFENSE SECTORS AND DISPOSITIONS OF MAJOR UNITS.

13

Japanese considered any White Beach landing possible was the laying of about 100 mines there. The few Japanese troops committed to defend that area indicates that Ogata expected only small landing parties there.

Basing his dispositions entirely upon the Sunharon and Asiga landing points, Colonel Ogata divided the island into three defense sectors (see Map 4): the northern sector embraced Tinian's northern point, Ushi Point Airfield and the Asiga Bay area; the southern sector included all of the area roughly south of Mt. Lasso; the western sector embraced the northwestern section of the island, including the White Beaches. To defend those sectors he assigned:

Northern sector_ 2d Battalion, 50th Infantry, plus one engineer platoon.

Southern sector_ 3d Battalion, 50th Infantry, plus one engineer platoon.

Western sector_ 3d Company of the 1st Battalion, 50th Infantry, plus one antitank gun squad.

Each of the battalions of the 50th Infantry was directly supported by a battery of four 75mm guns from the Mountain Artillery Battalion. Weapons of the latter organization, plus 70mm guns organic to the infantry battalions, constituted Tinian's "mobile artillery" and totalled 20 pieces of 70mm or greater.

Ogata designated reserves to counter either of the landings he anticipated:

Reserve_____ 1st Battalion, 50th Infantry (less 3d Company and one antitank gun squad). This unit dug in near Mt. Lasso.

Mobile
Counterattack
Force _____ 1st Battalion, 135th Infantry. This unit was located in the south-central portion of the island.

Commanders of these two reserves each reported directly to Ogata. He would have to issue two orders to set both in motion.

Ogata assigned and positioned other Japanese Army units as follows:

Tanks _____ Tank Company, 18th Infantry Regiment (12 tanks). This unit was held in reserve south of Mt. Lasso prepared to support a counterattack against a U. S. beachhead.

Headquarters
Unit_____ Supply company, signal company (plus one radio squad), engineer company (less two platoons), and a medical detachment. These elements were stationed generally east and southeast of Mt. Lasso.

Japanese naval units, under Captain Oya, appeared to have been stationed with more relation to convenience than to design. The 56th Naval Guard Force, one construction battalion, antiaircraft defense groups, and elements from two air groups disposed themselves in defense of airfields and harbor installations, with particular attention to Tinian Town and Ushi Point Airfield. Naval personnel manned the bulk of the island's "fixed artillery," which included: three British 6-inch coast defense, ten 140mm coast defense, ten 120mm dual purpose and four 76.2mm dual purpose. (For positions of these and other "fixed" weapons see Map 5.)

Commanders of the three sectors received an impossible directive from Colonel Ogata: " . . . be prepared to destroy the enemy at the beach, but be prepared to shift two-thirds of the force elsewhere." Just how sector commanders would perform this complex mission was not indicated in Ogata's plan. He ordered his "Reserve" to "maintain fortified positions, counterattack points, maintain antiaircraft observation and fire in its area." He told his "Mobile Counterattack Force" to be prepared to "advance rapidly to the place of landings, depending on the situation, and attack." The artillery battalion and the tank company Ogata enjoined to prepare to support counterattacks against U. S.

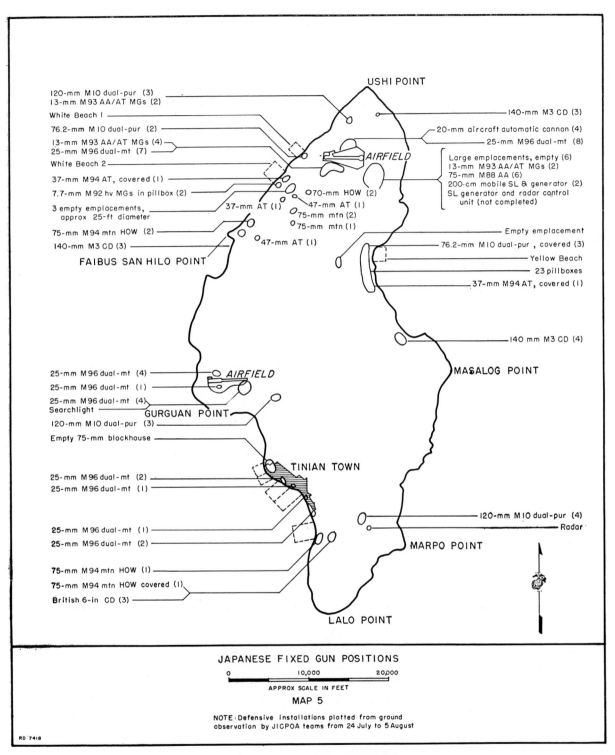

USHI POINT

120-mm M10 dual-pur (3)
13-mm M93 AA/AT MGs (2)

White Beach 1

76.2-mm M10 dual-pur (2)

13-mm M93 AA/AT MGs (4)
25-mm M96 dual-mt (7)

White Beach 2

37-mm M94 AT, covered (1)

7.7-mm M92 hv MGs in pillbox (2)

3 empty emplacements,
approx 25-ft diameter

75-mm M94 mtn HOW (2)

140-mm M3 CD (3)

FAIBUS SAN HILO POINT

37-mm AT (1)

70-mm HOW (2)
47-mm AT (1)
75-mm mtn (2)
75-mm mtn (1)

47-mm AT (1)

AIRFIELD

140-mm M3 CD (3)

20-mm aircraft automatic cannon (4)

25-mm M96 dual-mt (8)

Large emplacements, empty (6)
13-mm M93 AA/AT MGs (2)
75-mm M88 AA (6)
200-cm mobile SL & generator (2)
SL generator and radar control
unit (not completed)

Empty emplacement

76.2-mm M10 dual-pur , covered (3)

Yellow Beach

23 pillboxes

37-mm M94 AT, covered (1)

140 mm M3 CD (4)

MASALOG POINT

25-mm M96 dual-mt (4)

25-mm M96 dual-mt (1)

25-mm M96 dual-mt (4)
Searchlight

120-mm M10 dual-pur (3)

Empty 75-mm blockhouse

25-mm M96 dual-mt (2)

25-mm M96 dual-mt (1)

25-mm M96 dual-mt (1)

25-mm M96 dual-mt (2)

75-mm M94 mtn HOW (1)

75-mm M94 mtn HOW covered (1)

British 6-in CD (3)

AIRFIELD

GURGUAN POINT

TINIAN TOWN

120-mm M10 dual-pur (4)
Radar

MARPO POINT

LALO POINT

JAPANESE FIXED GUN POSITIONS

0   10,000   20,000
APPROX SCALE IN FEET

MAP 5

NOTE: Defensive installations plotted from ground
observation by JICPOA teams from 24 July to 5 August

RD 7418

Map 5. **JAPANESE GUN POSITIONS**

landings. Generally speaking, Ogata emplaced his artillery pieces so that they cross-sited on beaches at Tinian Town and Asiga Bay, although other strategic points along the west coast were also covered. A total of 20 "mobile" artillery pieces, with no more than two at any one place, assumed positions from which to deliver either the Tinian Town or the Asiga Bay fires but not both. Characteristically, the Japanese commander did not mass his artillery fires at Tinian. Such employment would have been feasible from positions about a mile south of Mt. Lasso, an area within range of all possible landing localities.

In the event of successful or partial landings, the defenders would "counterattack to the water and . . . destroy the enemy on beaches with one blow especially where time prevents quick movement of forces within the island." Colonel Ogata considered the airfields and the harbor area the key points of Tinian's defense and ordered a strong, determined defense of them; "but in the eventuality we have been unable to expel the enemy . . . we will gradually fall back on our prepared positions in the southern part of the island and defend them to the last man."[23] Ogata's subordinates had complete instructions—if they could understand them.

None of Ogata's orders or messages reveal his estimate as to the strength of the U. S. force ready to attack Tinian. But, since he had enjoyed good communications with his superiors on Saipan throughout most of the battle for that island, he should have been aware that as many as three U. S. divisions were available to strike him.

HIGH-LEVEL PLANNING

On high planning levels the Marianas were considered as a single strategic objective, so that, in all deliberations and meetings of the Joint Chiefs of Staff (JCS) and the Combined Chiefs of Staff (CCS),[24] the invasion of Tinian was under consideration simultaneously with that of Saipan and Guam.[25] Admiral Ernest J. King, a member of the JCS, spoke forcefully before the CCS in January 1943 of the desirability of seizing the Marianas, which he considered the "key" to the Central Pacific.[26] King, however, achieved no significant acceptance of this opinion until the summer of 1943 when, at the Quebec conference, the CCS noted that the Marianas might constitute a "necessary or desirable" campaign. But even that acceptance was qualified; for, in formulating a time schedule for projected Pacific operations, staff planners omitted the Marianas.

By late fall of 1943 events had made the pattern of victory clear enough to bring Admiral King an ally in his arguments for taking the Marianas. General Henry H. Arnold, Army Air Force Chief of Staff, was by then anxious to find bases from which his huge new bombers, the B–29's, could bomb the home islands of Japan. Arnold knew that airfields in China, though within bombing range of the Empire, were vulnerable to Japanese ground operations. He anticipated that the opening B–29 raids, scheduled for 15 June 1944, would precipitate ground attacks against B–29 China bases. General Arnold naturally wished for bases not vulnerable to the enemy's strength and yet within range of the enemy's home islands. As he later stated, "The Marianas, specifically Guam, Saipan, and Tinian, came closer to filling the bill than any other."[27]

Thus supported in his views, Admiral King won his point during the JCS deliberations of mid-November 1943.[28] Later in the month the U. S. chiefs met with their British counterparts at Cairo, Egypt. There a planning schedule for 1944 was approved; it included an operation for the "seizure of Guam and the Japanese Marianas" and the initiation of "very

[23] NTLF G–2 Report, 9.

[24] The CCS was composed of the American and British Chiefs of Staff meeting together. The JCS, though having representatives from the U. S. Army, Army Air Force and Navy, included no Marine officer.

[25] See Hoffman, *op. cit.*, for a detailed discussion of high-level planning leading to the Marianas campaign.

[26] CCS 56th Meeting, 14Jan43, at Casablanca.

[27] Henry H. Arnold, *Global Mission* (New York: Harper and Brothers, 1949), 476–480, 536.

[28] JCS 123d and 124th Meetings, 15 and 17Nov43.

long range bombing of vital targets . . . from bases in the Marianas." [29]

Only then was the Marianas campaign removed from the possibly-necessary-or-desirable category and listed among the definitely scheduled campaigns. Its acceptance had followed a slow, never-unanimous series of developments. Indeed, on command levels subordinate to the Joint Chiefs of Staff, ineffectual opposition continued for several months after the die had been cast at Cairo.[30]

On 23 December 1943, following the Combined Chiefs' meetings, the two principal U. S. area commanders in the Pacific (Admiral Chester W. Nimitz, Central Pacific; General Douglas MacArthur, Southwest Pacific) were apprised of the decisions reached.[31] Although the directive presented sufficient detail to enable the two commanders to mold their own campaign plans into a more or less finished shape, there necessarily would be many alterations during 1944.

Admiral Nimitz' campaign plan, code-named GRANITE, was published only four days after receipt of the CCS directive. The 27 December GRANITE plan, in reality a preliminary draft, scheduled the "Capture of Tinian, Saipan and Guam" for 15 November 1944. On 13 January 1944, only 17 days after the first draft, a smoother GRANITE was issued. In the short period between the two, discussions and developments indicated the desirability of making certain changes. The most significant of these pertained to Truk, against which island a landing had been tentatively set for 15 August in the first GRANITE plan. The new plan stipulated that, if Task Force 58's mid-February carrier attacks should indicate invasion unnecessary, Truk would be by-passed and subsequent operations (including the Marianas) would be accelerated.[32]

By 12 March 1944 the Joint Chiefs had decided that a speed-up of the entire Pacific War would be possible. Developments leading to that conclusion were: The economical and speedy execution of the Marshalls operation (30 January–20 February); advancement of General MacArthur's target date for the Admiralties operation from 1 April to 29 February; MacArthur's plan of by-passing the Hansa Bay and Wewak areas and moving directly to Hollandia; Admiral Nimitz' recommendation that a major amphibious operation be launched against either Truk or the Marianas in mid-June, followed by an assault against the Palaus about 1 October; General Arnold's urgent request for early capture of the Marianas; and, most important, Task Force 58's 16–17 February strikes, which had revealed Truk as considerably weaker than generally supposed and which supported the growing belief that by-passing Truk would be feasible.[33]

The Joint Chiefs' new directive was specific: the Southern Marianas would be seized, target date 15 June 1944, and B–29 bases and secondary naval facilities developed there.[34] The Marianas operation, so long a doubtful embryo, now had an expected date of birth.

The day after he received the JCS directive, Admiral Nimitz relayed instructions to his subordinate commands: stop Truk planning, concentrate all efforts on planning for the Marianas.[35]

Lieutenant General Holland M. Smith's V Amphibious Corps Staff immediately set to work polishing up previously conceived plans.

---

[29] "Specific Operations for the Defeat of Japan," CCS 397 revised.

[30] See George C. Kenney, *General Kenney Reports* (New York: Duell, Sloan and Pearce, 1949), 347–349.

[31] CCS 417/2, 23Dec43.

[32] GRANITE, 27Dec43 and GRANITE, 13Jan44.

[33] W. F. Craven and J. L. Cate, *The Army Air Forces in World War II*, Volume IV, The Pacific, Guadalcanal to Saipan (Chicago: University of Chicago Press, 1950), 553–554, 570; Naval Analysis Division, *Campaigns*, U. S. Strategic Bombing Survey (Pacific) (Washington: United States Government Printing Office, 1946), 194, 204; MajGen J. F. C. Fuller, *Second World War* (New York): Duell, Sloan and Pearce Publishing Company, 1949), 200, 205; Kenney, *op. cit.*, 218–370; Capt W. Karig, LCdr R. Harris, LCdr F. A. Manson, *Battle Report, The End of an Empire* (New York: Rinehart & Company, Inc., 1948), 138–155.

[34] JCS 714/4, 12Mar44. For other changes contained in the 12 March directive see Hoffman, *op cit*, 20.

[35] TF 56, G–5 Report, 1.

For the task of seizing the Southern Marianas, General Smith decided to form two landing forces: one, designated Northern Troops and Landing Force (NTLF), to seize Saipan and Tinian; the other, designated Southern Troops and Landing Force (STLF), to capture Guam. Over the two forces, which would be separated by 100 miles, an Expeditionary Troops Staff would exercise control. Holland Smith would command this over-all troop echelon and also the Northern Troops and Landing Force, a dual job made feasible because Guam would not be attacked until the Saipan operation was well underway.[36] The Guam invaders would be commanded by Major General Roy S. Geiger.

Meanwhile, the Navy's top command structure for the Marianas had also been established. Here again, two forces were necessary. The Northern Attack Force, under Vice Admiral Richmond K. Turner, would support and land the Northern Troops at Saipan and Tinian, while the Southern Attack Force, commanded by Rear Admiral Richard L. Conolly, would perform similarly for the Southern Troops' assault against Guam. A Joint Expeditionary Force Staff, headed by Admiral Turner (like General Smith operating in a dual capacity), would coordinate and control the two widely spread attack forces.

Both Holland Smith's Expeditionary Troops and Turner's Expeditionary Force were parts of the Fifth Fleet, commanded by Admiral Raymond A. Spruance. This fleet, with control over more than 800 ships, was the largest ever assembled up to that time in the Pacific. It would transport, land, cover, and support the Marines and soldiers who would assault the Saipan-Tinian-Guam beaches.

A bold, inspired thrust, of proportions never before attempted in the Pacific War, was soon to be undertaken. The target area lay 1,200 miles from the nearest U. S. base and about 4,000 miles from the area where the bulk of the troops would be embarked. The amphibious doctrine evolved by the U. S. Marines in the period between the two great wars would be tested again. Experiences in past campaigns gave every reason for confidence.

Landing force commanders at specific Marianas objectives (Saipan, Tinian, Guam) would command all troops ashore until such time as Admiral Spruance decided that the capture and occupation phase at a given island was completed, whereupon an island commander would take over. Tinian's island commander would be Major General James L. Underhill, whose responsibilities included base development, civil affairs, and all of the multifarious administrative matters attendant to governing a captured island.

Admiral Turner elaborated upon the island commander's duties as follows:

. . . these officers [island commanders] landed at each objective very early in the assault phase. They reported to the local Landing Force Commanders . . . [who assigned them] administrative duties in support of the assault troops similar in general to the duties they would perform after assuming command of the islands. . . . Then, when the Capture and Occupation Phase for each island was declared completed, the Island Commander assumed command and reported to the Commanding General Expeditionary Troops for the execution of the Defense and Development Phase. Thereafter, until the Commander Joint Expeditionary Force turned the islands and sea areas over to the Commander Forward Area, the Landing Force Commander and the Island Commander had coordinate status under Commanding General Expeditionary Troops. In turn, the latter was responsible to Commander Joint Expeditionary Force.[37]

To assist him in the exercise of his dual command, General Holland Smith split his V Amphibious Corps Headquarters into two parts. One group he called the "Red Staff," the other the "Blue Staff." The former eventually became the staff for NTLF, the latter for Expeditionary Troops. Since preliminary planning had been accomplished before the split (12 April 1944), there existed a high degree of coordination and like-thinking between the two echelons.[38]

Available to NTLF for the Saipan-Tinian landings were the 2d and 4th Marine Divisions,

---

[36] Actually, the Saipan operation was completed 12 days before the Guam invasion.

[37] Ltr from Adm R. K. Turner to CMC, 21Dec50, hereinafter cited as *Turner*. See Appendix II, Chronology, for dates upon which island commanders, and subsequently Commander Forward Area, took over at the various Marianas objectives.

[38] NTLF Report, 2–3.

commanded by Major Generals Thomas E. Watson and Harry Schmidt, respectively. The 3d Marine Division and the 1st Provisional Marine Brigade would comprise the Southern Troops and Landing Force.[39] In Expeditionary Troops reserve, prepared to reinforce any of these landings, was the 27th Infantry Division (Major General Ralph C. Smith, USA). A strategic reserve, the 77th Infantry Division bivouacked in Hawaii, could be brought into the Marianas area after D-plus 20.

Operation plans poured out in a steady flow. The time required for planning, from the highest echelon down, with each subordinate coordinating his own plan with that of his immediate superior, was drastically compressed by the procedure (normal for amphibious operations) of concurrent planning. This made possible the preparation, by the four principal command echelons, of highly detailed, inter-related operation plans, issuance dates of which fell within a three-week period:

Pacific Fleet	Operation Plan No. 3–44, 23 April 1944.
Central Pacific Task Forces	Operation Plan Com FIFTH Fleet No. Cen 10–44, 12 May 1944.
Joint Expeditionary Forces	Operation Plan No. A10–44, 6 May 1944.
Expeditionary Troops	Operation Plan No. 3–44, 26 April 1944.[40]

On 3 June 1944, nearly a month after publication of the last of the high-level operation plans for the Marianas, Admiral Nimitz issued a document to replace his campaign plan GRANITE (13 January 1944), which had been rendered out-of-date by the Pacific War's accelerated pace. Designated GRANITE II, the new plan listed the Marianas campaign as the first of the period and set the tentative target date for 15 June 1944. Other operations scheduled in GRANITE II were: Palau—8 September 1944; Mindanao—15 November 1944; South-

MAJOR GENERAL HARRY SCHMIDT, who had led the 4th Marine Division at Saipan, commanded the troops (V Amphibious Corps) who captured Tinian.

ern Formosa and Amoy or, as an alternative, Luzon—15 February 1945.[41]

TACTICAL PLANNING [42]

On the basis of the mission assigned in Expeditionary Troops operation plan, ". . . seize . . . Saipan, then be prepared to seize Tinian on order," NTLF planning for Tinian's capture commenced at the same time as that for Saipan. It was apparent, however, that Tinian plans would not need to attain the same degree of finality before departing from Pearl Harbor as would those for Saipan. One high-ranking naval officer described the Tinian planning at this time as "playing by ear." [43] This notwithstanding, several important Tinian planning

---

[39] The STLF Staff was composed of personnel from III Amphibious Corps Headquarters. The 1st Provisional Brigade was composed of two infantry regiments, artillery, antiaircraft, engineer and LVT groups.

[40] TF 56 G–5 Report, 5.

[41] GRANITE II, 3Jun44, 9–13 and 25–26.

[42] Unless otherwise indicated, this section is derived from the following sources: NTLF Report, 2–6; NTLF G–3 Report, 1–3; NTLF G–2 Report, App. A.

[43] Interview with VAdm H. W. Hill, 20Sep50, hereinafter cited as *Hill Interview.*

steps were taken: available maps, photos and charts were distributed to subordinate units, arrangements were made for loading resupply shipping, tentative plans were coordinated with the assigned Tinian Garrison Forces, and all available intelligence information regarding Tinian was disseminated.[44]

Enroute to Eniwetok, which served as a final staging area for the move to the Marianas, the NTLF Staff drew up a concept and a tentative operation plan for Tinian's capture. At Eniwetok (6–11 June) these were submitted to General Holland Smith, who decided to hold them pending further developments and completion of the Saipan operation. This first concept envisaged a shore-to-shore landing on *northern* Tinian in order that artillery might furnish support from positions on southern Saipan.[45]

During the Saipan operation the island of Tinian was scrutinized from almost every angle; frequent photographic missions were flown to detect changes of enemy positions and installations; information about the Tinian defenses as revealed by documents captured at Saipan was studied and evaluated. Intelligence held by NTLF before the Tinian operation exceeded in accuracy, completeness and timeliness that available for any operation up to that time in the Pacific War. U. S. commanders were almost as familiar with the Japanese strength and defensive preparations at Tinian as was Colonel Ogata.

Meanwhile a shift in command took place. Since early in the Marianas planning, General Holland Smith had operated as commander of Expeditionary Troops and of NTLF. Admiral Turner, likewise, had functioned as commander of the Expeditionary Force and of the Northern Attack Force. These dual roles had imposed no particular hardship until now because, of three chosen Marianas objectives, Saipan was the only island under attack. Soon, however, operations against Guam and Tinian

would proceed concurrently, and an alteration in the command structure became desirable.

General Smith therefore assigned command of NTLF to Major General Harry Schmidt at 1000, 12 July. As part of the same shift, Major General Clifton B. Cates relieved Schmidt as 4th Division commander.[46] Three days later Admiral Turner dissolved the original Northern Attack Force and formed a new one under Rear Admiral Harry W. Hill, who had served as second-in-command of both the Joint Expeditionary Force and the Northern Attack Force during the Saipan operation.[47]

Early in July, when it became evident that Saipan would soon fall, the NTLF Staff commenced reconsideration of the tentative plans for the Tinian attack in the light of additional information available; and Hill's Northern Attack Force staff also began solidifying plans that had remained fluid until now. Much midnight oil was burned by the two staffs in studying the problem of getting the Marines ashore and supporting them once there. Admiral Hill reported that "the more we looked at the Tinian Town beaches, the less we liked them. My staff was of one mind: land on the northern end of the island."[48]

Thus, the naval and Marine staffs, studying the situation from somewhat different points of view, arrived at a similar solution regarding the best place for landing. Through frequent conferences between the two staffs, information, opinions and advice were exchanged, and the planning progressed speedily. The presence of all interested commanders close at hand

---

[44] For information regarding NTLF training and rehearsals for the Marianas campaign, see Hoffman, *op. cit.*, 30–34.

[45] For a more detailed discussion of the origins of this concept, see Appendix VIII.

[46] TF 56 G–1 Report, 13.

[47] Actually, Hill had been alerted to this assignment earlier in the month. On 5 July Turner sent the following message: "Rear Admiral Hill hereby designated to command the naval attack force for the capture of Tinian. . . . This force will be designated TF 52 with reorganization to be effected later. Request proceed with plans subject to approval by originator of tactical scheme and allocation of forces." Quoted from Ltr from VAdm H. W. Hill to CMC, 16Jan51, hereinafter cited as *Hill Ltr*. To this, Admiral Turner adds: ". . . Hill was assigned to the exclusive duty of planning for the Tinian invasion on July 2, the day the Island Commander relieved him of the task of unloading all ships at Saipan." *Turner.*

[48] *Hill Interview.*

greatly facilitated planning, since recommendations and decisions could be obtained expeditiously.

Although all other principal commanders derived the definite impression that Admiral Turner strongly opposed the scheme of landing on the northern beaches and preferred an assault at Tinian Town (an impression they still shared over five years later), the admiral declares that:

I merely insisted that full study and consideration be given, before decision, to all possible landing places—all of them difficult, for more than one reason. And, in accordance with an invariable custom, I refused to give a decision until such studies had been made, and also until the main features of the landing plan had been developed.[49]

But the admiral's desire for "full study and consideration" was not his alone; nor had other commanders arrived at their preference for the northern beaches without carefully weighing advantages and disadvantages and finding the scales tipped toward the advantages. All commanders, however, reserved whole-hearted acceptance of the White Beach plan until they could be assured that a landing there could be supported. In the words of Colonel Robert E. Hogaboom, NTLF operations officer:

The whole success of such a landing depended upon determining to a high degree of accuracy the logistic feasibility of supporting a landing over the northern beaches.[50]

While admitting that the Tinian Town beaches had certain outstanding disadvantages (". . . Tinian's defenders would almost surely concentrate against a landing in Sunharon Harbor"), Admiral Turner pointed out two definite advantages:

1st, it did not have the extensive swamp and wide low-land back of it that had proved so troublesome at Saipan, but the land rise from the beach was short; and 2d, once a beachhead had been gained, there was quite a good small-craft harbor with a narrow entrance, and behind a very shallow protective reef, that would have permitted unloading in all but seriously heavy weather.[51]

As objections to the White Beaches, Admiral Turner pointed out that: First, it was necessary

REAR ADMIRAL HARRY W. HILL commanded the transports, warships, and aircraft that landed and supported the troops who captured Tinian.

to conclude the operation promptly, and an advance down the length of the island from the north would be too time-consuming; second, the White Beaches were too narrow to land a force of the size contemplated; third, logistic support over the tiny beaches would be difficult if not impossible; fourth, a change for the worse in the weather might jeopardize the entire operation; and fifth, if artillery could not be landed, "the troops would soon outrun their field artillery support given entirely from the southern end of Saipan."[52]

The flood of intelligence information pouring into U. S. hands appeared to confirm the practicality of the original landing force concept for the attack on Tinian. Every indication supported the belief that Colonel Ogata was less prepared to counter a landing on the northwestern beaches than any other. But these beach areas, designated White 1 and 2, were extremely poor, being very narrow [53] and

---

[49] *Turner.*

[50] Ltr from Col R. E. Hogaboom to CMC, 22Jan51, hereinafter cited as *Hogaboom.*

[51] *Turner.*

[52] *Ibid.*

[53] Intelligence sources reported that White 1 had only about 60 yards usable for passage of amphibian vehicles and White 2 about 160, of which only the 65-yard center section was free of coral boulders and ledges. 4th Mar Div Report, Sec III, 5–6.

having three- to ten-foot cliffs on their flanks. Never had such a large force attempted a landing over such narrow and restricted beaches. Could it be done? In addition, could amphibian tractors (LVT's) negotiate the hemmed in beach terrain and get far enough inland to unload, turn around and return to sea? Disturbing questions—that had to be answered before Jig-Day.

To supply answers, the Amphibious Reconnaissance Battalion, V Amphibious Corps (Captain James L. Jones), in conjunction with Underwater Demolition Teams 5 (Lieutenant Commander D. L. Kauffman) and 7 (Lieutenant Richard F. Burke), conducted physical reconnaissances of the White Beaches and the Yellow Beach on the east coast on the nights of 10–11 and 11–12 July.[54] These well-trained personnel debarked from the transport-destroyers (APD's) *Gilmer* and *Stringham* and quietly paddled rubber boats[55] to within 500 yards of the shore. There they slipped into the water and swam to the beach. While the Marines explored beach areas, the underwater demolition teams investigated shelving reefs in front of the beaches. Aside from the technical skill required, stout hearts were necessary equipment for men in these night reconnaissance undertakings.

Originally, reconnaissance of north-Tinian's beaches was scheduled for one night rather than two. Company A, Reconnaissance Battalion (Captain M. H. Silverthorn, Jr.), was to examine the Yellow Beach and Company B (1st Lieutenant Leo B. Shinn) the White Beaches.

Company A's search proceeded without a hitch. The Marines reconnoitered Yellow Beach and its flanks to the high water mark; then one officer, 2d Lieutenant Donald Neff, moved inland about 30 yards to locate beach exits for vehicles. Company A's explorations revealed several obstacles: floating mines in the approaches to the beach; a number of underwater boulders and pot-holes; almost insurmountable 20- to 25-foot cliffs on the beach flanks; double-apron barbed wire on the beach itself; and evidence of fortifications in the area behind the beach (". . . construction activity continued unabated during the time the patrols were ashore . . . ."). The Yellow Beaches appeared a poor choice.[56]

Meanwhile, men of Company B experienced complications. Powerful ocean currents swept them and men of the naval underwater demolition team so far off course that those scheduled for the White 2 reconnaissance landed instead on White 1 and the group intended for White 1 reached a point on the reef some 700 to 800 yards to the north. Only half the mission was completed on 10–11 July.

The task of investigating White 2 the next night was assigned to Company A, the unit that had executed the Yellow Beach mission. This time the current-drift problem was solved. The *Stringham* guided the detachment to White 2 by noting on her radar the course of the rubber boats and sending course corrections over an SCR–300. So assisted, Company A executed its mission successfully. While the Marines checked the beach, underwater demolition personnel conducted a reconnaissance of the reef fronting the beach.

Regarding the missions executed on the nights of 10–11 and 11–12 July, Admiral Turner commented:

> The first series of reconnaissances were made as secretly as possible; and, in order to avoid the disclosure of landing intention, positive orders were issued that any mines and obstacles found there were under no circumstances to be disturbed.[57]

---

[54] This mission was rehearsed on the night of 9–10 July off beaches in Magicienne Bay, Saipan.

[55] Another rubber boat landing on Tinian had been contemplated two years earlier. In mid-1942, while selection of a suitable objective for the 2d Raider Battalion was still under consideration, Admiral Nimitz had ordered Lieutenant Colonel Evans F. Carlson to investigate the possibilities of hit-and-run raids against Tinian, Wake, Hokkaido, Tulagi, and Attu. None of these plans were executed, however. In early July 1942) Makin, Gilbert Islands, was selected as the raid objective. Michael Blankfort, *The Big Yankee* (Boston: Little, Brown and Company, 1947), 37–38.

---

[56] AmphReconBn, V AC Report, Report of reconnaissance of Yellow Beach #1 Tinian, 11Jul44. NTLF Opn Order 27–44.

[57] *Turner.*

Reports on the first night's White 1 reconnaissance and the second night's White 2 mission confirmed much that had been assumed and, in addition, revealed several new facts. Both beaches, flanked by rough, rocky cliffs, offered extremely restricted landing areas for vehicles. But on the brighter side, the reconnaissance indicated that LVT's and waterproofed tanks or wheeled vehicles could safely negotiate the reef and land, and that troops could clamber over the low cliffs that flanked the beaches. Further, Marines disembarking from boats at the reef could wade ashore without encountering dangerous depths. The reconnaissance located no mines or man-made obstacles. In short, the White Beaches were neither better nor worse than planners had estimated.[58]

The report of Underwater Demolition Team 5 confirmed the Marines' findings and noted that:

No mines or man-made underwater obstructions were found. A sufficiently thorough search was made to insure that no lines of mines were present. Buried mines or an odd mine not in pattern would have been overlooked by this search. It is difficult to bury mines in coral but very possible in the gravel slopes at shore edge.[59]

Here, then, was a nod of approval for those who had favored the White Beaches from the outset. And for those who had been skeptical of the feasibility of landing there, here was evidence more favorable than unfavorable to the White Beaches.

The landing force operations officer, Colonel Hogaboom, summarized the work and results of the amphibious reconnaissance:

This was an extremely difficult operation that was almost perfectly executed and the perfection of the execution is due both to the high competence of the reconnaissance battalion and the underwater demolition team and to the detailed and careful manner in which the reconnaissance was rehearsed prior to its execution . . . in the absence of the detailed information which these reconnaissance units gave us on the extremely narrow and restricted beaches it would not have been sound to embark on this very risky operation.[60]

With the amphibious reconnaissance reports in, and the landing day less than two weeks away, the final decision regarding the place of landing still had not been made. With the purpose of clearing up this matter, Admiral Turner called a conference of all principal Marine and Navy commanders and their key staff officers. In anticipation of opposition from Admiral Turner, NTLF staff officers prepared themselves with ". . . a tremendous volume of evidence and information to support our plan . . ."[61]

The conference took place on 12 July aboard Turner's flagship, the *Rocky Mount;* top officers present were Admirals Spruance, Turner and Hill and Generals Smith and Schmidt. In Admiral Turner's words:

At the start of the conference, over which I presided, I made a preliminary statement, as I remember, outlining the general advantages of the various beaches from the naval viewpoint. I then called on Schmidt and staff, and Hill, to express their views. Both made excellent presentations.[62]

General Schmidt, who had that very day assumed command of the landing force, advanced the following in justification for his White Beach scheme: First, landing against the prepared Japanese positions at Tinian Town would prove too costly; second, Saipan-emplaced artillery could lend effective support to a landing on Tinian's northern beaches; third, the Ushi Point Airfield could be captured expeditiously and used for supply and evacuation; fourth, tactical surprise would be more probable of attainment; fifth, the operation would be more distinctively a shore-to-shore move and thus easier to execute; and sixth, supplies, for the most part, could be preloaded at Saipan and moved on wheels and tracks directly to selected inland dumps on Tinian.[63]

[60] *Hogaboom.*

[61] *Ibid.*

[62] *Turner.*

[63] LtCol R. K. Schmidt, Military Historical Study, "The Tinian Operation, A Study in Planning for an Amphibious Operation," prepared at the Amphibious Warfare School, Senior Course, Marine Corps Schools, Quantico, Virginia, 1948–1949, 10–11. Ltr from LtCol R. K. Schmidt to author, 30Jun50. Ltr from Gen H. Schmidt to BrigGen C. C. Jerome, 23Jul50.

[58] AmphReconBn, V AC Report, Report of reconnaissance of White Beach #1, Tinian, and Report of reconnaissance of White Beach #2, Tinian, both reports dated 12Jul44. NTLF Opn Order 27–44.

[59] Ltr from CO, UDT 5 to CTG 52.2, Reconnaissance of approaches to Beaches White 1 and 2, 13Jul44.

Admiral Hill, whose Northern Attack Force Staff had worked in close cooperation with Schmidt's Staff, agreed whole-heartedly with Schmidt and emphasized again his preference for the White Beaches. At the same time, Hill stressed—as he had on several occasions before and after this conference—the importance of the weather factor in the White Beach landings. He had maintained from the outset that the Navy could land the Marines providing that there were three days of good weather.[64] (Specific measures taken to prevent bad weather from seriously crippling the operation will be covered later in this chapter.) Following Hill's presentation, in Admiral Turner's words, "there was a rather short question and discussion period and then I announced my decision in favor of the White Beaches. . . . Spruance expressed his approval of my decision."[65]

Colonel Hogaboom later wrote regarding this: ". . . we were all surprised at the unexpected rapidity and ease with which the plan was presented and accepted."[66] It is apparent that Admiral Turner had already decided in favor of the White Beaches before the *Rocky Mount* conference. Admiral Turner later commented: ". . . before the reconnaissances of July 10 and 11 were made, I had (without announcement) tentatively decided to accept the White Beaches unless the reconnaissance reports were decidedly unfavorable."[67]

On 13 July, the day following the conference aboard the *Rocky Mount*, General Schmidt issued his NTLF Operation Plan 30–44.[68] The plan was notable in many respects; it incorporated, in varying degrees, the nine principles of war[69] but particularly emphasized three of them: *surprise*, *mass* and *economy of force*. Attention to *surprise* influenced the choice of landing beaches, the scheme of maneuver, the

employment of supporting arms, the formulation of various deception devices, and the functioning of logistical units. The corollary principles of *economy of force* and *mass* received recognition through the concentration of maximum strength and hitting power in the assault division and the centralization of most of the available artillery to fit the unusual circumstances of the situation. The NTLF solution to the Tinian problem was, in all respects, classic.

The plan, later adopted as an order, directed the assault division, the 4th (General Cates), to land at "How-hour, Jig-day" over the diminutive White Beaches, push inland and capture Objective O–1 (including Mt. Maga as its principal feature). Then, making its main effort toward Mt. Lasso, the division would seize the Force Beachhead Line (FBHL),[70] embracing Faibus San Hilo Point on the west, Mt. Lasso in the center, and Asiga Point on the east. (See Map 6, facing page 25.) This plan did not specify a definite date for the landing, noting that Jig-Day would "be announced." On 20 July, Admiral Spruance, Commander Fifth Fleet, confirmed the date that had previously been tentatively chosen for Jig-Day: 24 July. Admiral Hill then selected 0730 as How-Hour.

Consistent with General Schmidt's policy of placing maximum strength and resources in the assault division, the NTLF operation plan assigned 533 amphibian tractors—all those available—to the 4th Marine Division. To assure control and coordination, all these vehicles were organized into a Provisional LVT Group. Represented on the NTLF Staff by Major Henry G. Lawrence, Jr., the group was composed of two armored amphibian battalions and six amphibian tractor battalions; half of these units were Army, half Marine. (For detailed breakdown see Appendix VI, Task Organization.)

Because of the extreme narrowness of the selected beaches, only one company of armored amphibians would be used in the assault landing. This unit, Company D, 2d Armored Amphibian Battalion, would form the first wave,

---

[64] *Hill Ltr.*

[65] *Turner.*

[66] *Hogaboom.*

[67] *Turner.*

[68] Operation plans are numbered consecutively for the period of a year; thus, this was the thirtieth issued by NTLF in 1944.

[69] Cooperation, Objective, Offensive, Movement, Mass, Economy of Force, Security, Surprise and Simplicity.

[70] The FBHL was a line, possession of which denied the enemy the benefit of ground-observed artillery fire on the beachhead.

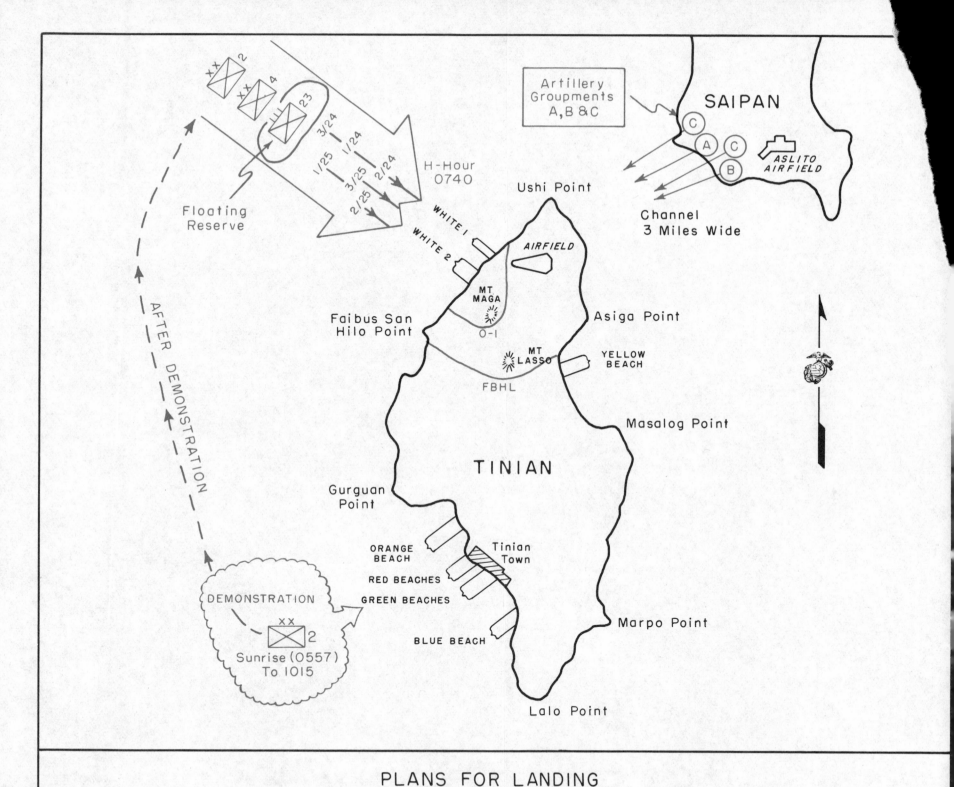

SAIPAN

Artillery Groupments A, B & C

ASLITO AIRFIELD

Channel 3 Miles Wide

XX 2
XX 4
III 23

3/24
1/25 1/24
3/25 2/24
2/25

H-Hour 0740

Floating Reserve

AFTER DEMONSTRATION

WHITE 1
WHITE 2

Ushi Point

AIRFIELD

MT MAGA

O-1

Faibus San Hilo Point

Asiga Point

MT LASSO

YELLOW BEACH

FBHL

Masalog Point

TINIAN

Gurguan Point

ORANGE BEACH

Tinian Town

RED BEACHES

GREEN BEACHES

Marpo Point

BLUE BEACH

DEMONSTRATION

XX 2

Sunrise (0557) To 1015

Lalo Point

PLANS FOR LANDING

0   2000   6000   10,000

YARDS

MAP 6

RD 7418

944790 O - 51 (Face p. 25)

one platoon preceding troop-carrying LVT's toward Beach White 1, while the other two platoons led the attack against Beach White 2. Fire from these vehicles would take up the slack from the time major-caliber supporting naval gunfire ceased until troops were nearly ashore. At a distance of 300 yards from shore, the armored amphibians would veer to either flank and fire into areas adjacent to the beaches. At that point the first wave of troop-carrying LVT's would open up with their forward-mounted .30-caliber machine guns and press on alone to the beaches.[71]

The artillery organization for battle as specified in the NTLF plan was unique (and will receive detailed treatment later). The 4th Division, though shorn of its organic 105mm howitzers, would have four battalions of 75mm pack howitzers (1st and 2d Battalions of the 10th and 14th Marines, respectively). So that the 48 howitzers, ammunition and other gear of the four battalions could be moved quickly from LST's to firing positions ashore, the 4th Division was assigned two amphibian truck (DUKW) companies.

Bolstering the armored fist for the assault unit's punch, General Schmidt attached the 2d Division's tanks to the 4th. To insure that the initial effort would receive constant and sufficient logistical support, the NTLF plan attached an Army engineer battalion (the 1341st) to the 4th Division. This battalion would function as a Shore Party on one of the beaches, while the division's organic shore party (2d Battalion, 20th Marines) would serve on the other. Other attachments to the 4th Division were routine: a provisional rocket detachment[72] and a joint assault signal company (JASCO).

The NTLF Operation Order directed the 2d Marine Division (General Watson) to "land on order in rear of 4thMarDiv . . . and move to designated assembly positions. . . ." More significant—initially—than the mission assigned in the NTLF operation plan, however, was the division's important role in the Jig-Day demonstration. While the 4th Division slipped ashore over the White Beaches, the 2d would execute, as part of a sizeable naval force, a feint off Tinian Town. Intelligence information pointed conclusively to the fact that the Japanese commander expected landings there, and a large deployment of ships off the town's beaches might appear a confirmation of his estimate. (See Map 6.)

General Schmidt's application of the principle of economy of force had built up the 4th Division and had greatly weakened the 2d. With its tank battalion and its entire artillery regiment (see below) detached, the 2d was at the lowest landing strength of any Marine division throughout the Pacific War. It had but two small reinforcing units: a joint assault signal company and a provisional rocket detachment. The NTLF organization for landing was keyed to one dominating idea: *mass* in the assault division sufficient combat power to facilitate its task of grasping and holding a beachhead under abnormal conditions.

In landing force reserve the 27th Infantry Division (Major General George W. Griner, USA), less its division artillery and one infantry regiment,[73] would "be prepared to embark in landing craft on four hours notice and land . . . on Tinian."

An important factor leading to selection of the White Beaches had been the practicality of furnishing artillery support from positions on southern Saipan. For the execution of this task, General Schmidt centralized all available Army and Marine artillery larger than 75mm under the XXIV Corps Artillery (Brigadier General Arthur M. Harper, USA). This powerful, 13-battalion organization would "support the landing on beaches White 1 and 2 on Tinian and subsequent operations from positions in the southern portion of Saipan. Mass of fires to be in support of assault units. Coordinate naval gunfire and air support with artillery fires."

[71] NTLF LVT Report, 1–3. Ltr from Maj H. G. Lawrence, Jr., to author, 16Jun50. Ltr from Maj F. A. Durand to CMC, 28Nov50.

[72] The Provisional Rocket Detachment was composed of 12 one-ton trucks, each mounting three 4.5-inch rocket launchers.

[73] The "one infantry regiment" was the 105th, which would remain at Saipan and continue mopping up Japanese.

To simplify control, General Harper split his large command into three parts: Groupments A, B, and C. Groupment A, commanded by Colonel Raphael Griffin, consisted of the 10th Marines (less 1st and 2d Battalions), the 3d and 4th Battalions, 14th Marines, and the 4th 105mm Howitzer Battalion, V Amphibious Corps. Groupment B, commanded by Brigadier General Redmond F. Kernan, USA, consisted of the 27th Division Artillery (less 106th Field Artillery Battalion). Groupments A and B were armed with 105mm howitzers. Groupment C, under General Harper's personal direction, included the 419th Field Artillery Group (145th and 225th Field Artillery Battalions), the 420th Field Artillery Group (531st and 532d Field Artillery Battalions), and the 106th Field Artillery Battalion. The 420th's two battalions manned the far-reaching 155mm guns, while the other three battalions of the groupment operated 155mm howitzers. (For firing positions of the three groupments see Map 6.)

Marine artillery units would displace to Tinian when ordered to do so by their respective division commanders. Army artillery units would receive displacement instructions from the NTLF commander.[74]

As already noted, the four 75mm pack howitzer battalions (two from each Marine division) would accompany the 4th Division in its assault landings on Tinian. The short range of these weapons made them poorly suited to firing from Saipan, and, in addition, planners were unanimous in the opinion that some artillery should be physically present at Tinian.

Immediately upon receipt of the NTLF plan (13 July), the divisions placed the finishing touches on their detailed plans for Tinian. On the basis of conferences and preliminary drafts, the divisions had been able to complete a large portion of their planning before actually having the finished NTLF document in their hands.

Major General Cates decided to land with two regiments abreast, the 24th Marines (battalions in column) on the left over Beach White 1, the 25th Marines (two battalions abreast)

on the right over Beach White 2. The division reserve, 23d Marines, would land on order on designated beaches. It would then be prepared either to pass through the 25th Regiment and continue to Mt. Lasso or to move in on the 25th's right and assist that unit in Mt. Lasso's capture.[75]

In keeping with its fluid mission to "land on order," the 2d Marine Division issued only very general instructions to its regiments. The 2d Marines would land over White 2, the 8th Marines over White 1, and the 6th Marines would be prepared to land over either.[76]

Since the 27th Infantry Division was not committed to the Tinian fight, its detailed plans will not be discussed here. The division's artillery, operating as part of the XXIV Corps Artillery, however, participated extensively in fire support of the operation.

The Tinian Garrison Forces (Major General Underhill) would prepare antiaircraft defenses, make necessary repairs of captured airfields, and execute base development functions.[77]

Though essentially a shore-to-shore movement, the Tinian operation also had many ship-to-shore characteristics. While some units and supplies moved directly in small craft from Saipan to Tinian, others embarked in ships, from which they came ashore in landing craft.

PERSONNEL AND LOGISTICS

A considerable burden was imposed upon the NTLF G–1 Section in its preparations for the Tinian operation. Many officers and men, wounded during the Saipan battle, were returning from hospitals to rejoin their units. In some cases, these were not yet fit for active front line duty and, in almost all cases, they had lost or had been separated from their equipment. It therefore became the G–1 Section's job to arrange for processing, quartering, messing and re-equipping these personnel. Thus saddled with a detailed task for which it was neither organized nor prepared, the section found it difficult to give normal attention to

---

[74] NTLF Opn Plan 30–44, Annex F.

[75] 4th Mar Div Opn Order 34–44.
[76] 2d Mar Div Opn Order 45.
[77] NTLF Opn Order 30–44.

other major problems requiring its consideration or action. This situation caused the NTLF G–1, Lieutenant Colonel Albert F. Metze, to recommend establishment of a corps or force rehabilitation and transient center if a similar problem arose in the future.

The two Marine divisions had suffered about 10,500 casualties in the Saipan operation, and there was no prospect of either reaching full strength before Tinian's Jig-Day. One replacement draft (1,268 officers and enlisted) joined the landing force on 11 July but fell considerably short of filling the vacancies. A second draft was on the move toward Saipan, but it did not arrive before Tinian's Jig-Day. Shortage of personnel, however, did not have a hampering effect upon planning.[78]

The morale of troops committed to the Tinian operation was generally high. This fact takes on significance only when it is recalled that the Marines involved had just survived a bitter, 25-day struggle and that, with only a fortnight lapse (as distinguished from a fortnight rest), they were again to assault enemy-held shores. More than one man, in more than one organization, wondered how long his luck would last. And yet, the spirit that pervaded the Northern Troops and Landing Force as it contemplated its coming battle was revealed more in a philosophical shrug, accompanied with a "here-we-go-again" remark, than in a resentful complaint that it should be called upon again so soon.

Because the time between operations was short, there was little opportunity for training or rehearsals. Indeed, commanders felt that a short period of relaxation would do their weary troops more good than would anything else. The only unit that actually rehearsed for its role was the Amphibious Reconnaissance Battalion, V Amphibious Corps. The specialized nature of its night reconnaissances of Tinian beaches had required a careful dress rehearsal.

One measure taken by the 4th Marine Division in the period between the Saipan and Tinian operations paid dividends: division staff officers, regimental and battalion commanders, and other selected officers, conducted careful re-

connaissances of Tinian from observation aircraft. The opportunity for pre-battle inspection of the objective seldom presented itself in the Pacific War because of the distances involved. Lieutenant Colonel Gooderham L. McCormick, 4th Division intelligence officer, described the results of the reconnaissance:

We all obtained . . . a view of the entire island. . . . The problems . . . of terrain and beaches were clearly seen. Another noteworthy observation was that the roads were all North-South and East-West and that the sugar cane fields were layed out in square blocks, again N-S and E-W. It was observed likewise that tree plantings, grown as wind breaks for the sugar cane, fringed the fields in the same N-S-E-W plan. This regular pattern . . . permitted a remarkably simple series of boundaries for the control of uniform advances by our troops.[79]

The shore-to-shore characteristics of the Tinian assault permitted a more flexible supply system than did other amphibious operations in the Central Pacific. This was true because the base of supply, in the form of the 7th Field Depot, was so close at hand on Saipan and because resupply ships were present in the target area. Detailed combat loading was not the restrictive factor that it was in over-seas operations such as the Saipan assault.

At the same time, a unique logistical problem was presented: Supply would have to funnel through the extremely limited White Beaches, where any congestion might seriously bottleneck the flow of supplies. To avoid any jam, the logistics plans provided that all supplies cross the beach on wheels and tracks and move direct to division dumps without rehandling. In effect, then, not a pound of supplies would be handled in the usual shore-party manner. The supply plan involved the shuttling back and forth of trucks and trailers between base supply dumps on Saipan and division dumps on Tinian and also the direct movement to inland dumps of all amphibian vehicles (LVT's and DUKW's) carrying supplies from ship to shore.

---

[78] NTLF G–1 Report, 4 and 7.

[79] Ltr from LtCol G. L. McCormick to CMC, 16Jan51, hereinafter cited as *McCormick*. Source credits Captain Charles D. Gray, S–2 of the 25th Marines, with originating the idea of air reconnaissance by unit commanders before Jig-Day.

On the Saipan end of the shuttle plan, much would depend upon the Saipan Island Command, under Major General Sanderford Jarman, USA, whose troops would perform the loading. According to Admiral Hill, "close harmony" existed between Jarman's Island Command and Navy and Marine logistical personnel.

Initial supply would be handled as follows: 32 LST's (landing ships, tank) and two LSD's (landing ships, dock), pre-loaded at Saipan, would furnish balanced amounts of water, rations and ammunition, plus minimum requirements of organizational and individual equipment and miscellaneous supplies, for the entire landing force for a period of four and a half days.[80]

This amount would be made possible by eliminating fuel items from the ship-to-shore move and by greatly reducing the amount of artillery ammunition carried. The gas and oil situation would be handled by placing floating fuel barges off the reef opposite the landing beaches; these barges would then be acessible to amphibian vehicles, which could pull alongside them. The planned reduction in artillery ammunition was possible because all artillery heavier than 75mm would deliver fires from Saipan and not land at Tinian initially.

Throughout the logistical planning, Marine and Navy commanders exerted all possible attention to carrying and landing only essential supplies. Then, in Admiral Hill's words:

We gathered up every cargo net in the Saipan area and top loaded the bare minimum of troop supplies on the LST's and LSD's. These supplies were in cargo nets and ready for immediate hoisting and each LST provided with two cranes so as to expedite the handling.[81]

In addition to the 32 LST's and two LSD's, the landing force was allocated 20 LCT's (landing craft, tank) [82] and 10 LCM's (landing craft, mechanized) for effecting the shuttle supply system. Eighty-eight cargo trucks and 25 trailers were loaded aboard these craft for the Saipan-Tinian shuttle. So that loaded vehicles could be discharged for the move inland, the logistical plan contemplated installation of two pontoon causeways, one for each beach. These prefabricated floating docks would be towed from Saipan and installed at an early hour after the H-Hour landings.[83] (For a discussion of the effectiveness of this device see page 134.)

The extreme narrowness of White 1 and 2 suggested to planners the desirability of extending those landing areas by providing some means of access over the three- to ten-foot coral cliffs on the beach flanks. But how could this be done? An ingenious answer, and an innovation in amphibious warfare, was the special portable LVT ramp, built at Saipan during preparations for the Tinian attack. The ramp, supported by two 25-foot steel beams, would support vehicles up to and including 35-ton medium tanks. The two beams were carried ashore on either side of an LVT, each beam uplifted to an angle of approximately 45 degrees from the angle of approach. Upon reaching the beach, the LVT would place the forward end of each beam against the top of the ledge, the aft end dropping and securing in the ground at the base. Two inclined girders from beach level to the island's terrain would thus be provided. Extending from the front of both beams and back over the top of the LVT were a series of 18 closely connected timbers which, as the LVT backed away, slid onto the steel beams and formed the ramp's deck.[84] LVT's carrying the special ramps would move ashore from an LSD 6,000 yards from the

---

[80] Most of the credit for working out the careful, detailed time-table for movement, loading and unloading of LST's in the Tinian operation goes to Captain Armand J. Robertson, USN, commander of the Tractor Flotilla.

[81] *Hill Ltr.*

[82] This craft designation was changed to LSU (landing ship, utility) on 10 October 1949.

[83] NTLF G–4 Report, 1–3. *Hill Interview.*

[84] TF 52 Report, Encl B. This ingenious, jury-rigged device was designed by Captain Paul J. Halloran, USN, Construction Officer, NTLF, assisted by Lieutenant W. B. Macrae, USNR. Actual construction was performed by the 2d Amphibian Tractor Battalion (Major Fenlon A. Durand) under supervision of Lieutenant Michael J. Sisul. Consultation was furnished by Colonel William W. Davies.

SPECIAL PORTABLE LVT RAMP was designed to provide access over the coral ledges flanking the landing beaches. After placing the ramp's forward end against the top of the ledge and securing the after end at the base, the LVT backed away, allowing the ramp timbers to fall into position on steel I-beams.

beach. Such movement would be executed on landing force order.[85]

A great imponderable hung like a cloud over all Tinian planning. Would the weather remain fair and friendly, or would it turn foul and hostile? Planners were well aware that the typhoon season had arrived and that even a storm several hundred miles distant might create a swell sufficient to stop unloading across the unprotected White Beaches.

To provide for this contingency, planners took the only two steps possible: they secured advance weather information and prepared to operate on an emergency basis if bad weather developed after the landing. Admiral Hill, the Northern Attack Force commander, who had stated the necessity for "three days of good weather," spoke to Admiral Spruance on this subject early in the Tinian planning. The latter gave his assurance that he would order a series of long-range patrol plane searches to westward and southwestward to watch for

swells or other indications of disturbance. Operating at a range from Tinian as great as 1,000 miles, aircraft could spot weather trouble brewing and provide Admiral Hill several days' warning. In addition, Commander in Chief Pacific's Weather Central and local aerologists kept a close check on this matter. Spruance gave Hill "full authority to alter Jig-Day as necessary, based upon these reports, to insure good weather."[86]

Plans were also evolved to cover the contingency of bad weather after landing. These included the preparation of approximately 30 tons of varied supplies for delivery by parachute drop and also for the employment of Saipan aircraft for delivery of about 100 tons daily as soon as Ushi Point Airfield had been captured and readied. In addition, a squadron of C–47's was alerted for possible movement from Eniwetok to Saipan.[87]

---

[85] Ltr from Maj F. A. Durand to CMC, 28Nov50.

[86] *Hill Ltr.*

[87] TF 52 Report, 1–3. *Hill Interview.*

On 20 July, with plans for Tinian reaching completion, Admiral Turner and General Smith decided to move to Guam where the Southern Forces were poised to strike. Before departing Saipan, Admiral Turner said to General Schmidt, "I'll give you two weeks to take Tinian." Schmidt replied, "Admiral, we will take that place in ten days." [88]

THE PREPARATORY BOMBARDMENT

Preparatory bombardment of Tinian started as early as 11 June 1944 (when Vice Admiral Marc A. Mitscher's Task Force 58 initiated the Marianas campaign) and continued steadily for 43 days. Even at night destroyers and Saipan-based artillery annoyed the Japanese. Under these circumstances it is not surprising that Japanese combat efficiency diminished somewhat.

---

[88] Ltr from Gen H. Schmidt to BrigGen C. C. Jerome, 23Jul50.

The U. S. bombardment plan followed a systematic pattern. Specific targets in the northern half of Tinian normally became the destruction responsibility of artillery, while air attacks were launched against enemy installations in the island's southern half; naval gunfire undertook destruction of targets unsuitable to air or artillery at any point on the island. As additional artillery units, planes and ships became available, the pace was gradually stepped up and the fire crescendo that would reach its climax on Jig-minus 1 began. Throughout this entire phase a target-condition record was carefully maintained; this chart showed a current evaluation of firing results and a detailed assignment of targets. By daily conferences between the supporting arms, a high degree of teamwork prevailed.

Naval Gunfire

On Jig-minus 2 (22 July 1944) the final intensification of naval bombardment prior to

READY FOR BUSINESS the special portable LVT ramp supported vehicles up to and including 35-ton tanks.

execution of scheduled Jig-minus 1 fires was undertaken by the *New Orleans*. From 0900 until her retirement for the night the heavy cruiser delivered main and secondary battery fires on selected Tinian targets.

During the day several Marine observers went aboard two gunboats (LCI(G)'s) to determine whether these craft were suitable for delivering close-support fires. The demonstration failed to impress the observers; the tiny craft lacked the stability necessary for point firing. The NTLF naval gunfire officer concluded that "employment of LCI(G)'s [for close support] would be unsafe. It was therefore decided to employ them, as heretofore, for deep support missions only." [89] These craft would be used at Tinian principally to deliver fires into cave entrances.

Other visitors aboard naval vessels on Jig-minus 2 were the naval gunfire officers and shore fire control parties of the landing force, who went aboard ships with which they would be working after the landings. By giving personnel concerned a chance to discuss mutual problems, these visits did much to smooth out call-fire procedures.

In the late afternoon Admiral Hill, commander Northern Attack Force, modified his previously distributed support plan. The change affected the firing times of some ships, a rescheduling made necessary by the planned employment of a new weapon, the napalm bomb (discussed later), against the beachhead area. At sunset ships retired with their assigned fire-support units in preparation for the scheduled bombardment that would commence at dawn the next day (23 July).

For the Jig-minus 1 and Jig-Day preparations, Admiral Hill divided Tinian into five fire-support sectors, assigned a fire-support unit to each, and designated Rear Admiral Jesse B. Oldendorf commander of the fire-support group. (For sectors and ships see Map 7.) The Tinian naval gunfire bombardment plan revolved about two fixed ideas: deception and destruction. And when there were conflicts between them, deception took priority.

Of the four ships specifically assigned to Sector 1 (which included the White Beaches), only the heavy cruiser *Louisville* participated in the Jig-minus 1 preparation, firing a mere 390 rounds into the 8,000-yard expanse between Ushi and Faibus San Hilo Points. The three destroyers of the task unit were instructed to "screen *Louisville*." [90] This penurious firing was intended to convince the enemy that the White Beach area was unimportant to U. S. plans. A great density of fire there might well have provided Colonel Ogata a clue to U. S. intentions. As will be seen, however, the battleship *Colorado*, though not a part of Unit 1, joined the *Louisville* (as scheduled) in pummeling the White Beaches during the afernoon.

Against Sector 2, which ran from Faibus San Hilo Point to Gurguan Point, the density of fire was much greater. Lying between Tinian Town and the White Beaches, this sector offered no landing beaches of any kind. Destruction fires there hinted nothing as to the real U. S. plans. All ships (one cruiser, three destroyers) of the task unit blasted their assigned area, firing a Jig-minus 1 total of 1,960 rounds.

Sector 3, which included the Tinian Town beaches as its principal target, deserved considerable attention. This it got. Here it was possible to achieve—at the same time—deception and destruction. U. S. planners hoped that heavy fires against the Tinian Town beaches would cause the Japanese to continue expecting the attack there. Of the five ships assigned to the sector, the battleship *Colorado* and the light cruiser *Cleveland* assumed the key roles. During the morning these two ships raked the Tinian Town beaches and the high ground that backed and flanked them. In the afternoon, while the *Cleveland* continued pounding the Tinian Town beaches, the *Colorado* made her scheduled move into Sector 1. There she levelled her powerful 16-inch guns against the White Beaches and surrounding areas, greatly increasing the tonnage thrown by the *Louisville* in the same general area.

Probably the most significant contribution of the *Colorado* on Jig-minus 1 was destruction of

---

[89] NTLF NGF Report, 3.

[90] Screening missions were designed primarily to protect against Japanese submarine attacks.

three Japanese 140mm coast defense guns on Faibus San Hilo Point. These three weapons, well-camouflaged and defiladed from Saipan-based artillery, were admirably sited to enfilade the White Beaches. Shortly after noon, when they were first spotted, the positions became a priority target for the *Colorado*, fires being directed by an artillery spotter in an observation plane (OY). Since the latter had no direct communication with the battleship, a complicated procedure was required in this situation: the observer in the plane sent his spotting corrections via his assigned radio frequency to the artillery command post, which passed them by telephone to the naval gunfire officer at NTLF Headquarters, who relayed them via medium frequency radio to the *Colorado*. The time consumed for this procedure was reasonably short, and the method, in spite of the relays, was effective. The battleship expended 60 16-inch shells and one hour and 45 minutes of time on the positions; this patient, systematic effort paid dividends, destroying all three of the big guns. Although the attention devoted to this single locality reduced somewhat the time originally allotted for fires directly upon the White Beaches, the landing force commander, General Schmidt, made it clear that he was willing to sacrifice some of the latter fires to insure destruction of the Faibus San Hilo Point positions.[91]

In addition to the *Colorado* and the *Cleveland*, the destroyer *Monssen* participated in the Sector 3 bombardment, firing 400 rounds during the day. Three other destroyers of the task unit were employed on screening missions, in the morning for Unit 3 and in the afternoon for the *Colorado*. Total rounds fired by Unit 3 (including those fired in Sector 1 by the *Colorado*) were 1,960.

Two battleships (the *Tennessee* and the *California*) assumed the Jig-minus 1 preparatory tasks in Sector 4, which stretched from Lalo Point to Masalog Point. Though ostensibly positioned for fires against the eastern coast, these two ships lent their efforts and shattering fire power to the bombardment of Tinian Town. Thus, while Unit 3 blasted the town and beaches from the front, Unit 4 struck from the rear. The *Tennessee* and the *California*, screened by three destroyers, fired 480 14-inch and 800 5-inch shells into Tinian Town during the day.

At 0952 Rear Admiral Howard F. Kingman, Commander Fire Support Unit 4, ordered his ships and those of Unit 3 to stop their scheduled bombardment and commence covering fires for Underwater Demolition Team 7 (UDT 7) as it reconnoitered the reef off Tinian Town. Since Tinian Town beaches would not be used for the initial landing, this particular UDT operation was intended primarily to deceive the enemy commander. Under a heavy blanket of fire, men of UDT 7 moved to the reef, performed their explorations, and returned to their ship (the transport-destroyer *Stringham*) shortly after 1100. No obstacles were located; no demolitions were performed; no casualties were suffered.

Sector 5, embracing the vast area from Masalog Point to Ushi Point, received light naval gunfire bombardment on Jig-minus 1. Although this sector included the Asiga Bay (Yellow Beach) area—which Ogata considered one of two possible major landing points—U. S. commanders did not order heavy pounding there. They feared that Ogata might be misled into moving reserves from the south to help defend the Asiga Bay coastline in the north. If this happened, U. S. planners would have out-tricked themselves—the White Beaches were also in the northern part of the island. The heavy cruiser *New Orleans* and the light cruiser *Montpelier* joined forces to send 980 rounds into Sector 5. The other three ships of the task unit (all destroyers), meanwhile, executed a screening mission.

Unfortunately, there was no yardstick by which naval gunfire's Jig-minus 1 achievements could be measured. In some instances—as with the *Colorado's* Faibus San Hilo Point mission—targets were definitely destroyed; but in the

[91] *Colorado's* efforts against enemy positions on Faibus San Hilo Point brought forth a message of personal thanks and congratulations from the Commanding General, XXIV Corps Artillery (General Harper), and a "well done" from the Commander, Northern Attack Force (Admiral Hill). *Colorado* Action Report for Guam and Tinian, 16 July–2 August 1944, 47–48.

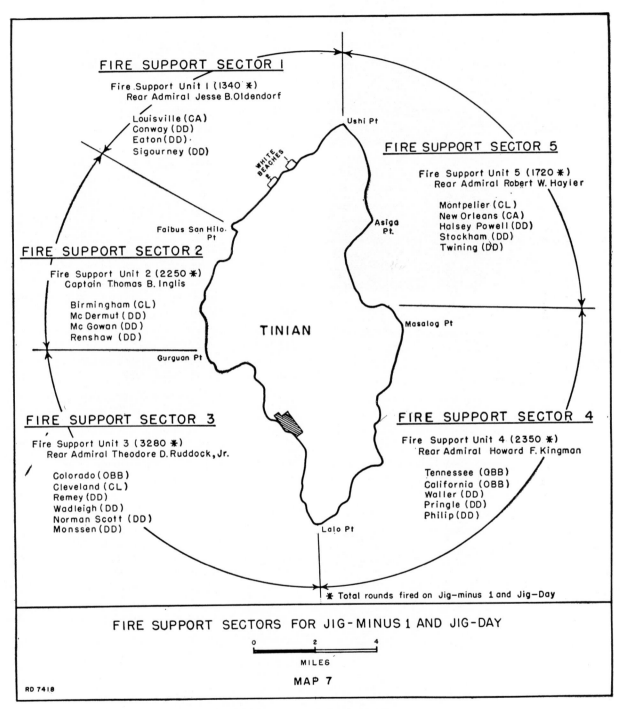

FIRE SUPPORT SECTOR 1

Fire Support Unit I (1340 ✱)
Rear Admiral Jesse B. Oldendorf

Louisville (CA)
Conway (DD)
Eaton (DD)
Sigourney (DD)

FIRE SUPPORT SECTOR 5

Fire Support Unit 5 (1720 ✱)
Rear Admiral Robert W. Hayler

Montpelier (CL)
New Orleans (CA)
Halsey Powell (DD)
Stockham (DD)
Twining (DD)

FIRE SUPPORT SECTOR 2

Fire Support Unit 2 (2250 ✱)
Captain Thomas B. Inglis

Birmingham (CL)
Mc Dermut (DD)
Mc Gowan (DD)
Renshaw (DD)

FIRE SUPPORT SECTOR 3

Fire Support Unit 3 (3280 ✱)
Rear Admiral Theodore D. Ruddock, Jr.

Colorado (OBB)
Cleveland (CL)
Remey (DD)
Wadleigh (DD)
Norman Scott (DD)
Monssen (DD)

FIRE SUPPORT SECTOR 4

Fire Support Unit 4 (2350 ✱)
Rear Admiral Howard F. Kingman

Tennessee (OBB)
California (OBB)
Waller (DD)
Pringle (DD)
Philip (DD)

Ushi Pt

WHITE BEACHES

Faibus San Hilo Pt

Asiga Pt.

TINIAN

Masalog Pt

Gurguan Pt

Lalo Pt

✱ Total rounds fired on Jig-minus 1 and Jig-Day

FIRE SUPPORT SECTORS FOR JIG-MINUS 1 AND JIG-DAY

0   2   4
MILES

MAP 7

RD 7418

Map 7. FIRE SUPPORT SECTORS.

LARGE CAVE, its entrance stripped of camouflage by concentrated pounding of U. S. supporting weapons, was one of a variety of targets struck before Jig-Day. Unless a cave were completely demolished, however, Japanese could move in as soon as the fire ceased.

majority of cases thick clouds of smoke and dust arose from areas fired upon and made it impossible to judge results with any accuracy. Ships' reports noted that missions were fired as scheduled or assigned but made no claims regarding the effects of their efforts. Many Marines at the time were inclined to be skeptical that naval gunfire had accomplished very much. After all, they pointed out, statistics had been more impressive than results at Tarawa and Saipan.

Air Support

While support ships executed their preliminary bombardment, Army, Navy and Marine aircraft delivered a series of strikes against Tinian targets. (See Chart 1 for organization of support aircraft at Tinian.) At three periods on Jig-minus 1 (0800–0840, 1200–1300, 1500–1600) all naval gunfire ceased against the southern portion of the island to allow aircraft full freedom in their attacks. In addition to these three periods, however, a number of other missions were flown at the direction of Commander Lloyd B. Osborne, USN, Commander Support Aircraft. A variety of targets were struck during the day: railroad junctions, antiaircraft guns, covered artillery positions, pillboxes, villages, cane fields, and the beaches at Tinian Town. The 358 planes participating in Jig-minus 1 strikes—231 fighters (VF), 73 bombers (VB), and 54 torpedo planes (VT)— dropped 500 bombs ranging in size from 100 to 2,000-pound and totalling in weight over 97 tons. In addition, 200 rockets, 42 incendiary clusters and 34 fire bombs (oil or napalm) were directed at the island.[92]

The fire bombs were an innovation. Only five days before their first use, Lieutenant Commander Louis W. Mang, USN, arrived at Saipan with a motion picture showing the effect produced by dropping jettisonable aircraft fuel tanks filled with napalm gel on land targets. Enthusiasm for this new weapon was instantaneous, and it was decided to utilize some of these preliminary to and during the Tinian attack. Since only a limited amount of napalm was available, Admiral Hill radioed a request to Admiral Nimitz for 8,500 pounds of this material. While waiting for it to arrive, substitute bombs, using a mixture of oil and gasoline, were employed.[93]

All "fire bombs" subsequently used at Tinian were dropped by Army Air Force P–47's based on Aslito Airfield, Saipan.[94] Colonel Lewis M. Sanders, USAAF, commanding the 318th Group's 194th and 73d Squadrons, described

---

[92] Planes for Jig-minus 1 came from the following sources: *Essex*—68 VF, 49 VB, 18 VT; *Langley*—38 VF, 8 VB, 17 VT; *Gambier Bay*—16 VF, 8 VT; *Kitkun Bay*—16 VF, 11 VT; 318th Air Group, Army Air Force—109 VF.

[93] An experimental fire bomb, using a mixture of gasoline and crepe rubber, was conceived in 1943 by Captain James R. Miller of the 23d Marines. The idea was not accepted because higher headquarters considered the mixture too combustible for safe handling. Ltr from MajGen L. R. Jones to CMC, 20Dec50 and interview with MajGen L. R. Jones, 25Sep50, both hereinafter cited as *L. R. Jones*.

[94] TF 52 Report, 85, 86, 93, 94, 101–104. *Hill Interview*.

CHART I

SUPPORT AIRCRAFT—TINIAN

Commander Northern Attack Force
                Rear Admiral Harry W. Hill
Commander Northern Support Aircraft
                Commander Lloyd B. Osborne
(a) *Task Group 52.14*
                Rear Admiral Harold B. Sallada
U. S. S. *Midway* (CVE 63)
U. S. S. *Nehanta Bay* (CVE 74)
U. S. S. *Gambier Bay* (CVE 73)
U. S. S. *Kitkun Bay* (CVE 71)
U. S. S. *White Plains* (CVE 66)
(b) *Task Group 59.1*
  Colonel William L. McKittrick, USMC
19th Fighter Squadron, 7th AAF
73d Fighter Squadron, 7th AAF
33d Fighter Squadron, 7th AAF
48th Bomber Squadron, 7th AAF
28th Photo Reconnaissance Squadron,
  7th AAF
VMF (N) 533, SUMC, Night Fighter
  Squadron
6th Night Fighter Squadron, 7th AAF
(c) *Task Group 58.4*
                Rear Admiral Gerald F. Bogan
U. S. S. *Essex* (CV 9)
U. S. S. *Langley* (CVL 27)
U. S. S. *Princeton* (CVL 23)
(d) *Task Group 59.3*
                Captain Clarence O. Taff
Patrol Squadron SIXTEEN (VP 16)
Rescue Squadron One (VH 1)

---

early difficulties in obtaining a correct mixture for the fire bombs:

A Navy commander came to Saipan . . . with napalm powder, but with an incorrect formula. We tried using Jap aviation gasoline, but that gave too much fire effect. Then we tried Jap motor gas and oil, with the napalm powder, and it was quite successful.[95]

The new "fire bombs" got their first trial run on 22 July (Jig-minus 2) when 18 P–47's at-

tacked Tinian targets, dropping 15 wing and belly tanks filled with a diesel oil-gasoline combination. Results of this first test were inconclusive. More extensive and more conclusive were the tests on the following day (Jig-minus 1) when 30[96] were dropped in areas immediately adjacent to the White Beaches. The bombs were well placed; flames seared the area. The effect on the Japanese was not definitely determined at the time, but the next day, when Marines of the 4th Division landed, several badly charred enemy bodies were found in open trenches behind the beaches.[97]

Artillery

While air struck from above and naval gunfire from almost every direction, the third member of the bombardment triangle—artillery—maintained a steady, 24-hours-per-day volume of fire on Tinian from positions on southern Saipan. The 13 artillery battalions (two 155mm gun, three 155mm howitzer, eight 105mm howitzer), by a careful assignment of zones of observation and an elaborate communication set-up, achieved a complete coverage of Tinian's northern half. Here again the proper balance between deception and destruction was maintained. It was desirable that artillery knock out as many known enemy installations as possible without furnishing the enemy any inkling of U. S. landing plans. As a positive guarantee that artillery would not divulge the chosen beaches by firing too many rounds there, the landing force authorized each battalion to shoot only 10 rounds for registration on or near the White Beaches but encouraged heavy shelling in other areas.[98]

Even though the 155mm guns could reach any point on the island (and some harassing fires were delivered by these weapons as far as

---

[95] Quoted in Vern Haugland, *The AAF Against Japan* (New York and London: Harper & Brothers, Publishers, 1948), 191.

[96] Most of these used only gas and fuel oil, while others also had portions of the precious napalm powder.

[97] TF 52 Report, 85, 86, 93, 94, 101–104; NTLF Opn Plan 30–44, Annex Dog.

[98] Ltr from LtCol C. A. Youngdale to CMC, 6Nov50, hereinafter cited as *Youngdale.*

POPULAR TARGETS for U. S. ships and planes before Jig-Day were these concrete and steel shelters near Ushi Point Airfield. Whether Japanese had occupied these shelters is not known. No bodies were found in these positions when Marines moved through the area.

Tinian's extreme southern tip), the greater accuracy realized against closer targets made employment of artillery against northern Tinian more remunerative. The south-Tinian bombardment could be delivered more conveniently and efficiently by ships and aircraft.

During the period of preliminary bombardment, artillery units depended almost exclusively upon the vulnerable little observation planes for spotting fire missions and evaluating results. In addition, however, artillery observers embarked in an LCI directed several missions against targets of opportunity. After the landings another means would be added: observers with front-line units.

As already noted, the three supporting arms achieved a high degree of coordination at Tinian. In their integrated effort the artillery (and specifically the XXIV Corps Artillery) became the controlling arm, being allowed to

select its targets first and to allocate remaining targets on the basis of their suitability to either air or naval gunfire. Never were these decisions made without consulting representatives of the other arms, however; target assignments represented the result of conferences and discussions and took into account the opinions of each participating arm.

The XXIV Corps Artillery alone fired 7,571 rounds against Tinian while the Saipan operation was still underway. During the period beginning when Saipan was declared secured (9 July) and lasting until Tinian's Jig-Day (24 July), the XXIV Corps Artillery, reinforced by battalions from the two Marine Divisions and the 27th Infantry Division, delivered a deluge of shells into northern Tinian.[99] Each

---

[99] Although statistics are not available for other artillery units during this period, the XXIV Corps Artil-

NAPALM BOMB EXPLODES near the White Beaches on 23 July (Jig-minus 1). Tinian saw the first extensive combat use of this bomb. All napalm bombs at Tinian were dropped by U. S. Army Air Force P–47's.

day's bombardment became more systematic and more thorough, until by Jig-minus 1 it reached a thundering climax. Artillery's contribution to the preliminary bombardment was significant indeed.[100]

By dark of 23 July Tinian looked much the worse for wear. Numerous fires at various points on the island sent up clouds of thick, black smoke. The increased tempo and intensity of the bombardment must have convinced Japanese commanders that the moment of U. S. landings was drawing very near. Under these circumstances a commander would make an effort to rally his forces, pass along last minute

instructions, check his defenses, repair any minor damage, and perhaps issue a "pep talk." If these activities were performed on the night of 23–24 July, they were done under the handicap of almost constant harassing fires delivered by Fire Support Unit 2. Much of this badgering was directed against Tinian Town and surrounding areas. A marked U. S. favoritism for this target had been evidenced throughout the day. Everything seemed to point to a landing there.

EMBARKATION AND MOVEMENT TO THE OBJECTIVE

In the words of the NTLF Transport Quartermaster (Captain Thomas W. McNeely), "Physical loading was accomplished . . . with a minimum of difficulty, the beaches and harbor facilities at Saipan proving adequate to

---

lery's organic battalions fired 24,536 rounds, an average of well over a round a minute for the entire 15 days.

[100] XXIV Corps Artillery S–3 Report, 8–13 and Annex 1.

handle . . . shipping easily and without delay."[101] The pier at Tanapag Harbor on Saipan allowed LST's to pull alongside for convenient and rapid loading. Using this means, six LST's daily received complete top-deck loads of rations, ammunition and water. Further, high ground backing the Tanapag Harbor coastline prevented Tinian observers from watching activities at the pier. After seeing hundreds of U. S. ships churning the waters about them for over a month, any small increase in naval activity would have created no special stir anyway. And, there was little they could have done about it even if they had known what was going on.

Ships, craft and vehicles employed by the Northern Attack Force for the Saipan-to-Tinian lift were:

Transports (APA's)—8
Landing Ships Dock (LSD's)—2
Landing Ships Tank (LST's)—37
Landing Craft Infantry (LCI's)—31
Landing Craft Tank (LCT's)—20
Landing Craft Mechanized (LCM's)—92
Landing Craft Vehicles and Personnel (LCVP's)—100
Pontoon Barges (loaded with drums of gasoline for LVT and DUKW supply)—14
Landing Vehicles Tracked (LVT's)—533
Amphibian Trucks (DUKW's)—130 [102]

The assault division (4th) was initially assigned all 37 LST's [103] so that most of its troops could be carried the short haul from Saipan to the assigned transport area off Tinian, whence they could move rapidly ashore aboard LVT's embarked in the same ships with them. This allocation simplified control and coordination during the island-to-island move and during the ship-to-shore move as well. The division embarked most of its personnel on 23 July (Jig-minus 1) from beaches near Charan Kanoa on Saipan, beaches within full view of Japanese on Tinian. But at that late date and in that situation, considerations of secrecy could be subordinated to those of convenience. Assault troops spent only one night aboard ship.

The bulk of the division's vehicles and heavy equipment (except tanks) were loaded in LCT's, LCM's, and LCVP's, which were then formed into groups and escorted to Tinian by Navy guide and control boats. Once there, they would remain in designated rendezvous positions until ordered ashore by unit commanders, orders to be transmitted through Beach Control Vessels and approved by Central Control.

The two LSD's [104] embarked most of the tanks assigned to the 4th Division, carrying the organic 4th Tank Battalion on the first trip to Tinian and the attached 2d Tank Battalion on subsequent trips.[105] Since the two LSD's did not have sufficient space to carry all of the tanks, the surplus was carried in LCT's and LCM's in a direct lift from Saipan to Tinian. Included in this group from the 4th Tank Battalion were Company D (light, flame-thrower tanks), one platoon from Company C, and several miscellaneous battalion vehicles. Only one platoon of light, flame-thrower tanks from the 2d Tank Battalion was carried to Tinian in LCT's and LCM's, the remainder of the battalion being transported in LSD's.[106]

The four 75mm howitzer battalions were loaded in one LST each. Since individual artillery pieces were loaded in DUKW's when taken aboard these ships, the move from ship to firing positions would be continuous.[107]

---

[101] NTLF Transport Quartermaster Report, 1.

[102] All totals except LVT's from TF 52 Report, 6. Latter report gave 537 LVT's as opposed to 533 in the NTLF LVT Report.

[103] This LST assignment applied only to personnel; top-deck loading was divided approximately equally between the 2d and 4th Marine Divisions. *Hill.*

---

[104] These were the *Ashland* (LSD 1) and the *Belle Grove* (LSD 2).

[105] Tanks were already in LCM's when taken aboard ship so that they could be transported from ship to reef without further handling.

[106] 4th Tank Bn Report, Enclosures A, B, C and D. 2d Tank Bn Report, 1.

[107] 4th Mar Div Report, 6–12.

TINIAN TOWN. Because U. S. commanders knew that the enemy expected landings on the beaches fronting the town, they directed a large share of the pre-Jig-Day bombardment into the waterfront and surrounding area, thereby fostering the illusion.

Allocation of all available LST's to the 4th Division left only eight transports [108] for the 2d Division's use. This number was sufficient to lift only two of its infantry regiments, the 2d and the 8th. The remaining regiment, the 6th, would wait at Saipan until 10 of the LST's carrying assault elements of the 4th Division returned. Then it too would proceed to Tinian.[109]

While the two divisions embarked for their short voyage, minesweepers of Task Force 52 covered the small area of mineable waters adjacent to Tinian's west coast. The sweeps, executed to within 500 yards of the shore, located no mines.[110] Ships of Task Force 52 could plough to assigned positions without fear of encountering floating or moored explosives.[111]

The trip from Saipan to Tinian was so brief,

[108] These vessels comprised a transport group under Captain Clifford G. Richardson. Ships were: *Cavalier, J. F. Bell, Heywood, Winged Arrow, Knox, Calvert, Fuller,* and *John Land.*

[109] 2d Mar Div Report, 1.

[110] In subsequent operations, encompassing all mineable waters adjacent to Tinian, 17 mines were swept from Asiga Bay off the Yellow Beaches on the east coast.

[111] TF 52 Report, 11.

inconsequential and unspectacular that it received no mention in any of the major action reports. For Marines, however, the voyage had at least one satisfactory feature: the food. Tired of their monotonous diet of "C," "K," and occasionally "10-in-1" rations, they partook of ships' fare with gusto. In most cases Navy personnel realized and appreciated this situation and made special efforts to provide interesting menus.

CHAPTER II   Jig-Day—24 July 1944

PRE-H-HOUR PREPARATIONS

It rained during the night preceding Jig-Day—for the Marines only water, for the Japanese shells and water. Apparently the spirits of neither were dampened. Many Marines aboard LST's and transports had been unable to find sleeping spaces below decks and, choosing the alternative, bedded down topside. Aside from the discomfort of this arrangement, no ill effects were noted. There was more to worry about than a mere drenching.

Wetter than either the Marines or the Japanese were the U. S. sailors of Underwater Demolition Team #5 who, during the early morning hours, departed the transport-destroyer *Gilmer* to perform a demolition mission on White 2, where reconnaissance-aircraft had spotted a number of Japanese mines. Rough water and heavy wind, however, scattered the swimmers and their raft-borne explosives and forced an abandonment of the mission. By 0516 the team reported back aboard their ship, having lost no personnel in the unsuccessful venture.[1] This failure posed a question: Would the mines cause trouble during the landings?

At 0530, 27 minutes before sunrise, control craft nosed into positions at the Line of Departure; observation planes and "call-strike" aircraft flew to their stations, the former to watch and report, the latter to wait for missions; Saipan-based artillery accelerated the tempo of fires and began pummeling scheduled areas; fire-support ships commenced pre-assault bombardment in assigned sectors. As the first streaks of daylight pierced the ashen sky, the bombardment mounted in fury.

At 0600 the tractor group, carrying assault Marines of the 4th Division, arrived in assigned areas off the White Beaches. Already the giant LST bow doors had creaked open, the massive ramps dropped, and the disgorgement of LVT's begun. Farther at sea the LSD's *Ashland* and *Belle Grove*, their tank decks filled with water, opened their stern gates to allow tank-carrying LCM's to float clear under their own power. The cruiser *Indianapolis*, carrying Admiral Raymond A. Spruance, Commander Fifth Fleet, arrived from Guam. Immediately, the *Indianapolis* took under fire a pillbox on Faibus San Hilo Point and an artillery position on Mt. Lasso's western slopes. Minesweepers began a pass through mineable waters off the White Beaches.[2]

---

[1] TF 52 Report, 16 and 30.

[2] *Ibid.*, 11 and 31.

After biding their time for nearly an hour, planes took over the principal role from 0620 to 0638, artillery and naval gunfire ceasing bombardment of the island's northern half to afford the planes safety from friendly shells. The target, though not pre-scheduled, was important: an estimated 14 mines on White 2. These could not be reached by minesweepers and, since the underwater demolition mission earlier in the day had failed completely, it was imperative that the mines be exploded by one means or another. The battleship *California* and the cruiser *Louisville* had attempted to detonate these same mines earlier in the day when they fired a number of rounds there, but evaluation of results had been impossible.[3]

Twelve fighters and two torpedo bombers strafed and bombed the area, achieving "successful" results, according to the Northern Attack Force's summary of daily air strikes.[4] This appraisal appears overly-optimistic, however, since three LVT's were subsequently blown up

---

[3] Ltr from Adm J. B. Oldendorf to CMC, 14Jan51. TF 52 Report, 64.

[4] TF 52 Report, Part VII, 106. Elsewhere in the same report (page 31) this strike was considered "partially successful."

SHIPS AND CRAFT, morning of Jig-Day off Tinian's White Beaches. Two airfields in picture were designated left to right: No. 1 (the main Ushi Point Strip) and No. 3. The White Beaches are generally along line of sight to Airstrip No. 3.

by mines on White 2, and since engineers later removed 100 antiboat mines from that beach, 15 of these buried between high and low water marks.[5]

As planes dived at their White 2 targets, the minesweepers reported that their pass had located no mines. When the last plane pulled out of its run, artillery and ships resumed the bombardment, scarcely a second being lost in the change-over. By 0700 the bombardment vehicle shifted into high gear. What had seemed a heavy rain of shells now became a deluge. Two battleships (the *California* and the *Tennessee*), one heavy cruiser (the *Louisville*), and four destroyers joined the 156 artillery pieces in a shattering bombardment of northern Tinian, paying particular attention to the White Beach area. Near the Line of Departure, 30 LCI gunboats waited impatiently to lead the amphibian tractors toward the beach.

Initial assault waves were not forming as rapidly as had been planned, and Admiral Hill, aboard his flagship, the *Cambria*, announced a ten-minute delay in How-Hour. New time— 0740.[6]

In an effort to deceive the enemy as to the real landing locality, the Demonstration Group had begun vigorous operations off Tinian Town at daybreak.[7] With typical pre-landing fury, the battleship *Colorado*, the light cruiser *Cleveland*, and the destroyers *Remey* and *Norman Scott* blasted the Tinian Town beaches and surrounding areas. Behind the men-of-war lay seven transports, carrying Marines of the 2d and 8th Regiments of the 2d Division. When, at shortly after 0600, transports actually lowered landing

craft and troops clambered down cargo nets into them, the Japanese probably thought that the issue would soon be contested on the Tinian Town beaches.

Landing craft moved to a randezvous area about four miles west of Tinian Town where they milled about as if attempting to gain control for the push into the beach; then, at about 0730, they headed full speed for the shore. The bait was dangled; the Japanese took it enthusiastically. Large-caliber mortars opened on the landing craft, keeping them under almost constant fire from their point of closest approach to the beach (2,000 yards) until they had countermarched and were out of range (3,500 yards). Many of the shells splashed close by, spraying shell fragments into some of the craft. Fortunately, however, neither boats nor men were hit, and all returned safely to their transports.

Ships supporting the diversion, however, were not so fortunate. The *Colorado* and the destroyer *Norman Scott* became preferred targets of a battery of three 6-inch guns emplaced in caves behind Tinian Town.[8] These enemy weapons had remained silent in their well-camouflaged positions waiting for just such an opportunity as presented itself on 24 July. Only 3,200 yards off shore lay a giant U. S. battleship, and closer yet a destroyer, both unaware of the blows that were about to strike. At 0740, as the landing craft began their feint toward the beach, the Japanese battery opened fire—not on the tiny landing craft, but on the larger "sitting ducks."

The first rounds found their mark; the *Colorado* trembled under the impact of enemy shells. Immediately she fired back, being joined in her retaliatory efforts by the light cruiser *Cleveland* and the destroyers *Norman Scott* and *Remey*. But while the U. S. ships sought their target, the Japanese battery hit the *Colorado* 22 times within 15 minutes, by which time she had moved out of range. Ship's officers estimated that about half the rounds fired at the battleship resulted in hits.

---

[5] 20th Mar Report, 4.

[6] TF 52 Report, 31.

[7] This account of the Tinian Town demonstration, unless otherwise indicated, is synthesized from the following sources: TF 52 Report, 32; *Colorado* Report, 2, 49–51, 69, 73, 85, 97–100, 124–144; TF 51 Report, Encl A, 19; 5th Fleet Report, 6; *Cleveland* Report, Encl A, 7; *Calvert* Report, 2–3; Richard W. Johnston, *Follow Me* (New York: Random House, 1948), 241; Fletcher Pratt, *The Marines' War* (New York: William Sloane Associates, 1948), 293–294; W. Karig, *Battle Report, End of an Empire* (New York: Rinehart & Co., Inc., 1948), 273; *All Hands*, Jan45, 57.

---

[8] TF 52 Report, page 66, identified the weapons as 6-inch guns made by Sir W. A. Armstrong and Whitworth Ltd, 1905.

6-INCH NAVAL GUN, one of a battery of three previously undiscovered guns that hit the *Colorado* and the *Norman Scott* on Jig-Day. Retaliatory ships' fire destroyed the Japanese battery on Jig-Day.

As the *Colorado* attempted to avoid the enemy fire, the *Norman Scott*, *Remey* and *Cleveland* bore in close to protect the larger ship. During this phase the *Norman Scott* received six hits, presumably from the same battery that fired on the *Colorado*.

While in its early minutes the duel favored the hidden enemy, the very volume of his fire soon stripped him of his only advantage—concealment. Once located by U. S. ships, the enemy position received a hammering series of salvos that (investigation later revealed) destroyed all weapons and killed all personnel.

On board the *Colorado*, meanwhile, a multitude of tasks was being performed: fighting fires, caring for the wounded, firing back at the enemy, directing the counterbattery efforts of other ships, and moving out of enemy range. At 0812, only 32 minutes after the first rounds had struck the *Colorado*, the cruiser *Indianapolis* reported off Tinian Town to relieve the damaged battleship of its fire mission. But the *Colorado* remained on her station until 1600, when she proceeded to Saipan anchorage for repairs.

The six rounds that struck the *Norman Scott* caused heavy casualties: 19 men killed (including her skipper, Commander Seymour D. Owens, USN) and 47 wounded. Damage to the ship was also extensive,[9] and Admiral Hill ordered her to discontinue fire-support duties and proceed to Saipan for repairs.

The 22 hits on the *Colorado*, while causing considerable damage,[10] "did not seriously affect the material fighting efficiency of the ship." But heavy personnel casualties, particularly on the antiaircraft battery, did seriously affect the fighting efficiency. The Japanese, in 15 minutes, inflicted the following: 43 killed (including 10 Marines), 198 wounded (including 32 Marines).[11]

---

[9] A 5-inch gun, a 40mm gun and a 35-inch searchlight out of action; the No. 1 stack demolished; gyro, radar, sound gear, and electrical circuits damaged; the superstructure riddled with several hundred holes.

[10] One 5-inch gun knocked out, two others damaged; the catapult (for launching spotting planes) destroyed; two blister fuel oil tanks flooded; one 40mm quadruple mount out of commission, one quadruple and one twin 40mm mount damaged; two 20mm guns knocked out; one director (Mark 51) out of action; and numerous shell holes at many points.

[11] These totals from detailed compilation in the USS *Colorado's* Action Report, 124–144. Of the 198 wounded, 97 required hospitalization aboard the USS *Tryon*, a transport fitted as a hospital ship, while the others remained aboard the *Colorado*.

Whether the demonstration was realistic enough to cause Japanese commanders to order any redeployment of troops is unknown, but the fact that defenders in the Tinian Town area remained there during the critical period seems to indicate that the ruse succeeded. Departure of the demonstration group caused at least one Japanese to indulge in some wishful thinking as he noted in his diary: "Up to 0900 artillery fire was fierce in the direction of Port Tinian, but it became quiet after the enemy warships left. Maybe the enemy is retreating." [12]

Off the critical northern beaches, meanwhile, there was much less excitement. The demonstration had held the center of Japanese attention, and preparations off the White Beaches

proceeded smoothly. At 0717 the first landing wave crossed the line of departure and began the 3,000-yard move to the beach. At about the same moment small-caliber fire—estimated variously as 50-caliber, 20mm and 40mm—began falling around the LST's. Its source could not be located because of the pall of smoke and dust that cloaked the island. Regarding this incident the logistics officer of the 2d Battalion, 23d Marines, aboard one of the LST's in the area, recalled:

The fire . . . wounded two or more Navy enlisted men of the crew of the vessel, and possibly a couple of Marines belonging to the landing team. . . . My recollection concerning the Marines who were wounded is hazy . . . the incident created a stir and speculation concerning the source of the fire, but everyone soon settled down to the business at hand. [13]

[12] 4th Mar Div Representative Translations Made on Tinian, Takayoshi Yamazaki.

[13] Ltr from Capt D. P. Libera to CMC, 23Dec50.

SUNHARON HARBOR and Tinian Town as seen from the Japanese 6-inch battery position. The U. S. Jig-Day diversion was realistic enough to draw the battery's fire.

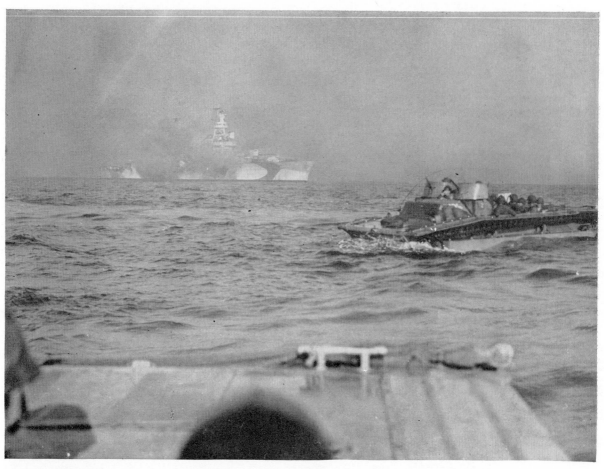

FIRE AND MOVEMENT. Troop-carrying LVT's churn toward the shore while a cruiser blasts beach areas. All 533 of V Corps' amphibian tractors were massed to land and support the 4th Marine Division on Jig-Day.

As LVT's carrying Marines of the 24th and 25th Regiments began the lengthy churn to the beach, fire-support ships made their finishing alterations on the beach landscape. The heavy cruiser *Louisville* lay between the White 1 and 2 boat lanes and delivered smashing frontal fires into the beach areas. The battleship *Tennessee* and the destroyer *Sigourney* (stationed north of the White 1 boat lanes) and the battleship *California* and the destroyer *Waller* (stationed south of the White 2 boat lanes) levelled enfilading fires against the beaches. From their flanking positions these ships continued bombardment until the LVT's were 1,000 yards from the shore in the case of major-caliber weapons and 300 yards for 5-inch. Ships in this disposition were stationed at minimum distances from the nearest reef or shoal: 2,000 yards for heavy ships, and 1,500 yards for light ships.

To prevent the enemy from directing artillery or mortar fire from high ground in rear of the beaches upon the advancing LVT's, the light cruiser *Montpelier* and the heavy cruiser *New Orleans* joined forces to work over the northeast side of the island, the latter employing 8-inch airburst shells for this mission. At the same time, the light cruiser *Birmingham* and four destroyers concentrated on Mt. Lasso's slopes. This relieved Saipan-based artillery and allowed it to focus fire from 11 of its 13 battalions directly on the landing beaches.

At 0730 a new voice rent the air: the LCI gunboats with their 20mm and 40mm guns and their 4.5-inch barrage rockets. Fifteen of these vessels participated in the initial beach assault,

WHITE BEACHES   AIRFIELD No. 3   USHI POINT AIRFIELD (No. 1)

OBSERVATION over northern Tinian was good from the Mt. Lasso-Mt. Maga heights, but U. S. supporting arms focused such a deluge of fire into this area that the Japanese saw very little of the Jig-Day landings from here. The 25th Marines seized this high ground on 25 and 26 July.

six against White 1, nine against White 2. Beginning at a range of about 2,000 yards and continuing until they turned to the flanks at about 100 yards from the beach, these craft maintained a heavy shower of shells into the beaches. After their swing to the outboard flanks, they delivered a steady stream of fire into areas adjacent to the beaches. At the Line of Departure, 15 more LCI gunboats waited their cue. At How-Hour they moved shoreward, six toward the area just north of White 1, nine toward the area just south of White 2. There they would unleash a barrage to isolate the immediate beach area from outside reinforcement.[14]

As had been anticipated, the cloud of smoke and dust raised by the intense bombardment was blown seaward by the east wind. This condition made it difficult for the LVT's to maintain direction, a task already rendered extremely difficult by a strong tidal current setting northward across the boat lanes. To remedy this situation, two plainly-marked P–47's indicated the direction of approach by flying at low altitude along the proper course. These pathfinding sweeps were continued until the LVT's reached the beaches.[15]

The LVT phalanx, meanwhile, crept shoreward. At 300 yards the armored amphibians turned toward the flanks, continuing their fires

[14] While on this mission LCI 460 became the only fire support vessel hit in the White Beach area. The result was two men seriously wounded and minor structural damage to the gunboat. The location and caliber of the enemy weapon causing the trouble was undetermined.

[15] TF 52 Report, 17, 31, 65.

against beach areas that could threaten the assault Marines. Now the tightly packed LVT's pressed alone to the beach. Soon the lengthy preparatory effort of U. S. ships, planes and artillery would be put to the real efficiency test. Were the numbers of rounds fired mere statistics? Or had the bombardment investment paid full dividends? The assault Marines, protected from enemy fire only by steel helmets and cotton dungarees, would soon have the answer.

At 0750, LVT's carrying men of Company E, 24th Marines, and Companies G and I, 25th Marines, clawed into the tiny White Beaches, growled to a vibrating halt, waited while troops debarked, then lurched back to sea. The restricted beaches demanded that no vehicles tarry and that traffic constantly keep moving. Other amtracs, carrying subsequent waves, were only four minutes behind.[16] (See Map 8, facing page 49.)

WHITE 1

Men of Company E, 2d Battalion, 24th Marines, scrambled from their eight LVT's on White 1 and found themselves in the midst of a small beach-defense detachment.[17] For a few

---

[16] 4th Mar Div Report, Section III, 16.

[17] Actually, White 1 was only wide enough to accommodate four of the eight LVT's on the beach proper; the

POINT OF THE AMPHIBIOUS SPEARHEAD; first two waves head for Tinian's shore.

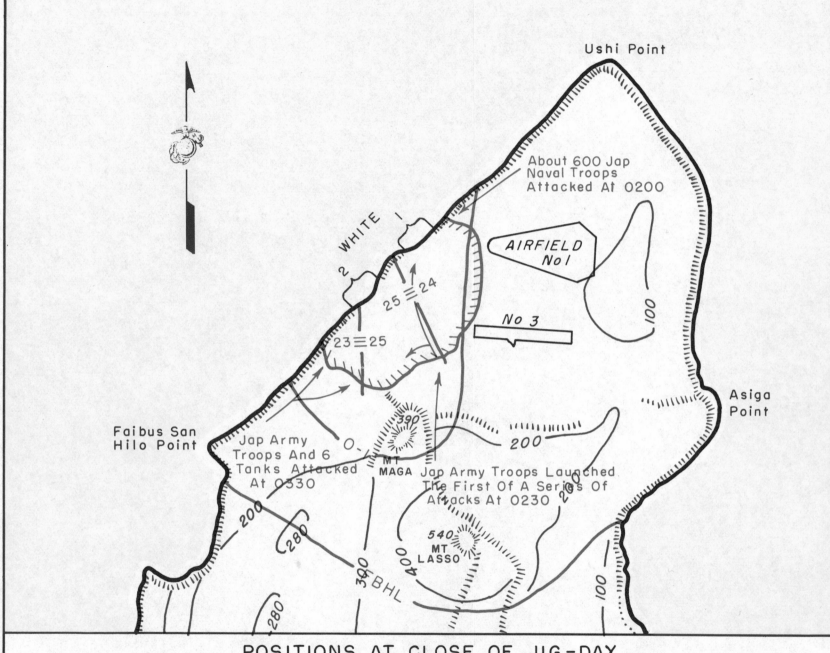

Ushi Point

About 600 Jap
Naval Troops
Attacked At 0200

WHITE 1

2

25 ≡ 24

23 ≡ 25

AIRFIELD
No 1

No 3

100

Asiga
Point

Faibus San
Hilo Point

Jap Army
Troops And 6
Tanks Attacked
At 0330

390
MT
MAGA

Jap Army Troops Launched
The First Of A Series Of
Attacks At 0230

200

200

280

540
MT
LASSO

400

200

100

390 BHL

280

POSITIONS AT CLOSE OF JIG-DAY
AND
POINTS OF JAPANESE COUNTERATTACK

0   3000

YARDS

moments the fighting was close-in and vicious, but such a skirmish could not last long. Its very nature demanded quick results. The outnumbered Japanese, fighting from crevasses in the jagged coral, were soon exterminated.

Here, then, was the 24th Marines' spearhead—a single rifle company, about 200 men, all that could be accommodated at any one time by the small beach. The unit would not be alone for long. On a fixed schedule, time between waves ranging from four to ten minutes, 15 more waves would follow; each would carry a company or an outfit of equivalent size. Even as Captain Jack F. Ross, Jr., reported that his company was pushing inland, eight more LVT's, carrying Company A of the 1st Battalion, ground into the beach.

Company A's mission was specific: execute a sharp left turn behind Company E, move to and protect the regiment's north flank. Captain Irving Schechter's men lost no time in performing this 90-degree wheel but immediately met a blast of small-arms fire as they dodged through the jagged rocks along the coast. Meanwhile, Company E also received small-arms fire that slowed its movement. Both companies had carried out assignments; they had snatched a small beachhead into which other elements of their battalions could land and deploy. Then, when the build-up of strength permitted, the push to O–1 could be undertaken with full vigor.

By 0820 the entire 2d Battalion, 24th Marines (Major Frank E. Garretson), was ashore. There, after following through the zone already cleared by Company E, it deepened and expanded that unit's front. While carving out its sector of the Jig-Day beachhead, the battalion lost 11 men killed, four of them officers. The first 200-odd yards' advance were the hardest; thereafter, in Major Garretson's words, "It was a cake walk to the O–1 line." [18]

Immediately following Garretson's unit, the remainder of the 1st Battalion (Lieutenant Colonel Otto Lessing) landed, swung to the left, and joined Company A on the regiment's north flank. Thus, by 0846, less than an hour after the first Marines hit the beach, two battalions had poured, company by company, onto and through White 1. Congestion had been at a minimum; all participants were well-indoctrinated with the importance of clearing the beaches. [19]

Japanese mortars and artillery pieces, as well as antiaircraft guns depressed for ground missions, dropped shells intermittently into the White 1 area. In addition, enemy small-arms fire, particularly on the regiment's left flank in the 1st Battalion's zone, slowed forward movement. This fire issued from thick brush and caves, and it was impossible—in most cases—to spot the source. [20]

Aside from the resistance encountered at the beach by elements of the 2d Battalion, 24th Marines, subsequent landings there progressed without special difficulty. The Japanese had failed to emplace effective obstacles to landings on White 1. Of a dozen horned mines subsequently removed from that beach, all had their horns bent flat from the weight of LVT's and other vehicles, but none had exploded. One officer who inspected these mines stated that they had become impotent because of deterioration. [21]

WHITE 2

Whereas White 1's limited facilities accommodated only eight LVT's abreast (including those nosed up against the flanking cliffs), the somewhat greater width of White 2 permitted simultaneous landing of 16 amtracs, providing that these grouped like peas in a pod and that

other four nosed up against the three- to ten-foot cliffs flanking the beach, where troops scrambled over LVT bows onto the shore.

[18] Ltr from Maj F. E. Garretson to author, 17Aug50, hereinafter cited as *Garretson*.

[19] Marines of the 4th Division did not land with packs at Tinian. In their pockets they carried emergency rations, a spoon, a pair of socks, and a bottle of insect repellent. Ponchos were carried folded over cartridge belts.

[20] 4th Mar Div Report, Section III, 16; 24th Mar Report, 4–7. 2d Bn, 24th Mar Report, 1; Interview with Maj J. F. Ross, Jr., 28Jun50, hereinafter cited as *Ross*. Interview with Maj I. Schechter, 2Jan51, hereinafter cited as *Schechter*.

[21] Ltr from Maj F. A. Durand to CMC, 28Nov50.

NOSED AGAINST THE CLIFF LINE, this LVT pauses while spray-wet Marines leap over the side and get drenched. Because the White Beaches were too narrow to permit all amphibian tractors to crawl ashore, many discharged passengers along the 3- to 10-foot flanking ledges. This picture caught one rifleman in mid-air, a radio operator wading shoreward with his SCR–300, and a bazookaman awaiting his turn to jump.

about half unloaded over the coral cliffs flanking the beaches.[22] Accordingly, the 25th Marines landed with two battalions abreast, 2d (Lieutenant Colonel Lewis C. Hudson, Jr.) on the right and 3d (Lieutenant Colonel Justice M.

Chambers) on the left. By scheduling waves to follow one another at brief time intervals, assault battalions came ashore as rapidly as limited beach conditions allowed.

The two assault battalions of the 25th Marines used different formations for the Tinian landings; Chambers' 3/25 moved ashore in a column of companies, while Hudson's 2/25 sent in one company in the assault followed by the other two abreast. Colonel Hudson explained this unusual landing formation, as follows:

In two previous assault landings it had been noted that the companies which landed initially had undergone certain control difficulties which actually had slowed them more than had enemy opposition (which

---

[22] The executive officer of the 3d Battalion, 25th Marines, commented on the over-the-cliff landing; "Usually two Marines stood at the bow of each LVT and assisted their comrades up to where they could secure a handhold on the jagged coral rim. Although this method was slow, it did relieve the congestion on the beach proper and permitted the assault units to advance rapidly inland, thus taking full advantage of the surprise gained." Ltr from LtCol J. Taul to CMC, 9Jan51.

was always light in the minutes closely following the lifting of the preliminary bombardment). Therefore it was planned that since enemy opposition would probably be light initially, one rifle company could take care of it, while the following could land in better order, receive a hasty orientation on the ground, and then push out at top speed. This plan was followed. It worked well. Control from the initiation of the landing was better at Tinian than on any other assault landing.[23]

The going was tougher on White 2 than on White 1. Here the Japanese had sprinkled a great number of horned mines, which proved troublesome to the landing. In addition to those mines designed to stop U. S. vehicles, the White 2 area contained a number of antipersonnel mines and booby traps. In the latter category were cases of beer, watches, and other souvenir items that had been wired to explode when disturbed. Recognizing these for what

they were, the Marines stayed clear and called the engineers to disarm them. Eventually, the engineer and pioneer companies, underwater demolition teams, and bomb disposal units collaborated to remove 100 horned mines from the White 2 area. Before the mine clearance could be completed, however, two LVT's were blown up about 30 yards inland from the shore, and a third was lost as it attempted to turn around at the beach. Even as late as 1400 a jeep ran over a mine on White 2 and lost all four of its tires.[24]

Mines were not the only difficulty: two enemy blockhouses (which the preliminary bombardment had failed to destroy), mounting antiboat-antitank weapons and protected by rifles and

[23] Ltr from Col L. C. Hudson to CMC, 29Dec50.

[24] One officer who witnessed the explosion said that the tires puffed into the air like "smoke rings." Fortunately, sandbags on the jeep's floor boards saved the driver. Ltr from Maj J. W. Sperry to author, 27Nov 50, hereinafter cited as *Sperry*.

DEMOLISHED LVT, one of three that ran over and detonated Japanese mines on White 2. One hundred horned mines, many of them unarmed, were eventually removed from White 2 and surrounding area.

machine guns, were situated to place interlocking bands of fire across the beach. The leading companies (G and I) by-passed these strong points and pressed the attack inland. The importance of clearing the immediate beach area had been justifiably stressed. Later waves undertook reduction of the two blockhouses, and both were shortly overrun, the Japanese having abandoned their supporting small-arms positions under the momentum of the U. S. assault. The two enemy strong points contained a total of approximately 50 dead Japanese. Other than these, few enemy bodies were found in the beach area.

By 0820 all Marines of the 25th Regiment's two assault battalions were ashore and attacking inland against resistance described as "strong" by the regimental report.[25] Intermittent artillery and mortar fire fell in the 25th Marines' area (and continued to do so for about the first 36 hours of the operation). Everyone agreed, however, that it was a mere sprinkle

---

[25] The 4th Division's basic report classified the resistance on White 2 as "moderate" and that on White 1 as "light."

compared to the Saipan D-Day deluge.[26] (See Map 8.)

RESERVE BATTALIONS LAND

While the assault battalions funneled into assigned beaches, reserve battalions of the 24th and 25th Marines readied for landing. By 0815 both were boated behind the Line of Departure, waiting for orders to start the 3,000-yard trek to shore. For Lieutenant Colonel Alexander A. Vandegrift, Jr., orders came at 0855 to land his 3d Battalion, 24th Marines, on White 1. After weathering a flurry of long-range small-arms fire en route, the unit reached the beach at 0925, whence it moved to an assembly area about 300 yards inland. There it awaited further instructions.

Lieutenant Colonel Hollis U. Mustain's 1st Battalion, 25th Marines, headed beachward shortly before 0900, and the entire unit was ashore by 0930. Here again, some small-arms

---

[26] 25th Mar Report, 2, 6–7, 9; 20th Mar Report, 4; 4th Mar Div Report, Section III, 16–17; 3d Bn, 25th Mar Report, 1–2; NTLF G–2 Report, Periodic Report 40.

MEDIUM TANK CRAWLS ASHORE from LCM that had dropped its ramp on White 1's reef. Other tanks, having followed the dozer-gouged beach path inland, have dropped their water-proofing gear and are moving on.

fire and a few rounds of Japanese mortar or artillery fire splashed menacingly around the LVT's as they neared the shore. This fire, which had caused "several casualties" in the 3d Battalion, 24th Marines, was "inaccurate and unobserved" against Mustain's unit. After its arrival ashore, the 1st Battalion, 25th Marines, moved to an assembly area and awaited orders.[27]

Meanwhile, regimental headquarters groups filtered ashore whenever the beach situation permitted. The 24th Marines' headquarters was particularly delayed by the landing endeavors of tanks and artillery. By 1230 both assault regiments had established advance command posts ashore, and two hours later the last elements of the 24th and 25th Marines had landed.[28]

TANKS AND HALF-TRACKS

It had been anticipated that beach conditions would be poor for the landing of tanks and half-tracks. They were. But, since there would be no automatic improvement merely by waiting, tank reconnaissance elements (which had accompanied leading infantry units ashore) recommended commencement of landing efforts. Two LCT's carrying bulldozers and other equipment for development of the limited beach facilities immediately headed for the shore. At about 1030 these craft arrived at the reef, one opposite each of the beaches. On White 1 the bulldozers crawled ashore without difficulty, but White 2 presented problems. After two bulldozers dodged through a maze of potholes and fissures (without benefit of marker buoys) and finally reached shore, a third, less fortunate, dropped beyond recovery in a pothole. After this mishap the LCT retracted and moved to White 1 where the remainder of the bulldozers landed. Once ashore, the bulldozers crawled slowly over the tortuous 1,000-yard interval to White 2. Work on that beach and on the routes of egress from it were delayed accordingly.

White 1 proved the better beach and was developed rapidly. The 4th Tank Battalion started debarking from LCM's onto the reef

there almost as soon as the first bulldozer landed. Initially, only one tank-bearing LCM could unload opposite White 1 at a time, but by 1300, improvements made by bulldozers and engineers allowed either two LCM's, or one LCM and one LCT, to unload simultaneously.

Because reports indicated that White 2 was now in better shape, one LCM debarked a tank for a trial run at 1100. Conditions were still not good; the tank's 100-yard trip from reef to beach consumed 45 minutes. Nevertheless, to relieve the congestion at the other beach, unloading at White 2 continued, one LCM at a time, until one entire tank company (A) had moved ashore there.[29]

Behind the tanks landing at White 1 came the 75mm half-tracks of the weapons companies of the two assault regiments. All were ashore and with their parent organizations by 1850. The tanks also moved directly to units which they had been directed to support: Company A tanks to the 25th Marines, Company B to the 24th Marines, Company C to the 23d Marines (division reserve, the landing of which will be discussed later). Company D, the light (flame-thrower) tank unit of the 4th Tank Battalion, was divided into platoons, each being attached to a medium tank company.[30]

Despite the arduous landing process for tanks and half-tracks, none were lost. At no time during landing of these vehicles were beaches seriously blocked to personnel in LVT's or artillery in DUKW's.[31]

---

[27] 3d Bn. 24th Mar Report, 1. 1st Bn, 25th Mar Report, 29.

[28] 4th Mar Div Report, Section III, 17.

[29] The 4th Tank Battalion Report, page 3, noted that "considerable delay" on White 2 was caused by "blocking of the beach exits by engineer equipment and apparent confusion on the White 2 Control Boat." Colonel Nelson K. Brown, 4th Division Shore Party Commander, described the other side of this situation: "When the construction equipment arrived, the normal conflict between constructor and user ensued over right of way. . . ." Ltr from Col N. K. Brown to CMC, 27Dec50, hereinafter cited as *Brown*.

[30] 1st Platoon to Company A, 2d Platoon to Company B, and 3d Platoon to Company C. The flame-thrower tanks used at Tinian were M3A1 light tanks that had their turret-mounted 37mm guns and ammunition racks removed and Ronson (Canadian) Flame-Throwers installed in lieu thereof.

[31] 4th Mar Div Report, Section III, 17–18. 4th Tank Bn Report, 3.

75MM PACK HOWITZER goes into action a short distance inland from the beach. Four battalions of these rugged little pieces landed at Tinian on Jig-Day. The other 13 battalions of U. S. artillery remained on Saipan, to provide support during the critical beachhead phase.

Although most of the 2d Tank Battalion arrived off Tinian in the afternoon (embarked in the same LSD's that had unloaded the 4th Tank Battalion earlier in the day), other activities on the crowded beaches prevented the unit from landing during daylight hours of Jig-Day. One platoon of four light (flame-thrower) tanks, however, came ashore during the evening of 24 July and early the next morning. Landing of these machines followed a channel crossing from Saipan in landing craft.[32]

ARTILLERY

The ship-to-shore movement of the four 75mm pack howitzer artillery battalions was painless. In all cases the individual pieces were carried in DUKW's (amphibian trucks) from LST's to firing positions without manhandling. The 1st Battalion, 14th Marines (Lieutenant Colonel Harry J. Zimmer), was the first artil-

lery unit ashore at Tinian. Landing at 1315 on White 2, it went into position about 300 yards inland from the beach's southern end and by 1430 was firing in support of the 25th Marines. Next ashore was the 2d Battalion, 14th Marines (Lieutenant Colonel George B. Wilson, Jr.), forced to move single file of DUKW's over White 1 because of other landing activities there. By 1515 the unit was prepared to support the 24th Marines from positions about 400 yards southeast of White 1.

Lieutenant Colonel Randall M. Victory, regimental executive officer, landed the 14th Marines' headquarters group at 1535 over White 2, set up a command post behind a small railroad embankment just inland and north of that beach, and established wire communication with the two artillery battalions ashore. Colonel Louis G. DeHaven, regimental commander, landed with the 4th Division command group the following day.[33]

---

[32] 2d Tank Bn Report, 1.

[33] Ltr from Col R. M. Victory to CMC, 22Jan51.

The two 10th Marines' battalions attached to the 4th Division were next, 1st Battalion (Lieutenant Colonel Donovan D. Sult) over White 2 and 2d Battalion (Major David L. Henderson) over White 1.[34] The former, in position 300 yards inland from the center of White 2 by 1635, reinforced the fires of the 1st Battalion, 14th Marines, while the latter, situated behind a railroad embankment about 800 yards inland from White 2, was prepared by 1630 to reinforce the 2d Battalion, 14th Marines' fires.[35]

While the four pack howitzer battalions conducted their ship-to-shore movement, Saipan-based artillery executed a number of missions in support of Marines in the Tinian beachhead. Forward observers, spotting many lucrative targets, experienced virtually no difficulties in transmitting fire requests to Saipan artillery. Within a matter of minutes shells crashed into target areas.[36]

23D MARINES LAND [37]

As early as 0730, Marines of the 23d Regiment, division reserve, received orders from division to occupy their assigned LVT's, parked track-to-track in the tank decks of LST's. As these machines simultaneously warmed their motors preparatory to launching, they emitted strong carbon monoxide fumes. Previous experience had taught that, when troops were cooped up under these conditions for periods in excess of 30 minutes, many became nauseated, nearly all got headaches. Since no instructions to launch LVT's were forthcoming, Colonel Louis R. Jones, the regimental commander, ordered the Marines to move topside awaiting further orders.

At 1030 the 4th Division ordered the 23d Marines to load troops in LVT's and commence launching. While this debarkation was underway, Colonel Jones received information that his regiment would land over White 2. But no definite time was specified for the move, and no instructions were given regarding what the unit would do once ashore.

Colonel Jones and members of his staff headed for the White 2 control boat at 1035. Unfortunately, the LVT assigned to carry this group was a mechanical wreck, engine failures being more the rule than the exception. At 1130, while his LVT wallowed helplessly in the choppy seas, Colonel Jones received a message (as information addressee) from the 4th Marine Division to Transport Group 52.2: "Request 23d Marines be landed White 2 as soon as ready prepared for action in zone of 25th Marines." Other than this, no instructions were received at this time.[38] It appears, however, that the lack of instructions resulted from communication difficulties rather than staff failures. The 4th Division Chief of Staff later wrote: "Division tried for hours to get 23d landed. Fortunately no serious harm was done by delay." [39]

Finally, at 1220 (an hour and 45 minutes after leaving the LST), Jones' vehicle limped to the control craft. There the control officer gave the colonel a confusing report: the first three waves of the 2d Battalion were already ashore, and the remainder of that unit was in the process of landing. A check proved this information false; no elements of the 2d Battalion had landed. In addition, it was discovered that the control vessel was 1,200 yards out of position.[40]

Meanwhile, the 2d Battalion commander, Lieutenant Colonel Edward J. Dillon, had been faced with a confusing situation: twice one of his company commanders received from a naval boat officer an order to land; each time the company commander requested instructions from

[34] The DUKWS involved in this move used a single-file, bumper-to-bumper formation to conserve the limited landing space available. Ltr from Capt S. J. Burich, Jr., to CMC, 26Dec50.

[35] 4th Mar Div Report, Section III, 18; 14th Mar Report, 1.

[36] Ross.

[37] General details regarding the 23d Marines' landing were derived from the 4th Mar Div Report, 18–19 and L. R. Jones. Specific details as cited.

[38] 23d Mar Report, 19.

[39] Ltr from Brig Gen W. W. Rogers to CMC, 20Dec50, hereinafter cited as Rogers.

[40] 23d Mar Report, 19.

Dillon who, in turn, requested clarification from Colonel Jones. The latter, still awaiting an order from division, told Dillon to hold up until definite word arrived.[41]

Another top officer of the 23d Marines also figured in the picture at this point. Lieutenant Colonel John R. Lanigan, regimental executive officer, aware of Colonel Jones' radio and LVT troubles, assumed that he and his advance command post group should take over control of the regiment until the command LVT began functioning properly again. While monitoring messages from division to the 23d Marines, Lanigan heard instructions for the regiment to commence landing and immediately attempted to pass along the order to the 2d Battalion.[42] This particular message failed to reach Dillon, however, and therefore did not affect the situation in any way at this time.[43]

At 1300 Colonel Jones received a specific mission, written 65 minutes earlier, from the 4th Division (probably the same message received by Lanigan): "On landing take over right sector zone 25th Marines . . . Reserve battalion in division reserve. . . ."[44] Jones immediately issued an order to the 2d Battalion (Lieutenant Colonel Dillon) to commence moving ashore. Here, however, communication difficulties further complicated the situation. The 2d Battalion could not be reached directly, and relays and delays eventually consumed 45 minutes.[45]

Dillon finally received his first definite order to land when division sent a message directly to him. He passed along the information to Jones, who had also received the division order and who was attempting to direct Dillon to start ashore. Jones told Dillon to execute "Plan A," a scheme of maneuver that would commit the 23d Marines on the right of the 25th. The 2d Battalion headed for the beach.[46]

Finally, at 1401, the first waves landed, followed rapidly by the remaining four waves. Once ashore, the unit moved to an assembly area near the extreme right (south) flank of the beachhead for a reorganization before moving into the attack. The beach was a scene of considerable congestion, what with the 25th Marines reserve (1/25) and elements of the right assault battalion (2/25) still in the immediate area. It appeared that an earlier landing of the 23d Regiment would only have increased the beach clog, so, despite the communication difficulties that might have had serious consequences under other circumstances, the late landing of the 23d Marines had no adverse effect upon the tactical situation.

The other two battalions followed over White 2, Lieutenant Colonel Ralph Haas' 1st Battalion beginning at 1415 and Major Paul S. Treitel's 3d Battalion beginning at 1500. Once ashore, Haas' unit moved up behind the 2d Battalion to support that unit and to protect the division right flank along the coast. Treitel's 3d Battalion, designated division reserve, moved to an assembly area about 500 yards in rear of the sector held by the 23d and 25th Marines.[47]

At 1535 Lieutenant Colonel Lanigan landed with his group, established the 23d Marines' advance command post, and undertook the task of determining the exact locations of the three battalions of the regiment.[48] Colonel Jones, meanwhile, experienced still more LVT difficulties. Setting out from the control vessel at 1649, Jones' LVT again broke down. This time the colonel and his headquarters group transferred to a DUKW that carried them to an LST where they embarked in another LVT. This vehicle

---

[41] Interviews with Col E. J. Dillon, 29Sep50 and 22Jan51, hereinafter cited as *Dillon*.

[42] Ltr from Col J. R. Lanigan to CMC, 6Nov50, hereinafter cited as *Lanigan*.

[43] *Dillon*.

[44] 23d Mar Report, 19.

[45] Ltr from CO, 23d Mar to CG, 4th Mar Div, 7Sep44. The short lapse between the end of the Saipan operation and Tinian's Jig-Day allowed insufficient time for proper servicing, repair and waterproofing of radio equipment. This, in the words of the regimental operations officer, was "a contributing factor to the breakdown of communications. . . ." Ltr from Maj W. E. Buron to CMC, 11Dec50, hereinafter cited as *Buron*.

[46] *Dillon*.

[47] 23d Mar Report, **21**.

[48] *Lanigan*.

was satisfactory, and the 23d Marines' staff reached shore at 1745.[49]

With the 23d Marines ashore, all nine infantry battalions of the 4th Division had landed; six of these deployed in the south half of the beachhead where trouble was expected.

1ST BATTALION, 8TH MARINES, LANDS

At 1515 General Schmidt, the landing force commander, received a message from General Cates, 4th Division Commander: "Request [that] one battalion landing team 2d Marine Division be ordered to land Beach White 1 this afternoon."[50] Acting on this request, General Schmidt sent a dispatch at 1526 to the Commander Northern Attack Force (Admiral Hill) and the Commanding General, 2d Marine Division (General Watson):

Request one battalion landing team designated by Commanding General 2d Marine Division be landed White 1 beginning 1600. 4th Marine Division reports landing can be effected in LCVP's or LCM's two at a time. Battalion landing team passes to control 4th Marine Division upon landing. Report battalion landing team designated and time landing completed.[51]

General Schmidt's dispatch, logged out at 1526, reached the 2d Marine Division at 1537. The "1600" landing hour was only 23 minutes away. General Watson passed instructions to the 8th Marines to land a battalion "immediately." Inasmuch as Colonel Clarence R. Wallace, the 8th Marines' commander, had previously designated his 1st Battalion as the leading unit in the ship-to-shore movement, no time was lost deliberating on this particular point. Again, however, time and space entered the picture. The time required to draft a message, send it, receive it, deliver it, read it, and act on it, was great and, to higher commanders waiting

for results, disappointing. Lieutenant Colonel Lawrence C. Hays, Jr., commanding the 1st Battalion, did not receive the order to land until 1615. The time consumed in filtering the message from 4th Division to NTLF to 2d Division to 8th Marines to Hays' Battalion was exactly one hour.

Still other delays were forthcoming before the battalion could land: the ship (*Calvert*) in which the unit was embarked had to close the distance to Beach White 1, a move completed at 1705. Then Hays quickly debarked his unit and the lengthy process began of sending two LCVP's at a time into White 1. In the meantime, more instructions channeled through the chain of command: upon landing, the battalion would become 4th Division reserve and would report to the 24th Marines. To determine exactly what employment was contemplated for his unit, Hays landed among the early waves and reported to Colonel Hart, commanding the 24th Marines. Hart instructed Hays to occupy an assembly area in rear of the 2d Battalion, 24th Marines. At 2000 the unit entered in its log: ". . . dug in assigned position."[52]

SHORE PARTY AND BEACH DEVELOPMENT

With the 1st Battalion, 8th Marines, ashore, landing operations ceased for the night. The number of men and the amount of equipment that had poured through the tiny White Beach funnels were impressive. The bulk of the 4th Division was ashore; and the remainder, including the command group and headquarters and service units, would follow the next day. From his command post aboard LST 42,[53] General Cates had excellent communications with

---

[49] 23d Mar Report, 21.

[50] This request was prompted by the situation on the left half of the beachhead, where the 24th Marines' assault battalions were spread thinly and where the reserve battalion would soon be committed. The battalion from the 2d Division would provide reinforcement there. *Rogers.*

[51] NTLF G–3 Operational Dispatches 23–25Jul44.

[52] 2d Mar Div D–3 Journal 17–24Jul44; G–3 Operational Dispatches 23–25Jul44; 4th Mar Div Report, Section III, 19; 24th Mar Report, 8; 1st Bn, 8th Mar Report, 1–2; 8th Mar Report, 1; 2d Mar Div Report, 2.

[53] This marked the first and only time in World War II that Marines used an LST as the location for a division command post. The principal advantage of this arrangement was the immediate availability of preloaded LVT's to expedite displacement of the CP ashore. Satisfactory communication resulted from use of a radio jeep on the LST deck. *Rogers.*

DARKNESS JIG-DAY found about 15,614 Marines of the 4th Division ashore, expecting any or all of the 9,000 Japanese defenders to counterattack. The American lodgement had been bought at a first-day cost of **77** killed, **470** wounded.

subordinate echelons and with his assistant division commander, Brigadier General Samuel C. Cumming, embarked in Patrol Craft 1080.

Priorities on use of the beaches conformed with the necessity of pouring sufficient troop strength ashore to repel any counterattack the Japanese might launch. These priorities did not permit the landing on Jig-Day of any of the 100 LCVP's carrying the division's light vehicles or the eight LCT's and five LCM's transporting heavy trucks. White 1, the only beach suitable for their use, had been fully occupied.

Throughout the day, the shore and beach parties trickled ashore. Advance detachments landed with the assault companies and remaining personnel and equipment came in during short lapses in the bustling beach operations. All men of these units were ashore by 1000 and all equipment by 1400. This unloading had been almost exclusively over White 1, with equipment intended for the other beach being moved from there overland. Since some soldiers and Marines of the Shore Party arrived ashore during the first minutes of the operation,

beach improvement commenced early, long before enemy resistance had been quelled in the area.[54]

The 4th Division Shore Party Commander, Lieutenant Colonel Nelson K. Brown, and the Group Beachmaster, Lieutenant Samuel C. Boardman, USN, were provided a radio-equipped craft from which they could supervise logistical activities on both beaches. These officers made frequent visits during the day to Central and Beach Control Vessels to apprise persons there of existing beach conditions. After spending the night aboard Submarine Chaser 1012 with the Force Beachmaster (Commander C. E. Anderson), Brown and Boardman went ashore the next morning and established their headquarters between the two beaches.

The 10 special portable LVT ramps arrived during the afternoon of Jig-Day on the second

---

[54] Shore Parties on the two beaches were provided as follows: White 1—1341st Engineer Battalion (Army), commanded by Lieutenant Colonel H. A. Gould, USA; White 2—2d Battalion, 20th Marines, commanded by Major J. H. Partridge.

trip of LSD's. Two were launched at about 1700 and sent in with plans to place them in position just south of White 1. One was lost when the LVT carrying it struck a coral head on the edge of the reef and turned over. The other ramp got ashore and was immediately installed, allowing tracked vehicles to negotiate the shore-line cliffs. The remaining eight were launched on Jig-plus 1.

Heavy beach activity emphasized the necessity for early installation of the two pontoon causeway piers, so that LST's and craft could pull alongside and discharge loaded trucks. The piers, towed from Saipan, arrived about dusk; and, under direction of the Force Beachmaster, work on their installation began. By the naval construction platoon's all-night labors, one of these (on White 1) was ready for use by 0600 the next morning. Work on the other, complicated by accurate Japanese artillery and mortar fire, proceeded slowly, and it was not ready until Jig-plus 3.[55]

The only hospital installation ashore on Jig-Day (other than battalion and regimental aid stations) was Company D, 4th Medical Battalion. This unit, together with headquarters and service personnel of the battalion, landed on White 1 at about 1630.[56]

DARKNESS JIG-DAY

By darkness of Jig-Day the Japanese on Tinian were greatly outnumbered. Of 40,000-odd U. S. troops that would eventually land to capture Tinian, about 15,614 were already ashore. The Japanese defenders, if they had not suffered a single casualty, would number only 9,162. U. S. forces, with good communications and superior mobility were under a single commander. The Japanese, on the other hand, had lost most of their communications to the U. S. bombardment, and Army and Navy forces were following the sometimes-dissimilar dictates of their respective commanders.

Tactical surprise, massive power, and hair-trigger control had made possible a completely successful landing over extremely limited beaches. The demonstration off Tinian Town confirmed the defenders' expectations during the crucial period. Japanese attention was focused on a point several miles from the spot where the landings were in fact progressing. By the time the truth became apparent to the enemy, 4th Division Marines had knifed through the narrow White Beaches and firmly established themselves ashore. Even had the Japanese not been fooled, however, their dispositions, inferior strength, and relative lack of mobility (imposed by U. S. supporting arms) would have precluded much early concentration at the north.

The landing force had taken a sizeable bite of Tinian on the first day and had suffered only light casualties (15 killed, 225 wounded).[57] The beachhead (see Map 8), 2,900 yards at its widest point, bulged inland nearly a mile in the center. Generally, the front lines rested upon defensible terrain. In fact, this had been the most important consideration in stopping the day's advance. Everyone expected a Japanese counterattack during the night; all felt confident that it could be stopped, providing sufficient time were available to prepare good positions. Accordingly, General Cates ordered the regiments to stop on defensible terrain at a reasonably early hour (1600–1630) so that lines could be well tied in, fires coordinated, barbed wire strung, and all hands prepared.

Colonel Hart's 24th Marines, manning the left half of the landing force front, moved steadily throughout the day, its 2d Battalion reaching the western edge of Airfield No. 3 and cutting the main road from Ushi Point to the central and southern parts of the island. This push placed the regiment's right along Objective O-1.

For the 1st Battalion, 24th Marines, however, the going had been slower. This unit, attacking northward along the coast, encountered a series of stubborn enemy groups hidden in

---

[55] The naval construction platoon working on the White 2 causeway suffered so many casualties from enemy fire that the Force Beachmaster replaced it with a fresh unit from Saipan. *Brown.*

[56] 4th Mar Div Report, Section III, 20–22.

[57] Figures from 4th Mar Div Report, Section IV, 24. The NTLF Report, 12, lists the same number killed but only 150 wounded.

caves near the water's edge. LVT(A)'s from the 2d Armored Amphibian Battalion, operating from off-shore, placed effective fire into these hideouts, and flame-thrower tanks burned away the matted vegetation; but the Japanese could not be routed. By 1600 when the 1st Battalion stopped for the night, it was still 400 yards short of O–1. More important than gaining O–1 was the preparation of good defenses for the night, and the Marines took entrenching tools in hand and set to work.[58]

Regarding the 1st Battalion's situation as it stopped for the night, Lieutenant Colonel Otto Lessing, the unit's commander, commented:

> . . . the right flank of the battalion had pushed forward vigorously and had reached the west edge of the airfield. . . . This push forward of the right flank seriously extended the battalion front, which would have been even worse had the left of the battalion moved on along the beach. . . . To partially compensate for this over-extension, attached half-tracks and 37mm guns were emplaced directly in the front line . . . the gun crews fought in the dual role of gunners and riflemen.[59]

The attacks of the 1st and 2d Battalions had diverged somewhat during the day so that a potentially dangerous gap developed between the two. Into this at 1630 went the 3d Battalion, which tied in the two interior flanks. As already recounted, the 1st Battalion, 8th Marines, reported in the 24th Regiment's area later in the day and dug in behind the 2d Battalion.[60]

Colonel Batchelder's 25th Marines, meanwhile, negotiated the mined exits from White 2 and pushed toward Mt. Maga's lower slopes. This regiment met somewhat greater resistance than did the 24th Marines. While it encountered no prepared defense positions after assault troops overran beach strong-points, small groups of Japanese remained active in the area, sniping at individuals who appeared in exposed areas and directing mortar and artillery fire upon any cluster of Marines that offered a good target. As the day wore on and the 25th Regiment pushed farther inland, the task of manning the ever-widening front became increasingly difficult. Like other regiments of both divisions, the 25th was operating at reduced strength, its battalions averaging but 565 men each. This condition contributed to the over-extension, and General Cates ordered the 23d Marines to assume a portion of the front, relieving the 25th Regiment's right flank units. (See Map 8.) Thus, with a reduction of its frontage, the 25th established a strong defensive position for the night.[61]

The narrow sector along the beach assigned to the 23d Marines required it to place only its 2d Battalion in the lines. Great depth in this area was accorded by the 1st Battalion, which dug in behind the 2d and gave full attention to this flank. This disposition was adopted because "this looked like [the] most probable counterattack zone."[62] The 3d Battalion, 23d Marines, as previously recounted, occupied an assembly area behind the 23d-25th Marines in division reserve.[63]

To bolster the 2d Battalion in its important position, the 23d Marines' commander, Colonel Jones, attached to it the 37mm platoon that had landed with the 3d Battalion.[64] The order to commence moving forward came at midnight, and the platoon reached its assigned positions at about 0220. Arrival of these guns doubled the number of 37's immediately available to the 2d Battalion. While the newly arrived platoon covered a coral-surfaced road that entered the left of the battalion's front, the other sited its weapons across a broad, flat field near the center

---

[58] 24th Mar report, 7–8.

[59] Ltr from Col O. Lessing to CMC, 11Dec50, hereinafter cited as *Lessing*.

[60] 24th Mar Report, 7–8; 2d Bn, 24th Mar Report, 1; 3d Bn, 24th Mar Report, 1.

[61] 25th Mar Report, 2; 3d Bn, 25th Mar Report, 2.

[62] *Rogers*.

[63] 23d Mar Report, 21.

[64] The 37mm platoons' parent unit was the regimental weapons company, which, in addition to three 37mm platoons, had a platoon of 75mm half-tracks. Normal assignment of 37mm platoons and the one generally used by all regiments at Tinian was: 1st, 2d and 3d Platoons attached to the 1st, 2d and 3d Battalions, respectively.

of the sector. Events would prove this employment wise.[65]

An important factor in the preparation of the division's defensive positions was the arrival of preloaded amphibian tractors at the front lines. These vehicles, carrying ammunition and barbed wire (plus standard loads of rations and water), placed important items where and when they were needed most. After the tractors arrived, Marines strung barbed wire forward of the entire division front to hinder enemy foot troops who might attempt an attack. Large amounts of ammunition were stacked near weapons in anticipation of rapid expenditure during the night. With fresh memories of the *banzai* attack at Tanapag Plain on Saipan, men of the 4th Division addressed full attention to preparing for another such thrust.

Along the front of the entire beachhead, Marines laid machine guns to insure interlocking bands of fire and assigned the 60mm and 81mm mortars target areas that would fill "dead spots," registered 75mm pack howitzers to cover the most likely routes of enemy approach, and ranged in weapons that could fire illuminating shells when and if the need arose for a lighted battlefield.

Front line Marines, well indoctrinated by Saipan experiences, needed no encouragement to dig their foxholes deep. They placed hand grenades and extra supplies of ammunition close to their positions so that there would be no fumbling in the dark.

In position astride the main road from the south to Ushi Point Airfield, the 2d Battalion, 24th Marines, took at least one significant security precaution. Expecting enemy forces to use the road in any counterattack effort, Major Garretson, the battalion commander, stationed a 15-man combat outpost about 400 yards to the front. This detachment would engage any small enemy groups seeking information and attempt to mislead them as to the actual main battle position. In the event of a large-scale attack, this outpost would withdraw and alert front-line Marines. Extremely close contact with the enemy frequently forbade use of such combat outposts in the Pacific War.

ENEMY OPERATIONS[66]

Anyone facing the bleak prospects that the Japanese did on 24 July 1944 would naturally embrace gratefully any good news—or, indeed, even any good rumor. Evidence that the Japanese believed that help would reach them is contained in the diary of Takayoshi Yamazaki (rank unknown), a member of the 1st Battalion, 135th Infantry Regiment:

24 July—We heard the story about the shift in the Cabinet [Premier Hideki Tojo and his entire staff resigned on 18 July 1944] and an order to complete the 4th Airfield (inland from Tinian Town . . .) by the 28th. It raised our morale to expect our planes. All the platoon rejoiced to the news.[67]

Colonel Ogata, commanding the Japanese defense force, had experienced a day of frustrations. From his command post atop Mt. Lasso, he got but infrequent glimpses at what was taking place. U. S. planes, artillery, mortars and naval gunfire maintained such a continuous hail of shells around his installation that to emerge from its protection was to invite death. Such information as funneled to him from subordinate echelons was sketchy and confusing; no part of the Japanese defense network was exempt from U. S. shelling. Many times, when there was important information that should have been sent or received by Ogata, communication failures prevented delivery. In other cases, messengers carried information to or from the colonel, arriving at their destination so tardily as virtually to nullify the news' value.

Captain Oya, commanding Japanese naval forces on the island, also found Jig-Day conditions difficult. His command post, located in a cave in the high ground behind Tinian Town, was the object of almost constant pounding by

---

[65] Ltr from Maj J. W. Sperry (with encl by Lt J. G. Tillis) to author, 16Oct50, hereinafter cited as *Sperry-Tillis*. Ltr from Maj D. S. Callaham to CMC, 27Dec50, hereinafter cited as *Callaham*.

[66] 4th Mar Div Representative Translations Made on Tinian, IX, Reconstruction of Enemy Movements from interrogation of six prisoners of war; NTLF G–2 Report, 9–10 and Periodic Report 40. Reactions of enemy commanders described in this subsection are the author's surmise based upon the above listed sources.

[67] 4th Mar Div Representative Translations Made on Tinian, VII, Diary of Takayoshi Yamazaki.

U. S. planes and ships. In the morning when his coast defense guns hit a U. S. battleship (the *Colorado*) and a destroyer (the *Norman Scott*) and his mortars discouraged a U. S. landing attempt at Tinian Town (the 2d Division's feint), Oya had reason to feel at least mildly elated. After that, however, the U. S. bombardment thundered monotonously around him, hour after hour, and his weapons seemed incapable of further retaliation. More frustrating than this, Oya received word of a U. S. landing on the tiny northwestern beaches, and he knew that most of his coast defense guns were positioned only for firing to sea, that the very nature of the installations would not permit these weapons to turn 90 degrees to strike the U. S. beachhead.

Presented with this situation, the two enemy commanders bent every effort to influence the course of the battle. With shattered communications, their hands were nearly tied. Ogata's operation plan, however, directing his units ". . . to destroy the enemy at the beach . . .," amounted to a standing operating procedure for Japanese in a situation such as this.[68] In the absence of further instructions, subordinate Japanese commanders would follow that dictate. There were four infantry battalions available to attempt that task.

The 1st Battalion, 50th Infantry, which had had some of its elements disposed on the landing beaches and the remainder in the Mt. Lasso area, was handiest to the U. S. beachhead. This unit had more time and better opportunity to observe U. S. defensive preparations than did other Japanese organizations. Also reasonably close at hand was the 2d Battalion, 50th Infantry Regiment, initially assigned to defend the Asiga Bay area. Most elements of this unit were disposed less than three miles from the U. S. beachhead. During daylight hours this distance would be extremely difficult to cover; after dark, with U. S. planes out of the sky, the march and deployment could be executed without excessive losses or tiring of troops.

The 3d Battalion, 50th Infantry Regiment, assigned to the Southern Defense Sector (see Map 4, page 13), remained in its area, presumably at Colonel Ogata's order. At this early time in the operation, the colonel could not abandon completely his deduction that an amphibious assault would come over the Tinian Town beaches. If he pulled the 3d Battalion from this area, no defense against U. S. landings there would be provided.

Besides, he had already issued orders [69] to his Mobile Counterattack Force (1st Battalion, 135th Infantry) to ". . . advance rapidly to the place of landings, depending on the situation and attack." From its assembly position in the Marpo area the unit began its long march to the U. S. beachhead. Movement along roads or through open areas was denied by American fire power and aircraft. The battalion had to dodge and straggle its way, column of files, along the sides of roads, where foliage provided concealment from the ubiquitous U. S. aircraft. At many points along the route, unobserved fire from ships and artillery thundered down upon the rambling column; but, faithful to his mission, the battalion commander (Captain Izumi) encouraged his men on to the north. That the entire move was observed at only one time by U. S. aircraft reflects creditably upon Captain Izumi's eye for terrain.

The only Japanese naval troops moving toward the U. S. beachhead at dusk were those assigned to various jobs around Ushi Point Airfield. Though not trained for an infantry mission, they had a fanatic will to close with the Americans, a will that compensated only in part for their shortcomings in technique. Armed with rifles, machine guns (in large part dismounted aircraft guns), and grenades, this conglomerate force avoided the bulging center of the U. S. beachhead, marched instead to a position from which it could strike the extreme left (north) U. S. flank along the coast.

THE COUNTERATTACKS [70]

At dark, Marines put aside shovels in favor of firearms. Though tired (they had never really

---

[68] Just as much S. O. P. was the Marine determination to defeat such enemy efforts—as they had on so many previous occasions.

[69] See Colonel Ogata's plan, page 14.

[70] General details on "The Counterattacks" were derived from the following sources: 4th Mar Div Report, Section IV, 25, and Annex B, 18–20; Carl W. Proehl, *The Fourth Marine Division in World War II* (Wash-

caught up on their rest since D-Day [15 June] on Saipan), Marines resisted the tendency for fatigue to induce carelessness. Their attitude of business-like caution reflected their Saipan slogan—"Stay alert"—a serious jest typifying the atmosphere of war.[71]

The Japanese commander dispatched several small reconnaissance groups at dusk to glean information regarding U. S. dispositions, information upon which he would base his counterattack plans. While most of these Japanese crept along just forward of the lines until chased by Marine fire, a two-man reconnaissance detail climbed up on a battered building forward of the 24th Marines and audaciously (or stupidly) commenced jotting notes about, or drawing sketches of, the front lines. This impudent gesture was rewarded with a thundering concentration of U. S. artillery fire.

At midnight Marines noticed a marked increase in the tempo of Japanese artillery fire falling in the beachhead area. Where previously they had endured only desultory mortar fire, midnight brought shells from Japanese field guns. This fire gradually increased in volume until the anticipated attack became reality. Between 0200 and 0530, the Japanese launched their assaults. The main spearheads came at three points: the extreme left flank, the extreme right flank, and near the center of the beachhead (see Map 8).

The Attack on the Left

The attack on the left came first and lasted longest. At 0200, men of the 1st Battalion, 24th Marines, straining their eyes through the black moonless night, suddenly saw a compact group of Japanese a short 100 yards away.[72]

The Marines opened fire. The compact group became a screaming mass of attackers as the first Marine bullets and shells found targets. Now the shadows were alive with about 600 leaping Japanese naval troops, loaded with aggressive spirit, requiring no instructions to make their screaming charge. Marines called flares into action; the battlefield became light. Marines needed no orders either: the 37mm guns sprayed canister; machine guns cut into the enemy area with grazing fire; rifles pounded out at sighted or suspected targets; mortars crunched into the defilade areas;[73] artillery crashed steadily behind the Japanese to shatter and destroy any reinforcement group.

The tightly packed foe was a choice target for all these weapons, and hundreds of shells lashed his ranks. At no time did the enemy penetrate the 1st Battalion; but extremely heavy pressure against Company A, the unit that bore the brunt, caused the battalion commander to reinforce it with engineers, corpsmen, communicators, naval gunfire liaison and shore party personnel.[74]

The fight continued hot and heavy until about 0545, when dawn and the vigor of the enemy effort broke simultaneously. Medium tanks from Company B, 4th Tank Battalion, entered the fray at this time and stopped all further thrusts at the Marines' lines. Many Japanese, convinced that all was lost, committed suicide with grenades. While armored amphibians afloat fired on enemy groups hiding along the coast, Marines of the 1st Battalion, 24th Marines, mopped up the area to their front, an activity completed by 0700. They counted 476 Japanese bodies, most of them within 100 yards of Company A's lines.[75] Although no figures are available for Marine casualties in this action, the battalion commander estimated that ". . . Company A was reduced to about 30 men with usable weapons before the enemy was repulsed."[76]

---

ington: Infantry Journal Press, 1946), 101–105; Capt John W. Thomason, III, "The Fourth Marine Division at Tinian," *Marine Corps Gazette*, Jan. 45, 7–8. Sources for specific details are cited at appropriate points.

[71] Never ones to allow a war to destroy their sense of humor, Marines amused themselves at odd moments following the Saipan battle by tossing half or whole bricks at one another, shouting an oft-repeated caution at the moment they let fly: "Stay alert." Most of the bricks were dodged or caught.

[72] The officer who commanded Company A in this action gave the opinion that the enemy troops were marching along the beach road, unaware that they were so close to U. S. lines. *Schechter*.

---

[73] "During the height of the action, over 1,500 rounds were fired [from two 81mm mortars], most of these during a 2 hour period." *Lessing*.

[74] *Lessing*.

[75] 24th Mar Report, 8. *Schechter*.

[76] *Lessing*.

The Attack on the Center [77]

Enemy movement to final assault positions and preparations for an attack against the beachhead center created such a stir that Marine units involved were at a 100 percent alert when the real trouble came. Shortly after midnight the 15-man outpost from the 2d Battalion, 24th Marines, returned with a breathless report that the Japanese were coming, and in great numbers. In addition, a number of "feeler" patrols had prodded the 25th Marines' lines for several hours, indicating by their behavior that a stronger thrust would come.

The first of a series of attacks against the center—near the boundary between the 24th and 25th Marines—began at 0230. This effort faltered and broke under a fusillade of small-arms, mortar and 37mm fire. But this was not the end. After bouncing off, recoiling, and re-organizing, the Japanese—elements of the 1st and 2d Battalions, 50th Infantry, and of the 1st Battalion, 135th Infantry—struck again. This time, though many of the attackers fell forward of the lines, others penetrated a weak spot at the boundary between the two Marine regiments. About 200 Japanese poured through this spot before the flow could be stopped. After pausing in a swamp behind the lines, the enemy force speared out in two prongs: one straight into the beachhead toward U. S. artillery positions, the other turning west into the 25th Marines' rear areas. The latter group of Japanese attained first contact when they met a well-prepared support platoon from the 3d Battalion, 25th Marines. Positioned to contain just such a penetration as had occurred, the Marines quickly eliminated this Japanese threat, killing 91 in a brief, violent skirmish.[78]

The other prong pushed deep into the rear of the beachhead, finally reached the 75mm howitzer firing positions of the 2d Battalion, 14th Marines. Battery D, firing a mission for the 24th Marines, suddenly found itself beset from the front by many determined Japanese. Marines not actively engaged in servicing the howitzers rallied to the defense of their positions with small arms, while the remainder continued firing an artillery mission for the 24th Regiment. Later, as pressure mounted, all hands turned to the task of stopping the Japanese close at hand.[79] At this juncture the .50-caliber machine guns of the other two batteries (E and F) of the battalion levelled a heavy volume of enfilading fire into the area forward of besieged Battery D. This fire, in the words of the battalion executive officer, "literally tore the Japanese . . . to pieces." [80]

To reinforce Battery D in its bitter fight, Company C, 8th Marines, arrived at 0445. But by then the situation was well in hand; the Japanese had faltered and stopped before the deluge of small-arms fire. Morning revealed about 100 dead Japanese in the area,[81] while the artillerymen had lost but two of their number—both killed manning a .50-caliber machine gun with Battery D. The only Japanese penetration of the night had shattered itself against a prepared rear area.

Up at the front, meanwhile, Marines of the 25th Regiment and the right (2d) battalion of the 24th Regiment, fought off a series of frontal rushes upon their positions. In each case the Japanese were stopped at the barbed wire forward of the Marines' lines. The all-night firing had taken a heavy toll of the

---

[77] Unless otherwise indicated, this section was derived from the following sources: 24th Mar Report, 8; 25th Mar Report, 2; 14th Mar Report, 2; 1st Bn, 8th Mar Report, 2; *Garretson; Ross.*

[78] One group of Japanese occupied a small wood near the lines of Company K, 25th Marines, causing the unit commander, Captain Thomas S. Witherspoon, to order his 60mm mortars to plaster the area. The mortar section leader, however, pointed out that the wood contained a Japanese torpedo dump, detonation of which might prove dangerous to the Marines. Witherspoon

answered in the best naval tradition: "Damn the torpedoes, fire away." Unpublished narrative of activities of the 3d Battalion, 25th Marines, at Saipan and Tinian, entitled "Saipan Saga" and "Tinian—An Encore," author not shown, 2. (Copy available in Marine Corps Historical Division.)

[79] Ltr from Lt Col G. B. Wilson, Jr., to CMC, 12Dec50. Ltr from Lt Col K. C. Houston to CMC, 15Nov50.

[80] Ltr from Maj W McReynolds to CMC, 8Jan51. Source indicates that Batteries E and F continued firing normal artillery missions throughout this fight.

[81] 14th Mar Report, 2 gives 99; Major McReynolds, 2/14's executive officer, says 110.

Marines' ammunition stocks, however, and by shortly before daylight there was concern along the lines that another heavy attack might exhaust supplies.

Dawn came first. Attached tanks moved up at once to range the area forward of the lines. They blasted points of resistance with their 75mm guns, killing or chasing such few Japanese as had survived the night melee.

Nearly 500 Japanese were killed in the attacks against the center of the beachhead and in the skirmishes behind the lines following the penetration.

The Attack on the Right [82]

The third and last major enemy effort struck the extreme right (south) flank of the beachhead at 0330. The 2d Battalion, 23d Marines, in position along the coast, bore the brunt of this thrust, although the 2d Battalion, 25th Marines, also figured prominently in the action. Moving north along the coastal road, the enemy force consisted of five or six light tanks (about half of those available to the Japanese at Tinian) with infantrymen riding and following on foot. [83]

First warning of the enemy move came when Marine listening posts stationed along the road a short distance forward of the lines reported enemy tanks rumbling in from the south. With the tanks an estimated 400 yards in front of the lines, Marine artillery opened up. The tanks came on. Ready for just this situation, U. S. ships began firing illuminating shells over the area, virtually turning night into day. Bazookas, 75mm half-tracks, and 37mm guns attached to three battalions now went into action. [84] One of the 37mm platoons, positioned astride the coral road, levelled point-blank fires into the enemy armor. [85] Even so, one fast-moving tank weathered a 37mm hit and drove through the front lines into rear areas before a Marine bazookaman finished it off. An officer present on the scene described the action as he saw it:

The three lead tanks broke through our wall of fire. One began to glow blood-red, turned crazily on its tracks, and careened into a ditch. A second, mortally wounded, turned its machine guns on its tormentors, firing into the ditches in a last desperate effort to fight its way free. One hundred yards more and it stopped dead in its tracks. The third tried frantically to turn and then retreat, but our men closed in, literally blasting it apart. . . . Bazookas knocked out the fourth tank with a direct hit which killed the driver. The rest of the crew piled out of the turret, screaming. The fifth tank, completely surrounded, attempted to flee. Bazookas made short work of it. Another hit set it afire, and its crew was cremated. [86]

Thus, five tanks stood immobile on the field of battle. [87] If a sixth accompanied this incursion, it escaped, since there was no trace of it the following morning when Marines moved through the area.

Despite the fact that their armor was gone, enemy foot soldiers from the 1st and 2d Battalions, 50th Infantry, and the 1st Battalion, 135th Infantry, pressed toward the Marines. The fighting that ensued was close-in and savage, but the Japanese never cracked the tight

---

[82] Except as otherwise indicated, this section derives from the following sources: 23d Mar Report, 21; *L. R. Jones; Dillon; Sperry-Tillis; Callaham;* Memo from Maj W. L. Dick to author, 25Sep50, hereinafter cited as *Dick.*

[83] Although most sources (including the 4th Division's Intelligence Report) gave six as the number of attacking Japanese tanks, the battalion commander of 2/23, who had reason to know, had stated that only five tanks participated. *Dillon.*

[84] Though the principal thrust was against 1/23, and 2/25, several of the tanks could be seen from the right flank of 1/25, and the attached 37mm platoon opened up and scored hits on three of the tanks. Ltr from Maj H. D. Strunk to CMC, 21Dec50.

[85] The commander of this platoon, Lieutenant James G. Tillis, noted that "our armor piercing shells penetrated the tanks from side to side in the upper body and turret."

[86] Lt Jim G. Lucas, Assistant Division Public Relations Officer, quoted in Proehl, *op. cit.,* 101.

[87] One Marine bazookaman, Corporal Bascom J. Jordan, achieved hits on two Japanese tanks. After missing with his first round, Jordan drew the fire of two tanks in his direction. His second shell found its mark, striking and disabling one of the machines. The other tank then turned and maneuvered away. Afraid that the kill might be denied him, Jordan jumped from his foxhole, pursued the tank halfway across an open field and achieved a hit. Three rounds, two tanks. *Dillon. Sperry.* Ltr from Maj H. V. Joslin to author, 17Dec50. Bronze Star citation for Corporal B. J. Jordan for service at Tinian, 25Jul44.

THESE FAITHFUL JAPANESE were ordered to "destroy the enemy at the beach." By issuing this impossible order, the Japanese Island Commander lost about one-seventh of his total strength in a scattered series of aggressive but poorly coordinated counterthrusts on the first night.

defense. The few who seeped through the lines met a quick end at the hands of the 23d Marines' reserve (1st Battalion), positioned to provide depth in this precise area.

The operations officer of the 2d Battalion, 23d Marines, described the weird termination of the Japanese activities:

. . . as it began to get light, Jap bodies began to fly ten to fifteen feet in the air in the area in front of our lines. . . . We knew that hand grenades did not have the power to blow a man's body that high and could not figure out what was happening. [Later] we moved out to mop up. . . . It turned out that about fifty percent of the dead Japs carried magnetic mines and had obviously been ordered to break through our lines and destroy the tanks in the rear of us. . . . The Japs who

were wounded and unable to flee were placing the tank mines under their bodies and tapping the detonators. . . .[88]

Daylight revealed that the enemy had expended 267 men and five tanks (of 12 on the island) against the right flank of the beachhead with no success.

[88] *Sperry*. Two minor mishaps accompanied the mop-up in the 23d Marines' sector. One medium tank of Company C, 4th Tank Battalion, ran over a dead enemy soldier who still clutched a bangalore torpedo. The resulting explosion blew six blocks off the tank's left track but did not harm the crew. Another tank incurred minor damage when a Japanese rose from the dead around him and attached a magnetic mine. A hail of Marine fire dropped him almost where he had lain before. Co C, 4th Tk Bn Report, 3.

During Japanese attacks against the left, center and right, naval supporting ships assisted the Marines by illuminating the battle area. The destroyer *Monssen*, for example, fired a solid hour of starshells forward of the 2d Battalion, 24th Marines, during the critical period of the counterattacks. In addition to the illumination fires, ships executed several important neutralization missions. At 0450, the cruiser *Cleveland* placed ten minutes' fire on Mt. Lasso's eastern slopes where enemy muzzle flashes had been observed. At 0500 (when the 4th Division was most vulnerable because of depleted ammunition stocks) two destroyers and a cruiser delivered supporting fires without benefit of shore spot on areas requested by Headquarters, 4th Division.[89]

A night action involving several hundred attackers supported by tanks cannot, by its very nature, be described with chess-like clarity. No two pairs of eyes saw the battle in exactly the

----

[89] TF 52 Report, 68–69.

same way; and, though the vital features of the engagement fit neatly together, the various marginal details present a jig-saw puzzle with too many pieces. For example, a bazookaman who hit an enemy tank, which shortly afterward burst into flame, would naturally claim the kill, never realizing that another bazookaman and two other 37mm guns had scored on the same tank at the same time. So here, in this constructed instance, destruction of one tank could have been reported four times—with four slightly different versions of how it was done. Unit commanders are often modest about their own exploits but seldom about those of their subordinates. A total of the various units' claims exceeds by many times the actual number of tanks committed to the attack. This fact comes as no disparagement of the Marines' excellent efforts. They were trained, equipped and prepared to stop the Japanese. They did.

The counterattacks were over. Strewn along the 4th Marine Division front were the bodies of 1,241 Japanese, of which about 700 belonged to organized infantry units. Thus in one frantic

JAPANESE TANK, one of five knocked out during the first night's battle. All Japanese tanks on Tinian were light models mounting 37mm guns and 7.7cm machine guns.

night, Colonel Ogata lost over one-seventh of his total defense force and over one-fifth of his organized infantry strength.[90] In addition to those killed in the night counterattacks, it must be presumed that some Japanese were wounded but managed to get away.[91]

Marine identification of enemy dead on the morning following the counterattacks revealed that a large portion of the known organized infantry strength had participated in the night thrusts and had suffered a costly defeat. In particular, the tremendous number of bodies identified as belonging to the 1st Battalion, 135th Infantry (the Mobile Counterattack Force), indicated that this unit had sustained especially heavy losses,[92] an evaluation confirmed on 26 July by a Japanese prisoner who stated that the battalion had been "practically annihilated." [93] The 4th Division intelligence officer attached importance to the appearance of the 1st Battalion, 135th Infantry:

Captured documents and interrogation of POW's indicate that [the unit] was scheduled for defense in the Tinian Town area. Commitment of this unit to this morning's counterattack is an indication that the enemy's reserves are being depleted.[94]

The 4th Marine Division's post-operation evaluation—"It was there and then that [we] broke the Jap's back in the battle for Tinian" [95]—appears accurate. It is pertinent to note, however, that this fact was not realized on the morning after the counterattack. Over six years later the division intelligence officer wrote: "We still believed the enemy capable of a harder fight . . . and from day to day during our advance expected a bitter fight that never materialized.[96]

Marines had fought and won an important, decisive fight. The Japanese commander had spent a large, irreplaceable portion of his garrison, while Marine losses were extremely light.[97] Considerable time and effort had been invested profitably in preparations for the Japanese counterattack. The disposition and strength of the Marine defense foredoomed Colonel Ogata's plan to failure. The Marines hoped for more such night attacks, since previous experience had taught that this type of fighting was altogether easier than digging the Japanese from their final retreats. With all the excitement, screaming and local crises, the *banzai* attacks were invariably cheaper and more decisive than the so-called "mopping-up" operations.

---

[90] Both of these fractions are based upon the original known strength of Japanese units on Tinian and do not take into account the number of casualties they suffered during the U. S. bombardment phase or during the 4th Division's landing and initial advance inland.

[91] The 4th Division's Unit History estimated the total of wounded Japanese as 700 to 800. In this battle the Japanese used sheets of corrugated tin as stretchers upon which to evacuate their casualties. Handling of these improvised litters made a racket audible to everyone thereabouts.

[92] 4th Mar Div Periodic Report (1800, 24 July, to 1800, 25 July).

[93] 4th Mar Div Periodic Report 73 (1800, 25 July, to 1800, 26 July).

---

[94] 4th Mar Div Periodic Report 72 (1800, 24 July, to 1800, 25 July).

[95] 4th Mar Div Report, 25.

[96] *McCormick.*

[97] Although no figures are available for this phase alone, the number of killed and wounded in the entire division is estimated at less than 100.

CHAPTER III

Surge to the South

JIG-PLUS 1—25 JULY 1944

Land the 2d Marine Division, expand the beachhead; these were the principal Northern Troops and Landing Force plans for 25 July. The 4th Division had fought most of the night; some reorganization and considerable resupply of ammunition would be necessary before it could continue the attack. Accordingly, the attack hour was delayed from 0700 to 1000. The 2d Marine Division, in the meantime, would pour ashore as rapidly as the meager beach facilities permitted. Then it would "be prepared to conduct offensive operations on NTLF order in a zone of action to be designated." Further, the division would "attach elements of RCT 8 [the 8th Marines] upon landing to 4thMarDiv." [1]

The 8th Regiment, which already had its 1st Battalion ashore, was first. Colonel Wallace and his headquarters landed on White 1 at about 0630, followed by the 2d Battalion (Lieutenant Colonel Lane C. Kendall) at 0922 and the 3d Battalion (Lieutenant Colonel Gavin C. Humphrey) at 1107. Japanese artillery shells, fired at long range, splashed sporadically and ineffectively around the double column of boats (LCVP's) carrying men of the 8th Regiment.

At the reef off White 1, the landing craft dropped their ramps to allow the Marines to splash the final 100-odd yards ashore.

Lieutenant Colonel Hays' 1st Battalion, 8th Marines, meanwhile, began the day under control of the 24th Regiment, in which capacity it received orders to relieve the 1st Battalion, 24th Marines, along the coast on the extreme left flank of the beachhead. This shift was accomplished at 0920, almost the same moment that Hays' unit reverted to its parent regiment, the newly landed 8th Marines. The latter, now attached to the 4th Division, assumed the northernmost sector of the front. [2]

The 2d Marines (Colonel Walter J. Stuart) commenced debarkation from transports (APA's and AP's) at about noon and began landing on White 1 as soon as the 8th Regiment's last units had cleared. Battalions landed in the sequence, 2d (Lieutenant Colonel Richard C. Nutting), 1st (Lieutenant Colonel Wood B. Kyle) and 3d (Lieutenant Colonel Walter F. Layer). As elements of the regiment splashed ashore throughout the afternoon, each successive group moved directly to an assembly area about 500–600 yards inland from White 1 where the unit spent the night. [3]

---

[1] NTLF Report, 12. NTLF Operation Order 31–44.

[2] 8th Mar Report, 1.

[3] 2d Mar Report, 1.

WADING ASHORE. Two regiments (2d and 8th) of the 2d Division splashed ashore from landing boats at the reef's edge on 25 July. Leisurely attitude is explained by the absence of resistance.

Unlike the 2d and 8th Regiments, which had been lifted from Saipan to Tinian in APA's and AP's, the 6th Marines made the move in LST's. By mid-morning of 25 July the regiment was alerted to the possibility of landing one of its battalions over White 1 during the afternoon. As the day dragged on, however, and the flood of men and equipment over White 1 continued, the plans were changed: at 1622 the battalion was ordered to land on White 2. Colonel James P. Riseley, commanding the 6th Marines, passed the directive to the 2d Battalion, which immediately started its long column of LVT's toward the beach. By 1930, long after sunset, Lieutenant Colonel Edmund B. Games reported his 2d Battalion completely ashore and assembled in division reserve about 700 yards inland from White 2.[4]

Earlier in the day, while elements of the 2d Division engaged in their long, measured movement from transports to White 1, the advance command group of the 4th Marine Division moved ashore over White 2. General Cates and the remainder of his headquarters group followed over the same beach and, by 1115, less than half an hour after leaving LST 42, opened

the 4th Division command post about 400 yards inland, midway between the two beaches. This was the signal for General Cumming, the assistant division commander, to head shoreward from Patrol Craft 1080 with his group. The latter landed at 1330.[5]

The 2d Tank Battalion, attached to the 4th Division, landed over a three-day period. One platoon of light (flame-thrower) tanks from Company D, after a direct move from Saipan in landing craft, had come ashore during the evening of Jig-Day and early on the next morning. Two mediums from Company C executed the LSD-to-shore move on the morning of 25 July, followed in the early evening by all except two platoons of the battalion. Finally, at 0630, 26 July, the last of the 2d Tank Battalion reached the beach. With the exception of two medium and two light (flame-thrower) tanks that operated with the 1st Battalion, 8th Marines, on the left of the beachhead, machines of the 2d Tank Battalion did not participate in the Jig-plus 1 attack.[6] The 4th Marine Di-

---

[4] 6th Mar Report, **1.**

[5] 4th Mar Div Report, Section III, 20 and Section **IV**, 26. *Rogers.*

[6] 2d Tank Battalion Report, 1, and page 1 of Companies A, B, C and D Reports.

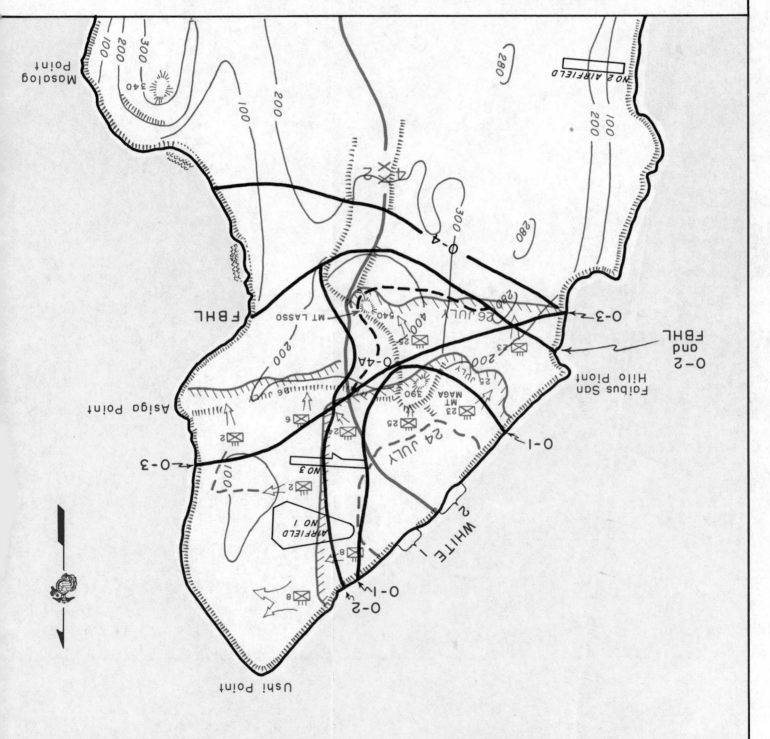

vision had not speeded the landing or employment of attached 2d Division tanks because: First, the situation did not require their use; and second, the beaches were fully occupied with the landings of matériel and personnel deemed more important to the early effort.

At 1430, 25 July, General Watson, commanding the 2d Marine Division, closed his command post aboard the *Cavalier*, embarked with his headquarters group in four landing craft, and headed for the beach. During the movement, the column of boats was bracketed by shells from an enemy artillery piece but no rounds actually found their intended mark. General Watson opened his command post ashore at 1600 only 75 yards southeast of General Cates' 4th Division installation. The 2d Division, less the 8th Marines (attached to the 4th Division), was now in position as landing force reserve.[7]

The congestion resulting from moving so many troops and so much equipment over limited beaches precluded displacement to Tinian of the NTLF command post. Until 28 July, therefore, General Harry Schmidt remained at Charan Kanoa on Saipan, from where he directed over-all landing force activities.

Expansion of the Beachhead

While elements of the 2d Division filtered ashore, the 4th Division expanded its holdings as ordered by General Schmidt: ". . . seize division O-2 line and be prepared to seize FBHL on NTLF order."[8] (See Map 9, facing page 71.) The division pushed forward at 1000. "Forward" varied from southwest, south, southeast, east, to northeast. The right regiment (23d) pressed southwest toward Faibus San Hilo Point; the left regiment (8th) struggled northward toward Ushi Point; the two center regiments (24th and 25th) fanned out to the south, southeast and east. Until the northern third of the island could be cleared, the Force Beachhead Line secured, and the attack

reoriented to the south, the front would retain its crescent-like shape.

In the 23d Marines' zone of action only one battalion had been committed during the previous night. That battalion, the 2d, had spent a busy, sleepless night. Therefore, to give maximum momentum to his Jig-plus 1 attack, the regimental commander ordered the 1st Battalion to relieve the 2d. The 2d Battalion when relieved would pass to NTLF reserve, replacing Major Treitel's 3d Battalion, which would shift to 23d Marines' reserve.

The 23d Marines' zone remained sufficiently narrow throughout the day to permit it to attack with the 1st Battalion in the assault, 3d Battalion following in regimental reserve. Using tank-infantry action to good advantage, the 1st Battalion swept through heavy cane fields and dense underbrush in its assigned zone along the coast, mopping up Japanese stragglers who remained active following their unsuccessful counterattack. Opposition on the 23d Marines' front was characterized as "light," and by 1637 the lines had moved just past Objective O-1 (see Map 9). To tighten the lines for the night, the 3d Battalion moved up on the left of the 1st, relieving some of the latter's elements in the process. The enemy's decisive defeat of the preceding night did not discount the possibility that he might try again, and the Marines addressed full attention to preparation of a firm battle position.[9]

On the 23d Marines' left, the 25th Regiment faced one of the most formidable terrain obstacles on Tinian: the sheer, half-moon-shaped northern cliff face of 390-foot[10] Mt. Maga. But the abruptness of this approach came as no surprise to the Marines. All regimental, battalion, and many company commanders had made a detailed air reconnaissance over Mt. Maga (and other Tinian features) before Jig-Day. The hill's complex features were so well fixed in these leaders' minds that the good and

---

[7] 2d Mar Div Report, 2. Ltr from Col J. T. Wilbur to CMC, 6Dec50.

[8] NTLF Opn Order 31-44. This was the first reference to O-2. The landing plan had designated but two objectives: O-1 and the FBHL.

[9] 23d Mar Report, 21. *Dick.*

[10] This elevation is from a captured Japanese map, which, presumably, was more accurate than the 440 feet shown on U. S. maps. Action reports of the 1st and 3d Battalions, 25th Marines, refer to this height as Hill 440.

bad approaches were known. Avoiding the precipitous northern approach, Colonel Batchelder ordered his 1st and 3d Battalions to swing to left and right, respectively, and envelop the heights from the more gradual east and west approaches. The 2d Battalion, meanwhile, by holding a position facing directly into the cliff line, would hold some enemy attention on the frontal approach.

The 1st Battalion's move via the eastern route was attended with some difficulty. After an easy maneuver into position preparatory to the final ascent, the Marines suddenly received a shower of Japanese small-arms fire. An unsupported infantry assault of the slopes in the face of this fire seemed unnecessary, so the battalion commander, Lieutenant Colonel Mustain, ordered the attached tanks (a platoon of mediums and three lights) to move to the top, locate and blast the enemy riflemen. The only route suitable for such a climb was a road, the lower portion of which had been mined by the defenders. Engineers of Company A, 20th Marines, immediately began clearance operation and in a short time reported the road ready for use. Tanks then drove alone to the heights, found no Japanese, and returned to the base of the hill with their negative report. But when the infantry again prepared to start up the slope, Japanese (who had lain low during the tanks' probes) again rained down fire.

This time, however, the Marines spotted the fire's source. Immediately, Mustain employed his 81mm mortars and tanks (firing from the hill's base) for delivery of heavy concentrations on the enemy positions. These measures were adequate; shortly after noon, Mustain's men swept unopposed to the top.

Here, however, the unit was alone. The 3d Battalion had not yet appeared on the western flank, and elements of the 24th Marines had not come abreast on the east. When apprised of this situation, the regimental commander ordered the 1st Battalion to hold its advance.

At this juncture, as Marines of the 1st Battalion reorganized after their ascent, Japanese rifles and machine guns positioned on a plateau to the south suddenly opened up. When enemy mortars joined the small-arms weapons in laying down a hail of shells and bullets, the assault

companies withdrew about 200 yards to an area affording better cover. Again, Marine tanks and mortars went to work; the enemy was killed or chased, and the battalion retook its former positions.

The other claw of the 25th Marines' pincer, meanwhile, closed on the hill from the west. Preceding the 3d Battalion's 1000 jump-off, 12 Army Air Force P-47's strafed and bombed along the chosen route to Mt. Maga. Although well performed, this strike neutralized only part of the enemy positions. Almost as soon as the battalion—in a formation of companies on column—started along its envelopment route, enemy riflemen hidden along the hill's lower slopes issued a stream of bullets that threatened to impose heavy casualties. In answer to this challenge, the battalion commander, Lieutenant Colonel Chambers, sent attached tanks and combat engineers (carrying flame-throwers, bazookas and demolitions) to assist the leading unit (Company L). This combination proved effective, and resistance soon became only sporadic.

The 3d Battalion then continued its advance but soon stopped when the battalion commander received word of a gap between his unit and the 23d Marines.[11] While waiting for re-establishment of contact, Colonel Chambers requested and received naval gunfire (the battleship *California*) and artillery (1st Battalions, 10th and 14th Marines) bombardment of suspicious areas to his front. The situation was far from static; even though the battalion held its front lines more or less stationary, combat patrols from Company L searched along Mt. Maga's western slopes with the object of destroying enemy weapons that might later impede the advance. These activities bore fruit; by 1500 the patrols had destroyed three unmanned 47mm guns emplaced along the hill's base.

After the 23d Marines came abreast, the 3d Battalion, 25th, resumed its push, following through the area cleared by its leading company. The swing to the top and establishment of contact with the 1st Battalion there proceeded without unusual incident. (See Map 9.)

---

[11] The 3/25 Report blames the gap on "the failure of the 23d Marines to come abreast."

Twenty-five Japanese civilians found in the area were sent to the rear for internment.

Thus, the 25th Regiment secured an important objective. Looming even more conspicuous 2,000 yards to the southeast was Mt. Lasso, but its approaches were slightly gentler and the routes to it somewhat less exposed. As the Marines dug in for the night, concertina barbed wire was strung forward of the lines. The value of this type of obstacle had been well illustrated on many occasions.

For the purpose of establishing combat outposts for the night, Company A, V Amphibious Corps Reconnaissance Battalion, sent one platoon to the 23d Marines, another to the 25th. Neither platoon functioned in the intended manner, however, both being ordered into front line positions. They rejoined their parent company the following morning.[12]

While the 25th Marines engaged in its double envelopment of Mt. Maga, the 24th Regiment concerned itself with a two-direction attack. While the right (2d) battalion swung south,

the left (3d) battalion pushed eastward. Both had easy going and reached Objective O-2 without difficulty. (See Map 9.) The regiment set an attack pattern on 25 July that it used for the remainder of the operation: skirmishers, following closely behind tanks, deployed over the entire front. The 1st Battalion, 24th Marines, after being relieved by the 1st Battalion, 8th Marines, from its zone on the extreme left of the beachhead, spent most of the day in regimental reserve. By 1500, however, the divergence in directions of attack between the 24th and 8th Regiments developed a gap between them. To fill this for the night's defense, the 1st Battalion moved in.

A comparison of casualties suffered on 24 and 25 July by the 2d Battalion, 24th Marines, indicated statistically that resistance had slackened: on the first day the unit had 50 casualties, on the second, 19.

Long before dusk the 24th Marines tied its flanks securely to the 25th Regiment on the right and the 8th Regiment on the left and settled down for whatever the night might bring.[13]

---

[12] 25th Mar Report, 2–3; 1st Bn, 25th Mar Report, 30–31; 3d Bn, 25th Mar Report, 3. V Amph Corps Amph Recon Bn Report, 1 and Annex A, 2.

[13] 24th Mar Report, 9; 2d Bn, 24th Mar Report, 1–2; 3d Bn, 24th Mar Report, 1.

USHI POINT was cleared on the second and third days by Marines of the 8th Regiment and supporting tanks. Well-coordinated tank-infantry action was used to good advantage throughout the operation.

HANGER AND ZEKE (Japanese fighter plane), were useless when captured on 25 July (Jig-plus 1), but Ushi Point field was repaired and employed by U. S. aircraft almost immediately.

Over on the corps' left flank the 8th Marines, attached to the 4th Division, had begun the 25 July attack with only its 1st Battalion in the lines. Using the same tactics employed along the beach by the 24th Marines on Jig-Day, the 1st Battalion, supported by armored amphibians afloat and tanks ashore, inched slowly through the gnarled coastal terrain and snare-like undergrowth. Marines found the zone littered with bodies—Japanese counterattackers of the night before—that required careful examination lest some turn out to be alive.

At first there was no opposition. But, as the unit pressed farther to the north, resistance began to develop along the coast. There, survivors of the counterattack, holed up in the craggy coral, fired occasional challenging bursts at the Marines. By 1115 the advance had bogged to a virtual standstill in the face

of an especially knotty core of opposition near the water's edge. The rugged terrain around the strong-point forbade effective use of supporting tanks, and the armored amphibians, because of the shore's configuration, could not hit the area. To relieve the deadlock, Lieutenant Colonel Hays ordered his battalion to pivot on the left and wheel in an arc to the beach. This maneuver, striking the enemy at right angles to the original direction of advance, was successful. Within 15 minutes a pocket of 20 to 25 well-concealed riflemen had been reduced.[14]

As the 8th Marines advanced, their front expanded, and at 1130 the commander, Colonel Wallace, ordered his 2d Battalion up on the 1st Battalion's right to attack eastward.

---

[14] Interview with Maj H. G. Gunter, 15Sep50.

74

This zone included the built-up area around Ushi Point Airfield as well as the strip itself. Since most of the Japanese troops originally assigned to this area had expended themselves against the 1st Battalion, 24th Marines, on the night of Jig-Day, they could oppose this attack only with occasional, ineffective small-arms fire. The advance swept rapidly through the area.

The 1st Battalion, too, gained momentum after destroying the beach strong-point and pushed northeastward along the coast. By dark the 8th Marines, having pushed about 200 yards past Objective O–2 (see Map 9), stopped and carefully tied in lines for the night.

The 2d Battalion stretched its lines about 400 yards south of Ushi Point Airfield to make contact with the 1st Battalion, 24th Marines. Rearrangement and adjustment of the 8th Marines' front continued until after dark, the greatest change being necessitated by a huge oil fire that burned very close to the 2d Battalion's positions and silhouetted the Marines to would-be attackers.[15]

Artillery Activities

For Colonel Louis G. DeHaven's 14th Marines, 25 July was by far the worst day of the operation. Indeed, from these artillerymen's viewpoint, never since D-Day at Saipan had they suffered so heavily. Troubles had begun the previous night when enemy mortars and field guns opened against the rear areas of the beachhead—particularly against the pier being installed at White 2 by "Seabees" (naval construction battalion personnel).[16] Artillerymen manning 75mm pack howitzers in this general area received their share of this fire.

At 0920 came the worst blow: An enemy shell hit the Fire Direction Center of the 1st Battalion, 14th Marines, killing the battalion commander (Lieutenant Colonel Harry J. Zimmer), the intelligence officer, the operations officer, and seven assistants. In addition, 14 other Marines of the battalion headquarters were wounded. Major Clifford B. Drake,

battalion executive officer, assumed command of the unit.

In retaliation, U. S. artillery blasted caves in Mt. Lasso's northern face, the suspected source of the enemy fire. An attack by strafing and bombing planes on the same area appeared to achieve excellent results, with observation aircraft reporting that the strikes destroyed two guns. The quiet that followed caused many to believe that the two guns destroyed had caused the earlier trouble; but some doubts arose in the afternoon when enemy artillery again registered on beach areas. The second shelling, although inflicting a "few" casualties and setting one DUKW afire, hit no important installation.

Of the 14th Regiment's total casualties for the entire Tinian operation (14 killed, 29 wounded), most were lost on 25 July (13 killed, 22 wounded).[17]

Meanwhile, General Harper's artillery continued to render support from positions on Saipan. Front lines had not as yet progressed to a point demanding displacement of guns from Saipan to Tinian. For the most part, response to requests from Tinian observers was quick and accurate. The one major exception came at a critical time: during the early morning hours of 25 July when the Japanese counterattacks were in full tilt. Then, the time lapse between request and delivery of fire seemed interminable. In his report to the landing force commander at 0534, 25 July, General Cates, the 4th Division Commander, observed that "it took about 35 minutes for [the XXIV Corps Artillery] to open fire" following his request.[18]

At 1513 the landing force commander, General Schmidt, sent a message to General Cates requesting more information regarding the "35 minute delay" in the "Corps Artillery opening fire."[19] General Cates, in a mailbrief, indicated that, although he had requested fire at 0437 and

---

[15] 8th Mar Report, 1–2; 1st Bn, 8th Mar Report, 2–3.

[16] Two "Seabee" battalions participated in the Tinian Operation: the 18th and the 121st.

[17] 14th Mar Report, 2–3. The 14th Regiment was composed of the following units on 25 July: 1st and 2d Battalions, 14th Marines; 1st and 2d Battalions, 10th Marines; and a Headquarters and Service Battery.

[18] NTLF G–3 Operation Dispatches 23–25Jul44.

[19] Ibid., 25–27Jul44.

again at 0442, no rounds were forthcoming as late as 0510.[20]

When General Harper received a copy of General Cates' mailbrief, he addressed a letter of explanation to General Schmidt, excerpts of which follow:

> The undersigned [General Harper] was personally aware of a high state of tension in the CP of the Corps Artillery beginning at about 2200 July 24, when urgent and repeated requests to silence enemy shelling began to be received. Between the hours of 0200 and 0542 July 25, 2010 rounds were fired by the Corps in 92 missions.

General Harper continued in his letter to note that the request from the 4th Marine Division (General Cates) had come at 0435, but that two minutes later another request was received through normal artillery channels (14th Marines) that included the urgent notation, "Break up counter attack." Harper pointed out that "under normal circumstances an artillery operations section must give precedence" to the latter type of call. Finally, "at 0507," after having fired the other mission first, the XXIV Corps Artillery executed part of General Cates' request.

General Harper closed his letter to General Schmidt with the statement that:

> The personnel of the XXIV Corps Artillery have all been imbued with a strong obligation to spare no effort to destroy the enemy and support our assault forces. Any warranted criticism of the Corps Artillery is a matter of deep concern and regret.[21]

General Schmidt could well be pleased with the progress of his landing force during the first two days at Tinian. Not only had the difficult beach situation been mastered, but the build-up of forces on Tinian had proceeded so rapidly that, quite apart from the 4th Division's decisive victory of 24–25 July, there could be no doubt of the operation's ultimate outcome. Now, with the bulk of two divisions firmly established ashore, the Japanese counterattack capability caused no apprehension. For individuals and units caught in even a small-scale

thrust, the fighting could still be rough; but judged from the over-all picture, the Northern Troops and Landing Force could not be pushed off Tinian by the troops available to the enemy commander. Seldom was the victor of any of the Central Pacific conquests so unmistakably identified so early in the fight. Admiral Nimitz, Commander in Chief Pacific, commented at this time: "The situation is well in hand."[22]

The second night saw no repetition of the first. Marines were just as ready. The Japanese were not. The night of 25–26 July was marked only by minor infiltration attempts at several points along the beachhead and one violent, small-scale skirmish between a Japanese patrol and a combat outpost positioned at a road junction near the 24th Marines' right flank. Manning the outpost was a platoon from the 4th Division Reconnaissance Company, attached to the 24th Regiment to assist in establishing security.[23] The commander of the reconnaissance platoon, Lieutenant Victor Maghakian, described the action in part as follows:

> After getting the men in position . . . near the road junction . . . I went on a reconnaissance. . . . I spotted a large enemy patrol coming down the road with a scout out in front.

> After seeing that they moved into position in a cane field about 50 feet from my platoon, I crawled back and told Captain Key [commanding the division reconnaissance company] what I planned to do.

> In the meantime the Japs were digging in and were making a lot of noise talking and did not suspect that we were so close. . . . I passed the word down the line to open up and fire rapid fire into the cane field, knee-high grazing fire, upon my signal.

> . . . we opened up and let them have it as fast as we could pull our triggers. They began screaming . . . and making awful noises. Then after a few minutes I ordered my platoon to fall back to the division lines because I was afraid that maybe our own division might fire on us.

> After falling back, I reported what happened, and our troops opened up . . . with mortar and machine gun fire.

> Next morning I took my platoon back to the road junction and the cane field and found between 35 and 40 dead Japs in that area. I did not lose a man that night.[24]

---

[20] *Ibid.*, The XXIV Corps Artillery's "Log of Requests and Fires" lists the two 4th Division requests at 0435 and 0450 respectively.

[21] Ltr from BrigGen A. M. Harper, USA, to CG, NTLF, 27Jul44, subj: Slow response to requests for fire.

[22] *Chevron*, 29July44.

[23] 24th Mar Report, 9.

[24] Ltr from Lt V. Maghakian to author, 16Oct50.

Related Naval Activities

Admiral Turner, Commander Joint Expeditionary Force, and General Holland Smith, Commander Expeditionary Troops, arrived early on the morning of 25 July in the *Rocky Mount*, which then anchored off Saipan (but within visual signaling distance of Admiral Hill's flagship at Tinian). Turner and Smith had left Saipan on 20 July to observe the first days of the amphibious assault against Guam. With his reappearance, Turner became senior officer present afloat (SOPA) at Saipan, but his presence altered in no way the command structure for the Tinian operation. Also, because Hill had under his command virtually all combat ships and planes in the area, he retained responsibility for offensive and defensive surface and air action for both Saipan and Tinian.[25]

Meanwhile, as Marines expanded their holdings at Tinian, soldiers and Marines of the Southern Troops and Landing Force (Major General Roy S. Geiger) had clawed firm beachheads at Guam, 88 miles to the southwest. It was important that troop activities on these two islands, as well as the construction and base development work at Saipan, proceed without interference from Japanese long-range bombers flying from bases in the western Carolines and in the Volcano-Bonin Islands. To keep the enemy off balance in his dispositions and planning, Vice Admiral Marc A. Mitscher led his Task Force 58 in a series of strikes on those bases considered most dangerous.

With U. S. planners actively considering the seizure of Yap, Ulithi and Palau, Mitscher's fast carriers initiated a three-day reconnaissance-in-force of the western Carolines beginning on 25 July. This completed, six carriers of the force ploughed northward for the third raid of the Marianas campaign on the Volcano-Bonins. Since enemy air strength at Iwo Jima had now come under the neutralizing power of planes based at Saipan, the carriers met virtually no opposition in this raid. The planes, shifting their attention to a number of shipping targets in the area, achieved excellent results.

U. S. losses of 16 aircraft were balanced against Japanese losses of five ships sunk, others damaged, and 13 planes destroyed.[26]

JIG-PLUS 2—26 JULY 1944

The highest point in the northern half of the island, Mt. Lasso, faced the landing force on 26 July. U. S. possession of this 540-foot feature would deny the enemy his best observation post for control of mortar and artillery fires against the U. S. beachhead. General Schmidt directed this day's main effort in the center of the force zone of action—against Mt. Lasso—and ordered the two divisions to "seize the O–3 line. Reorganize and prepare to seize the O–4 line." [27] (See Map 9.)

Shortly before noon, 26 July, General Schmidt supplemented his previous order and gave the divisions more leeway:

At discretion assault division commanders, continue advance south of O–3. . . . Keep this headquarters

---

[25] TF 51 Report, Encl A, 19. *Turner. Hill.*

[26] Joint Army Navy Assessment Committee, "Japanese Naval and Merchant Shipping Losses During World War II by All Causes," February 1947, 14. Fleet Admiral Ernest J. King, Second Report to the Secretary of the Navy, 27Mar45, *U. S. Navy at War* (Washington: Government Printing Office, 1945), 112, gives Japanese losses as follows: 11 ships sunk, eight ships damaged. A. R. Buchanan, *The Navy's Air War, A Mission Completed* (New York: Harper & Brothers, 1946), 215, gives enemy losses at 32 ships sunk, 10 planes destroyed.

[27] NTLF Opn Order 32–44. This was the first operation order reference either to O–3 or O–4. Both were designated to conform with the situation that had developed after two days' fighting. Omission of O–2 and the FBHL from the day's order is worthy of examination. Objective O–2, the northern half of which had already been reached on 25 July, no longer constituted a suitable Corps objective. Prospects of the 2d Division reaching the east coast indicated the desirability of specifying an objective (O–3) that would orient the entire Corps' direction of attack for the drive to the south. The FBHL, laying between O–3 and O–4, was omitted because it did not fit into the Corps' plans for "elbowing"—allowing first one division and then the other to forge rapidly ahead supported by the bulk of the artillery. In this case, the maximum distance from O–3 to O–4 in the 2d Division's zone (on the extreme left) was about 5,000 yards; the minimum distance in the 4th Division's zone (on the extreme right) was about 200 yards.

DIVISION COMMANDERS, General Watson (left) of the 2d and General Cates (undershirt) of the 4th, examine operation maps and discuss the situation on Jig-plus 2 (26 July).

advised [regarding] location of front lines, composition and location division reserves. Division reserves not to be employed without informing NTLF.[28]

The situation now permitted a two-division attack, 4th on the right pushing southward, the 2d on the left moving straight east to the coast where it too would turn south. Since both divisions now had similar missions, there was no longer reason to have the 4th Division reinforced by 2d Division armor and light artillery. General Schmidt ordered "all organic units 2dMarDiv ashore" to pass to parent control at 0630, 26 July. This instruction affected the 1st and 2d Battalions, 10th Marines, the 8th Marines, and the 2d Tank Battalion.

---

[28] NTLF G–3 Operational Dispatches, 25–27 July (1148, 26 July).

At 0755 the XXIV Corps Artillery, still 13 battalions strong, commenced a five-minute preparatory bombardment forward of the Marine lines. Since Mt. Lasso lay in the 4th Division's zone, the bulk of fire supported that unit.

This preparation was reinforced by fires from the *Tennessee, Cleveland,* and two destroyers. In addition, six destroyers were available for direct support missions as requested by assault battalions. The naval gunfire support had been consistently excellent during the first days and nights at Tinian. It would remain so throughout the operation.

The 4th Marine Division moved out at 0800, just as the final shells of the preparation blasted the terrain to the front. The right

(23d) regiment had conducted a minor line-straightening move an hour before with the purpose of making the 0800 attack easier to coordinate. Pushing forward with its 1st Battalion on the right along the coast and 3d Battalion on the left, the 23d Regiment made steady progress. The absence of effective Japanese resistance allowed the Marines to move just as fast as the thick cane fields, with their oppressive muggy heat, would permit. While the two assault battalions pressed steadily forward, the 2d Battalion, released from division reserve, searched out suspicious areas. By noon the 23d Marines had advanced to O–3 (see Map 9).

After a quick reorganization, the unit pushed on again. Almost immediately, Marines of the 3d Battalion encountered a store of enemy torpedoes in a wooded area, a cache deadly enough to shatter the unit. The battalion commander, Major Paul S. Treitel, requested the services of Lieutenant William Bellano, a bomb disposal officer from Headquarters and Service Company, 20th Marines, who disarmed the deadly obstacles within half an hour. Treitel's battalion then resumed its advance. By 1430 the regiment, having met only occasional Japanese machine-gun and rifle fire, reached commanding ground in the vicinity of Objective O–4, where it consolidated its positions for the night.[29]

On the left of the 4th Division front, the 25th Marines pushed along three distinct ground levels in its assigned zone of action. In addition to its three organic battalions, the regiment was reinforced by the 2d Battalion, 24th Marines, which remained on the division left flank to maintain contact with the 2d Marine Division and to clear a series of caves in a cliff line in that area.

The 25th Regiment's double envelopment of Mt. Maga on 25 July had left the northwestern face untouched. The 2d Battalion began mopping up this face almost as soon as the other two battalions reached the crest, but darkness found the task unfinished. The unit resumed its task on the morning of 26 July and completed it at noon.

[29] 23d Mar Report, 22. *Dick.* Ltr from LtCol P. S. Treitel to CMC, 18Dec50, hereinafter cited as *Treitel.*

MT. LASSO was steep and rugged. The enemy abandoned the hill with its excellent defensive possibilities and allowed the 1st Battalion, 25th Marines, to capture it without a fight.

From front lines on Mt. Maga's southern slopes, the two battalions (1/25 and 3/25) that had seized the hill the day before jumped off for the 26 July attack. The key terrain feature, Mt. Lasso, lay entirely within the 1st Battalion's zone of action. The hill afforded excellent possibilities to a defender, having long fields of observation and difficult approaches. The Marines expected a fight there. But, unaccountably, the Japanese abandoned Mt. Lasso, allowing the Marines to climb it without opposition.

There, at 1630, the 1st Battalion formed a circular defense around the summit, placing its front lines generally along 4th Marine Division Objective O–4A. Lieutenant Colonel Mustain felt natural concern about his lines along the mountain's eastern slopes, because units of the 2d Marine Division had not as yet come abreast and the 2d Battalion, 24th Marines, was some distance to the rear. Accordingly, he requested that an additional company be attached to his battalion for the night defense. Colonel Batchelder concurred and Company E, 25th Marines, moved to Mt. Lasso and dug in.

The 3d Battalion, 25th Marines, also advanced virtually unopposed. By mid-afternoon Objective O–4A had been seized and the next objective (O–4), 1,000 yards farther south, appeared possible of attainment. Permission to proceed there, however, was denied by the regimental commander, who felt that the contact problem would be too great if one of his units advanced that far ahead of the others. Since the 3d Battalion's sector of Objective O–4A was in a depression and very unsatisfactory for defense, the unit pulled back about 450 yards to establish itself for the night (see Map 9).

Just before dark, Marines of the 3d Battalion observed several enemy tanks on the ridge line to their front (Objective O–4). These vehicles were beyond effective range of antitank weapons available to the unit, so an air strike was requested and delivered. Outcome of this was undetermined, since ground troops were "unable to observe the results" and air unit reports made no mention of it.

The 24th Marines, less 2d Battalion (attached to the 25th Regiment), reverted to 4th Division reserve after relief by elements of the 2d Marine Division. The regiment spent the day mopping up rear areas and reorganizing. At 1555 the 1st Battalion, 24th Marines, was designated as NTLF reserve.[30]

The 4th Division's artillery employment for the day's advance was standard: 1st and 2d Battalions, 14th Marines, in direct support of the 25th and 23d Regiments, respectively. The first artillery heavier than 75mm to land at Tinian were the 105mm howitzers of the 3d Battalion, 14th Marines (Lieutenant Colonel Robert E. MacFarlane). This unit completed

its displacement from Saipan by noon, 26 July, and began firing general support missions at 1315. An indication of the inactivity of the enemy's mortars and artillery: the 14th Marines suffered no casualties on 26 July.[31]

To the East Coast

The 2d Marine Division moved out toward the east coast at 0806, 26 July—8th Marines on the left, 2d Marines on the right (see Map 9).[32]

The 8th Marines swept rapidly across the Ushi Point flats. The airfield had been abandoned, but the Marines carefully searched each position to make certain that none of the enemy were lying doggo. By noon Colonel Wallace, the 8th Marines' commander, reported his assault battalions (1st and 2d) on the east coast. The 3d Battalion, which had followed the assault across the island, then became 2d Division reserve, with a mission of clearing a built-up area about 500 yards east of Ushi Point Airfield. The remainder of the 8th Regiment, also designated division reserve, began seaching for enemy stragglers west of Objective O–3.[33]

On the 8th Regiment's right, the 2d Marines pressed rapidly across the island, arriving on the east coast at 1230. There the unit quickly reoriented its direction of attack to the south and moved out, 1st Battalion on the left along the coast, 2d Battalion on the right. Immediately after changing direction, the 1st Battalion was confronted with a precipitous cliff-line across its front. Scaling this was out of the question, so Lieutenant Colonel Kyle, the battalion commander, requested and received the regimental commander's permission to detour the steep portion of the cliff line. After the 2d Battalion had pushed far enough ahead to permit it, Kyle's battalion left a small force to contain any Japanese in the escarpment, swung to the right through the zone already cleared, by-passed the cliff, and turned back to resume its former frontage.

[30] 25th Mar Report, 3; 1st Bn, 25th Mar Report, 31–32; 3d Bn, 25th Mar Report, 3-4; 2d Bn, 24th Mar Report, 2. 24th Mar Report, 10.

[31] 14th Mar Report, 3–4.

[32] The 2d Regiment relieved the 24th Regiment and assumed its assigned zone before the attack hour.

[33] 8th Mar Report, 2–3.

TO THE EAST COAST move Marines of the 2d Division on 26 July (Jig-plus 2). Though the enemy had all but abandoned this portion of the island, Marines combed the area carefully, thereby reducing the number of by-passed Japanese. Mt. Tapotchau on Saipan looms in the distance.

At 1700, with this accomplished and firm contact established between the two assault battalions, the regiment stopped for the night. The Marines strung barbed wire along their front lines in preparation for whatever might develop. The 3d Battalion, in regimental reserve, established a secondary defense line to add depth to the defense.[34]

Meanwhile, as the 2d and 8th Regiments spurted toward the east coast, the 6th Marines completed landing on White 2. Arriving at the beach with his leading units, Colonel Riseley, the regimental commander, reported to the division command post for instructions. There he found that his unit would move into the lines on the right of the 2d Marines and fill a gap between that organization and elements of the 4th Division. Thereafter, the 6th Marines would occupy the right half of the 2d Division front and attack to the south.

By 1135 the 1st and 3d Battalions, commanded by Lieutenant Colonels William K. Jones and John W. Easley, respectively, had moved into the lines prepared for the push to the south. At noon the 2d Battalion, which

after landing the previous evening had been designated as 2d Division reserve, reverted to the 6th Marines. The attack to the south began at about 1300; progress was excellent. Within an hour the regiment swept to commanding ground about halfway between Objective O–3 and the Force Beachhead Line (see Map 9). There, to allow the 2d Regiment time to detour the cliff in its zone and come abreast, the 6th Marines held up the advance. Patrols were immediately dispatched to the front to scout out suspicious areas, while the rest of the regiment dug in for the night.

At 1450 a patrol from the 1st Battalion encountered a "large column" of Japanese approaching the Marine lines. In the fire fight that followed, the enemy point and connecting file were annihilated, the remainder of the column dispersed. Observation aircraft soon appeared over the scene and verified the patrol's report: considerable activity in front of the 6th Marines. Artillery and mortars immediately registered and chased the enemy from the area. The 6th Marines neither saw nor heard any more from these Japanese during the day.[35]

---

[34] 2d Mar Report, 1–2.

[35] 6th Mar Report, 1–2.

When the 2d Marine Division stopped for the night, long gains had been made. Its 2,500-yard push to the east coast now made it possible for the landing force to attack in a single direction—south (see Map 9). Opposition had been light and scattered, as reflected by the day's casualties in the 2d Division: 2 killed, 14 wounded.[36] Saipan had never been like this.

One incident marred the smoothness of the day's operations in the 2d Marine Division's zone of action. During the early afternoon while the 2d and 6th Marines were negotiating the cliff line that cut through their areas, friendly Saipan-based artillery thundered down upon them. "Not only had they figured wrong on their mask clearance," commented one of the officers exposed to this fire, "but we were standing on the mask! . . . since there were no FO's [forward observers] on the ground controlling this fire, we had a hell of a time getting it called off."[37] Happily, this was one of a very few such instances at Tinian. Records show no casualty statistics on this episode.

Meanwhile, Ushi Point Airfield was already in use by artillery observation planes. Since relatively little of the preparatory bombardment had been directed against the field, damage was minor. An air observer, after viewing the field on 26 July, dispatched a message to NTLF headquarters informing that the field was "excellent" and could be landed upon after a few hours' work.[38] Work was initiated at once by the 121st Naval Construction Battalion. A few enemy artillery shells fell ineffectively on the strip, but this gesture failed to interrupt either construction work or the operations of observation planes.

[36] 2d Mar Div Report, 2. NTLF G–3 Report, 9–10.

[37] Ltr from LtCol H. K. Throneson to author, 28Jan51, hereinafter cited as *Throneson.*

[38] NTLF G–3 Operational Dispatches, 25–27Jul44. Interview with Maj R. Fuller, 20Jul50.

USHI POINT AIRFIELD, wet from one of Tinian's frequent downpours. Since relatively little of the U. S. preparatory bombardment was directed against the field, damage to it was minor. By 29 July the strip extended 4,700 feet in a single, hard-surfaced runway.

On 27 July the 4th Division engineer officer (Lieutenant Colonel Nelson K. Brown) and air officer (Lieutenant Colonel William C. Wendt) reconnoitered the field to determine how much improvement it required. On the basis of their findings, General Cates informed General Schmidt in part as follows: "10 hours needed to prepare strip 150 feet [wide] by 2,500 feet [long], 14 [hours] for strip 75 feet by 5,000 feet."[39] This estimate was close: by the next day, red flags marked a usable strip 150 feet wide and 3,000 feet long. The work continued, and by 29 July the strip measured 4,700 feet in length.[40]

Ushi Point Airfield would later provide facilities for the United States' largest bombers in their attacks against the Japanese home islands. At 0730, 28 July, a U. S. Army Air Force P–47 set its wheels down on the white coral runway, the first plane heavier than the observation planes to land there. Within 13 months this same field would hold a B–29 called *Enola Gay*, which would carry its fateful bomb to Hiroshima.[41]

The two Marine divisions had landed at Tinian considerably understrength. The 1,268 officers and men who had joined on 11 July (Jig-minus 13) filled some of the Saipan-created vacancies, but all units were still understrength. On 26 July a sizeable replacement draft arrived at Saipan for the Northern Troops and Landing Force. With the exception of 70 officers and men temporarily needed for activities on Saipan,[42] the entire draft of 1,782 was transferred directly into the divisions on Tinian: 2d Division—35 officers and 827 enlisted; 4th Division—32 officers and 818 enlisted.[43]

[39] NTLF G–3 Operational Dispatches, 25–27Jul44.

[40] *Ibid.*, 27–29Jul44.

[41] TF 52 Report, 38.

[42] Most of these later joined the divisions on Tinian.

[43] NTLF G–1 Report, 4. Plans from the beginning had contemplated transfer of 4th Division replacements to the 2d Division at the end of the Tinian operation. This was planned because the 4th's rehabilitation area (Maui, Hawaii) would be closer to the United States and therefore more convenient for a personnel build-up than would that of the 2d Division (Saipan). Incident

Engineers and Shore Party

The flow of supplies, equipment and personnel over the White Beaches remained heavy, considering the small size of the beaches and the restricted routes of egress from them. That no serious clog developed at any time was a credit to shore party functioning. Early on Jig-Day the 1341st Engineer Battalion (USA) and the 2d Battalion, 20th Marines,[44] operating on White 1 and 2, respectively, had commenced the task of keeping supply traffic steady and systematic. Initially, these shore party battalions had operated directly under the assault regiments, but on the afternoon of Jig-plus 1 (25 July) the 4th Division Shore Party Commander (Lieutenant Colonel Nelson K. Brown) took over. At 1000 the next morning (26 July), control of the Shore Party shifted to NTLF, Colonel Cyril W. Martyr assuming command. This move merely superimposed an NTLF Shore Party Headquarters on that of the 4th Division.[45]

The 2d Marine Division did not operate a Shore Party at Tinian, because there was no need for more personnel on this job. Following its landing at 0800, 26 July, the 2d Battalion, 18th Marines (which had functioned as the 2d Division's Shore Party at Saipan), moved to an assembly area to await orders. At 1310 NTLF Shore Party ordered the unit to send one platoon to assist in the operations at White Beach 2; at 1500 Colonel Robert J. Straub, 2d Division logistics officer (D–4), ordered the remainder of the battalion to work in the division dumps, a task it performed throughout the

to the 4th Division's departure from the Marianas, 916 officers and men moved to the 2d Division.

[44] The 20th Marines was the engineer regiment of the 4th Division. The 2d Division's engineer regiment was the 18th Marines. Tinian was the last operation in which engineer regiments were designated. The 1st Battalions of the 18th and 20th Marines later became the 2d and 4th Engineer Battalions, respectively.

[45] 20th Mar Report, 1–4. The NTLF Shore Party Headquarters was formed from the Regimental Headquarters, 18th Marines, plus two officers from Headquarters, V Amphibious Corps. The strength was six officers and eight enlisted men. NTLF Engineer and Shore Party Report, 1.

SUPPLY TRAFFIC was heavy over the White Beaches, but Army and Marine Engineers kept it moving at a steady pace. Extreme narrowness of the beaches demanded the mobile loading of all materiel coming ashore, so that it could be transported directly from vessels, across the beaches to inland dumps or combat units. By such all-out, round-the-clock effort, logistical personnel moved two-day reserves of water, ammunition and rations into Tinian dumps before bad weather curtailed beach operations on the afternoon of Jig-plus 4.

remainder of the operation. Later, when Ushi Point Airfield became operable for cargo planes, the unit shouldered the additional job of unloading aircraft.[46]

Of the two pontoon causeways planned for the beaches, only the one at White 1 was initially successful. The White 2 pier had suffered damage from Japanese artillery fire during installation and accommodated very little traffic during the first three days. White 1's pier, on the other hand, was subjected to much less fire during the installation period and by the morning of Jig-plus 1 received a heavy volume of traffic. Preloaded trucks and trailers began their LCT trip from Saipan to Tinian on Jig-plus 2, landing over the White 1 causeway. This routing continued on Jig-plus 3 (27 July) until 1400 that date, when the White 2 causeway was also in commission and began receiving LST's and craft for unloading.[47] The speed of the causeway method of unloading was impressive: one LST discharged her cargo of 30 ration-loaded trucks on the White 1 pier in only six minutes. A few empty trucks and trailers re-embarked over the causeways, to return to Saipan for a second load, but the majority had to await capture of Tinian Town and its protected docks before making the return trip.[48]

The 1st Battalions of the two divisions' engineer regiments (18th and 20th Marines) had, before the operation, been split into companies and these attached to infantry regiments. This arrangement remained constant throughout the battle.[49] Their duties focused about demolition of enemy pillboxes and caves, a job for which they were prepared by training and experience. The daily employment of these attached combat engineers contributed materially to the advances.

---

[46] 2d Bn, 18th Mar Report, 1.

[47] "The incipient typhoon that some days previously had been beginning to show east of Guam had by the 27th begun to increase in energy and had shifted to a position 50 miles west of Tinian." *Turner.*

[48] NTLF G–4 Report, 3.

[49] Attachments: A/18—2d Marines; B/18—6th Marines; C/18—8th Marines; A/20—25th Marines; B/20—24th Marines; C/20—23d Marines.

WHITE 2 CAUSEWAY, delayed in installation because of Japanese artillery fire, finally became operative on the afternoon of Jig-plus 3 (27 July). This prefabricated pier and the one at White 1 enabled LST's, LCT's, and LCM's to pull alongside and unload cargo. Unfortunately, the causeways had a short life, both being wrecked by the storm on the night of 29–30 July.

The night of 26–27 July was relatively quiet at all but one point along the front. The exception, however, was pronounced. In the sector occupied by Lieutenant Colonel Richard C. Nutting's 2d Battalion, 2d Marines, the enemy remained active from dusk to dawn. Why he showed such preference for this particular sector was never revealed. None of the skirmishes took on counterattack proportions, but all were troublesome. Along the battalion's entire front, groups of Japanese prodded and jabbed as if looking for a weak spot through which to pour.[50]

Nor was this the only direction from which trouble came. Even as men of the battalion strained their eyes toward the dark shadows to their front, they heard enemy activity to their rear. Almost as suddenly, they found themselves beset by attackers who apparently had been by-passed and who were bent upon moving through the Marine lines to rejoin their comrades. Here was a fresh twist: Japanese attempting to get out of Marine rear areas. This

particular effort centered against Company F, whose commander (Captain Warren Morris) notified the battalion commander that "about 60 Nips" had hit him from the rear. Bullets snapped back and forth briskly for a while; then the attackers fell silent—dead silent.[51]

Such activity, front and rear, kept men of the 2d Battalion awake all night, killed two and wounded two of their number. But morning revealed 137 dead Japanese sprawled in front of, behind, and in, the battalion's lines.[52]

JIG-PLUS 3 AND 4—27 AND 28 JULY 1944

Lack of large-scale contact with the enemy (dead or alive) after the first day and night

[51] Interview with LtCol M. P. Ryan, 19Dec50.

[52] 2d Mar Report, 2. During this action one Marine spotted a Japanese wearing an aviator's jacket and shouted, loud enough for many to hear, ". . . I want that jacket." When the Japanese in question fell forward of the lines, the Marine only awaited the coming of daylight to secure his prize. But, at dawn, when he went out to claim the souvenir, he found that someone had already been there—the jacket was gone. *Throneson.*

[50] 2d Mar Report, **2.**

at Tinian complicated Marine intelligence officers' tasks of gathering accurate information regarding Japanese dispositions and intentions. Such information as was obtained was in most cases sketchy and inconclusive and only served to caution the divisions against lowering their guards. By evening of 26 July, for example, the landing force disseminated the following results of an interrogation of a prisoner captured the day before by the 24th Marines: Remnants of the 1st Battalion, 50th Japanese Infantry, had moved into a small village about a mile forward of the 4th Division's front; the shattered 2d Battalion, 50th Infantry, had occupied high ground on Masalog Point, far to the 2d Division's front; the 3d Battalion and tanks were still in or near Tinian Town. Furthermore, the prisoner warned of a counterattack scheduled for 26 July (which failed to materialize).[53] This information, uncorroborated by any other source, probably presented a true picture of the situation as the prisoner knew it at the time of his capture but hardly provided any basis for specific deductions by the Marines. Actually, the enemy had already moved farther south and had postponed his counterattack.

The NTLF G-2 (Lieutenant Colonel Thomas R. Yancey, USA) came to a conservative conclusion on 27 July that summarized not only that day's enemy situation but the entire operation's enemy situation as well. Without saying so, he seemed to indicate the importance of all units conducting aggressive patrolling far to the front:

To date there have been no indications that our front line units have encountered the 50th Infantry Regiment in force [since the first night's counterattacks]. It is believed that this unit is largely intact and it is known that they are well equipped and seasoned troops. They are capable of intervention *at any time* [author's italics] and may be expected to offer a strong opposition when encountered.[54]

Elsewhere in the same report, Yancey noted that the "most likely enemy capability" was: "To fight a delaying action, withdrawing to,

and organizing further defenses in, the high ground in the southeastern end of the island."[55]

Faced with this enigmatic enemy situation, General Schmidt formulated his scheme of maneuver and assigned his objectives on 27 and 28 July to facilitate an irregular "elbowing" advance.[56] From the front lines held on the morning of 27 July, Objective O-4 was near for the 4th Division, far for the 2d Division; once Objective O-4 had been reached, the emphasis would shift—Objective O-5 would be near for the 2d Division, far for the 4th Division. (See Map 10, facing page 87.) The Corps' attack on these two days, then, would find the 2d Division carrying the ball on 27 July, the 4th Division on the 28th. On the first day the 2d Division would push forward at 0730, the 4th Division at 1000; on the second day the 4th Division would attack at 0700, the 2d Division at 1000. Variations in these attack hours was consistent with plans to punch first with the left, then with the right. Principal advantage of this arrangement was that the bulk of the supporting fires could be allotted first to one division, then to the other. Not only did the XXIV Corps Artillery mass its fires to support the main effort, but two 105mm howitzer battalions of the division executing the secondary attack were also made available to support the principal thrust in each case. In the absence of specific enemy targets, artillery fired on areas that appeared to offer good defensive positions to the Japanese.

Following a thundering five-minute preparation fired against suspicious-appearing areas to the front, the 2d Division moved out at 0730, 27 July—2d Marines on the left along the east coast, 6th Marines on the right. Capably assisted by attached tanks,[57] the assault regiments

---

[53] NTLF G-2 Periodic Report 42, 1800, 25 July, to 1800, 26 July.

[54] NTLF G-2 Periodic Report 43, 1800, 26 July, to 1800, 27 July.

[55] *Ibid.*

[56] The NTLF commander, General Schmidt, explained that "the tactics and technique employed by the Corps . . . were necessary because of two such small divisions being required to fight on a very broad front. . . . the employment of tactics known as 'elbowing' [helped solve the problem]." Ltr from Gen H. Schmidt to CMC, 17Apr47.

[57] 2d Tank Battalion attachments: Company A—8th Marines (in reserve); Company B—6th Marines; Company C—2d Marines. Platoons of Company D, the light (flame-thrower) tank unit, were attached one to each of the three medium tank companies.

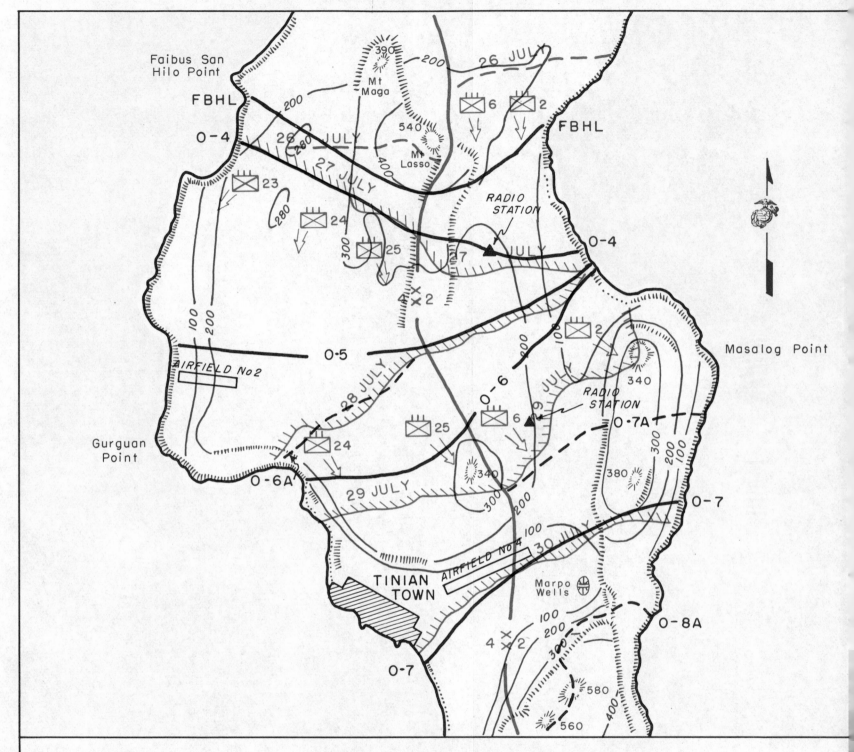

Faibus San
Hilo Point

FBHL

O-4

Mt
Maga

390

540

Mt
Lasso

26 JULY

FBHL

O-4

Masalog Point

RADIO
STATION

O-5

AIRFIELD No 2

Gurguan
Point

O-6A

29 JULY

O-6

RADIO
STATION

O-7A

340

380

O-7

AIRFIELD No 4

TINIAN
TOWN

Marpo
Wells

O-8A

580

560

O-7

PROGRESS LINES FOR 27, 28, 29 AND 30 JULY 1944

0   2000   4000

YARDS

MAP 10

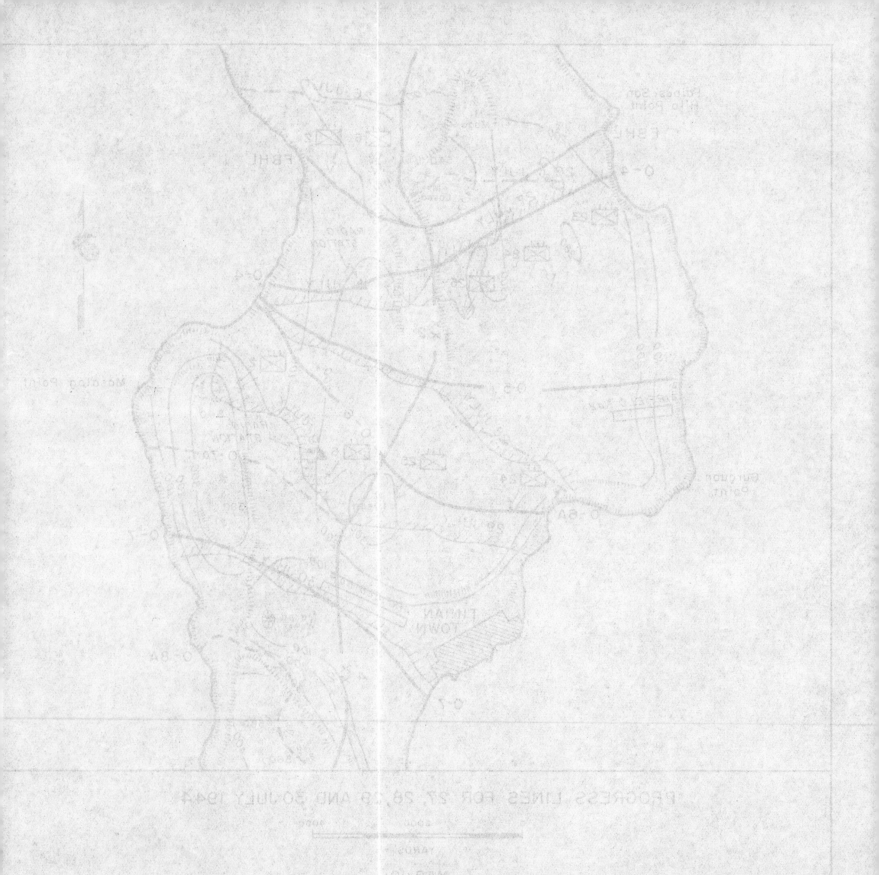

LINE OF SKIRMISHERS was the formation normally used at Tinian even when there was no enemy contact. Here a platoon from the 2d Marines pushes forward while an observation plane (OY) cruises overhead. High ground in distance is part of a long spine extending almost straight south from Mt. Lasso.

advanced rapidly, encountering only scattered machine-gun and rifle fire. By 1345 the 2d Division was in firm possession of Objective O–4. There the two assault regiments prepared their defenses for the night. The 2d Marine Division in six hours and 15 minutes on 27 July had gained about 4,000 yards. Immediately after stopping, both regiments dispatched patrols to scout the area about 500 yards to the front. All of these, except one, returned with a negative report: no enemy located. The exception, a patrol from the 2d Battalion, 2d Marines, encountered five Japanese, two of whom were killed before they could escape.

After a quiet night, disturbed only by an occasional exchange between front line Marines and snooping Japanese, the 2d Division attacked at 1000, 28 July, as scheduled. Where on the previous day the extreme left flank unit (1st Battalion, 2d Marines) had travelled 4,000 yards along the coast of Asiga Bay, its 28 July advances totalled only about 350 yards. This reduction on the second day had nothing to do with resistance encountered, it rather followed the NTLF order to move from Objective O–4 to O–5, a distance of only 350 yards on the left flank. Other 2d Marine Division units had to move farther, progressively increasing in distance from left to right (see Map 10).

By early afternoon on 28 July, after advancing against "light resistance," the division reached O–5 and began consolidating its positions for the night. Patrols immediately moved out to investigate areas within 600 yards of the front. All returned to report no enemy located. For the night defense, front line regiments placed outposts at important tactical localities to their fronts. No important actions occurred during the night, although two small enemy patrols were chased from cane fields forward of the 6th Marines' lines shortly after dark, and two Japanese soldiers lost their lives trying to infiltrate the 2d Marines' lines.[58]

While the 2d and 6th Regiments made the long push to O–4 and the short jump to O–5, the 8th Marines remained in reserve. The regiment displaced three times on 27 July, twice to keep reasonably close behind the rapidly moving assault regiments and the last time in response to an order at 1600 detaching it, less 2d Battalion, from 2d Division control and placing it in NTLF reserve. In the latter capacity the unit moved about two miles to the rear, a move harder on the disposition than the legs, inasmuch as trucks provided shuttle service from one area to the other. The 2d Battalion, 8th Marines, remained in division reserve, about 2,000 yards behind the front lines.

On 28 July the 8th Marines continued its pawn-like moves. In the early afternoon its 1st Battalion was under NTLF control behind the 4th Marine Division; the 2d Battalion was attached to the 2d Regiment; the remainder was in the 2d Division zone of action under NTLF control. Later, at 1750, the 8th Marines, less 3d Battalion, reverted to division reserve; the 3d Battalion remained in NTLF reserve. Even this change had a condition: the 2d Battalion would be detached the following morning and again placed under operational control of the 2d Marines.[59] The regiment's status changed so often that most low-ranking Marines knew little and cared less about which

headquarters issued them orders. To those unfamiliar with the reasons for all the attachments and detachments, the frequent moves seemed like a carefully conceived plan to make life unpleasant. One 8th Regiment Marine observed: "I'll sure be glad when we get back in the assault where it's comfortable again." [60]

The Longest Advance [61]

On 27 July (Jig-plus 3) the 4th Marine Division played its assigned secondary role and girded itself for the next day. With the 23d Marines on the right along the west coast and 25th Marines on the left, the 4th Division moved out at 1000, 27 July, and reached Objective O–4 by noon, having encountered virtually no opposition. Both assault regiments immediately sent combat-reconnaissance patrols about 1,000 yards to the front, but all returned to report no contacts with the enemy. Marines of the 4th Division spent a quiet night.

Facing the division on 28 July was a panorama of gently undulating hills, precisely surveyed into rectangles and squares by the cane plantings. Only occasional wooded patches disturbed the patchwork-quilt design of the landscape. South of Objective O–4 the island bulged to its greatest width, increasing the division front near O–5 to between 4,000 and 4,600 yards.

The 4th Division's attack, which commenced at 0700, produced the longest single day's advance of the entire operation. Massed artillery laid a shattering preparation against dominating terrain features during the 10 minutes preceding the jump-off, one 5-minute effort 1,500 yards forward of the lines, another of the same period 2,000 yards to the front. The advancing Marines met negligible resistance, and by 1250 the division held O–5.[62]

[58] 2d Mar Div Report, 2–3; 2d Mar Report, 2–3; 6th Mar Report, 2; 2d Tank Bn Report, page 2 of all company reports.

[59] 8th Mar Report, 3–4.

[60] Ltr from M/Sgt J. E. Van Alstyne to author, 24Dec50.

[61] This account of the 4th Division's 27–28 July attack is derived, unless otherwise indicated, from the following sources: 4th Mar Div Report, Sec IV, 27–28; 23d Mar Report, 22; 24th Mar Report, 10; 25th Mar Report, 3–4; L. R. Jones; Dick.

[62] Level terrain within the division zone offered few vantage points for observation posts. The 3d Bat-

PAST A SILENCED BUNKER move Marines on 27 July. Straight tree lines separating cane fields from one another provided convenient orientation and reorganization points for the attackers. Marine at end of column carries a 60mm mortar complete with base plate (weight: 42 pounds) in addition to his other gear.

In anticipation of a future tactical advantage, General Cates, the division commander, requested and received General Schmidt's permission to push on to the south so that a narrower part of the island could be reached. About two miles beyond O–5 a bay indentation would narrow greatly the division zone of action. This point the 4th Division designated as Objective O–6A. Activities to reach it began at

1325, following a 10-minute preparation fired by the cruisers *Louisville* and *Montpelier* and the destroyers *McDermut* and *Halsey Powell*. Like the artillery, ships hit areas that, if occupied by the enemy, could prove obstacles to the advancing Marines.

To fill the expansive front, General Cates committed the 24th Marines, less its 2d Battalion,[63] in the center between the 23d and 25th

---

talion, 23d Marines, solved this problem by establishing its OP on top of a medium tank. This OP, perhaps the most unusual in the operation, offered several satisfactory means of communication, including the tank radio, the commander's SCR–300 mounted atop the tank, and a wire-laying jeep following at about 75 yards. *Treitel.*

[63] The 2d Battalion was still under 25th Marines' control, having been attached on the morning of 26 July. At 1800, 28 July, the battalion was detached from the 25th Marines and assigned as NTLF reserve. The unit's regularly assigned commander, Lieutenant Colonel Richard Rothwell, who had missed the first three days

Regiments. In this formation the 4th Division surged forward.[64] By 1730, after encountering only scattered "knee mortar"[65] fire, the division reached O–6A, pinching out the 23d Marines in the process. The latter regiment then became division reserve and set about mopping up scattered Japanese on Gurguan Point, particularly around Airfield No. 2 (see Map 10).

The 23d Regiment, which moved the farthest (7,300 yards) during the day, made free use of available vehicles to lessen the strain on tired legs and feet. Marines clustered upon every tank and half-track in the zone, and the regiment's action report described the advance as a "blitz." Midway in the day's move one rifle company and two tanks streaked ahead on a reconnaissance-in-force. Their mission covered an area as far south as the airstrip at Gurguan Point, a move that encountered only sporadic and ineffective fire from Japanese small-arms and light-automatic weapons.[66] This patrol action provided a screen for the main body, which itself was moving very rapidly.

The greatest work load was imposed upon the communicators, who had to exert themselves to the maximum in order to maintain wire lines between the frequently displacing command posts and the racing assault elements.

The 4th Division's rapid advance caught up with a number of Japanese civilians who had been withdrawing under U. S. pressure; a total of 185 men, women and children were interned during the day. Only two military prisoners were taken, and their interrogation indicated that the Japanese had fallen back to the southern end of the island. At 1325, 14 U. S. aircraft strafed an area described by prisoners and internees as Colonel Ogata's command post, but Ogata lived to fight another day.[67]

Re-groupment of the Artillery

The 4th Division's artillery regiment, the 14th Marines, had been split into a Tinian and a Saipan echelon since the beginning of the operation. It was destined never to get together completely during the entire Tinian operation. The 1st and 2d Battalions, which had landed on Jig-Day, were followed by the 3d Battalion on 26 July. This left only the 4th Battalion (Lieutenant Colonel Carl A. Youngdale) and the attached 4th 105mm Artillery Battalion, V Amphibious Corps (Lieutenant Colonel Douglas E. Reeve).[68] The latter unit landed at Tinian on the afternoon of 27 July and was ready to fire at 1810. But Youngdale's battalion was delayed in its displacement when the causeways fronting the beaches were wrecked by rough seas. After waiting aboard the *Cambria* for several days, 4/14 finally landed over Tinian Town beaches on 1 August, the final day of the operation. The unit did not occupy firing positions on Tinian.[69]

---

of the operation, returned from the hospital and rejoined the battalion on 27 July.

[64] "After passing the O–5 line the 3d Battalion [23d Marines] captured a large warehouse loaded to the rafters with beer and liquor. It took a great deal of leadership and persuasion by platoon leaders and company commanders to get their men to continue the attack without stocking up." *Treitel.*

[65] The knee mortar, actually a 50mm grenade discharger, was not fired from the knee as its small size and curved base plate suggested. Since the weapon was commonly referred to by this nickname throughout the Pacific War, however, knee mortar is used in this narrative.

[66] *Buron.*

[67] Actually, at least one captured Japanese claimed that Ogata had been killed at Mt. Lasso on Jig-Day. But Sergeant Major Tadami Ushiyama of the 50th Infantry's Medical Unit, a person in a position to know the truth, stated that he saw the colonel during two successive command post displacements from the Mt. Lasso area. The sergeant major was sure that Colonel Ogata survived until the night of 2–3 August. Similar testimony from four other prisoners (two superior privates, one corporal and one lance corporal) further strengthens the sergeant major's statement. 4th Mar Div Representative Translations Made on Tinian.

[68] This unit was often referred to as the 5th Battalion, 14th Marines, its original title when organized on 1 March 1944. The following month (16 April) it received the title used at Saipan and Tinian. The organization operated under yet another title at Iwo Jima in February 1944: 4th 155mm Howitzer Battalion, V Amphibious Corps. This came as a result of a change in the unit's armament from 105's to 155's. Ltr from LtCol D. E. Reeve to CMC, 17Nov50. Ltr from Maj M. R. Burditt to author, 5Jan51.

[69] *Youngdale.* The regimental commander of the 14th Marines comments pertinently in connection with 4/14's displacement: "Before our departure from Saipan I was given to understand that the battalion

Units of the 14th Marines were assigned missions as follows: 1st and 2d Battalions in direct support of the 25th and 23d Marines, respectively; 3d Battalion and 4th 105mm Artillery Battalion, V Amphibious Corps, in general support. When the infantry's advance demanded a displacement on 28 July, all artillery organizations moved up close enough behind the front lines to provide effective support for the final push.[70]

under Lt. Col. Douglas E. Reeve was detached and would not rejoin the regiment. I was therefore unable to understand their arrival on Tinian on the 27th of July. At that time inquiry was made as to the whereabouts of 4–14; no explanation was forthcoming, but my personal opinion is that . . . the similar (4th Battalion) designation of the two battalions was responsible for the erroneous displacement of the 4th 105mm Howitzer Battalion, V Amphibious Corps." Ltr from Col L. G. DeHaven to CMC, 19Dec50.

[70] 14th Mar Report, 4–6.

Meanwhile, the 10th Marines (2d Division) finally got together under the command of Colonel Raphael Griffin on 27 July. The 1st and 2d Battalions of this regiment had been ashore since Jig-Day, when they landed under 4th Division control. The 3d and 4th Battalions, however, had remained at Saipan from where they rendered island-to-island fires in support of the landings and expansion of the beachhead. By 26 July, with assault troops moving rapidly, the time for displacement from Saipan to Tinian had arrived. The next day, therefore, after remaining aboard LCT's overnight awaiting beach availability, the units landed, 3d Battalion (Lieutenant Colonel William C. Capehart) at 1500, 4th Battalion (Lieutenant Colonel Kenneth A. Jorgensen) at various times from 0130 to 1330.

Colonel Griffin and his headquarters group established a command post and assumed control of his firing battalions prior to 1600, 27

GROUNDED LST off Beach White 2. After unloading 24 trucks on the pontoon causeway and taking aboard a load of 200-odd casualties, the ship attempted to retract. Then, during a sudden squall, she broached on the reef. Casualties aboard her were transferred the next day to another ship.

July. Initial assignment of units: 1st Battalion (75mm pack howitzer)—direct support of the 2d Marines; 2d Battalion (75mm pack howitzer)—direct support of the 8th Marines; 3d Battalion (105mm howitzer)—direct support of the 6th Marines; 4th Battalion (105mm howitzer)—general support of the 2d Marine Division. These assignments obtained for most of the operation, although needs for massing fires at particular points sometimes demanded alterations.[71]

An unusual incident occurred a few days after the 4th Battalion's arrival at Tinian. In the words of the battalion executive officer:

> . . . an air spotter reported that a Japanese tank had stopped on a crossroads on the southern plateau. This crossroads was the base point on which the battalion had registered. 4/10 fired one volley of eight howitzers and scored one direct hit on the tank. This tank was thus destroyed by one volley at a range exceeding 6,500 yards.[72]

Progress of the Tinian attack by 27 July indicated the desirability of displacing the XXIV Corps Artillery's 155mm howitzers from Saipan to Tinian so that these pieces would not be required to fire at such great ranges. Accordingly, the 419th Field Artillery Group began the move at 1500, 27 July; and, at dawn of 28 July, one of its battalions, the 145th, commenced firing from Tinian positions. The group's other battalion, the 225th, began its Saipan-Tinian move early on the morning of 28 July and by mid-afternoon began executing fire missions.

The 106th Field Artillery Battalion, a 155mm howitzer unit organic to the 27th Infantry Division but which had operated as part of Groupment C, XXIV Corps Artillery, since initiation of the Tinian bombardment, embarked on 27 July for displacement to Tinian. Only one battery actually landed there, however; the other two returned to their Saipan positions after being deterred by wrecked pontoon causeways from landing on the White Beaches.[73]

The XXIV Corps Artillery's 420th Field Artillery Group, capable of reaching any point on Tinian with its long-armed 155mm guns, remained at its Saipan positions, whence it delivered support throughout the Tinian operation.

With his 155mm howitzer group on Tinian and his 155mm gun group on Saipan, General Harper obviously could not personally supervise both. In this situation he decided that Tinian was the logical site for his command post and made the move with his headquarters group by 0715, 28 July.[74]

Bad Weather and Its Effects

By picnic standards, the weather at Tinian had been unpleasant. Nearly every day featured rain squalls, gusty winds, and ominous clouds. And yet, for Jig-Day and three days following, the seas remained calm enough for reasonably convenient shore activities. The "three days of good weather" that Admiral Hill had considered vital had already expired. On the afternoon of 28 July the weather got worse—much worse. This condition resulted from the effects of a typhoon that built up west of the Marianas and sent its swells and winds against Tinian's west coast. The seas surrounding Tinian changed to a dirty gray-blue as the winds mounted and the waves boiled over one another and grew into larger, uglier masses. Surf roaring against the tiny White Beaches and their rocky flanking shelves forced temporary suspension, at 1800 on 28 July, of all unloading over the beaches.

The next day efforts were resumed. But in the afternoon LST 340 broached and went hard aground on the reef when struck by a squall during her attempted retraction from White 2.[75] In the same squall, LCC (landing craft control) 25473 washed up on the reef north of White 1. Thereafter, only DUKW's could operate through the angry surf, and even these with great difficulty.

During the night of 29–30 July the two pontoon causeway piers became victims of the

[71] 10th Mar Report, 1–3.

[72] Ltr from Maj W. P. Oliver, Jr., to CMC, 12May47. Interview with Maj Oliver, 19Sep50. Exact time of this occurrence not known. Probably 31 July.

[73] 27th Inf Div Arty Report, 31.

[74] XXIV Corps Artillery S-3 Report, 12.

[75] Salvage operations continued until 13 August 1944 when she was finally pulled off. Taken to Tanapag Harbor, Saipan, on 25 October 1944, LST 340 was beached, after which she served as a receiving station. She was then decommissioned, designated the USS *Spark*, and assigned to Commander Naval Base Saipan.

RAIN fell on Tinian almost daily, dampening clothing, weapons, equipment and spirits.

rough seas. The pier at White 1 broached after its anchor chains parted; the one on White 2 broke into two parts.

Because it was apparent that the DUKW's alone could not shoulder the entire supply and evacuation task, Admiral Hill ordered his emergency air-supply plan put into effect. Immediately, a previously alerted squadron of transport planes (C–47's) [76] began the move from Eniwetok to Saipan, where it would engage in air supply for the Tinian attackers. Planes already available at Saipan, including several Curtiss "Commandos" of Marine Transport Squadron 252, immediately went to work on the air lift. By 31 July planes had delivered 33,000 rations (99,000 meals) to Ushi Point Airfield. Though these were the only items carried by air during the assault phase (24 July–1 August), the assistance so rendered was great. On return trips planes transported wounded men to Saipan hospitals.

But for the seaworthiness and efficiency of the amphibian trucks (DUKW's) and a tailor-made emergency air-supply plan, the supply situation may have become serious. [77]

The same bad weather that complicated the logistical situation made life unpleasant for the troops who had to plod wet and uncomfortable through Tinian's muck. And when they stopped for the day, the nightly misery of preparing a foxhole in the spongy mud began. Jokes about running water in each foxhole grew as tiresome as the unremitting deluge. More than one Marine spent more than one rainy night in a sitting or standing position, preferring to have the water run off him than around him. [78]

---

[76] This was the U. S. Army Air Force's 9th Troop Carrier Squadron.

[77] DUKW units at Tinian, which in the words of the NTLF G–4 "performed an astounding feat of supply," were as follows: 477th Amphibian Truck Company, U. S. Army; 27th Division Provisional Amphibian Truck Company, U. S. Army; 1st Marine Amphibian Truck Company; 2d Marine Amphibian Truck Company. A total of 140 DUKW's participated in the Tinian operation.

[78] TF 52 Report, 20–21; NTLF G–4 Report, Sec B, 2–3.

With the weather getting worse and worse, General Harry Schmidt decided on 28 July to move to Tinian. He had remained at Charan Kanoa on Saipan during the first days of the operation. But now, with the two divisions surging to the south, lines of communication were getting progressively longer. Displacement would relieve this situation. After an uneventful island-to-island trip, General Schmidt opened his new NTLF command post just south of Mt. Maga at 1315, 28 July.[79]

Feeling confident that, despite bad weather, the Tinian operation would continue as scheduled, Admiral Spruance, Commander Fifth Fleet, and General Holland Smith, Commander Expeditionary Troops, departed at 1800, 28 July, for a return trip to Guam.[80] Admiral Turner, Commander Joint Expeditionary Force, remained at Saipan aboard the *Rocky Mount*. Before departing the area, General Holland Smith sent a message to General Schmidt: "Magnificent work. Keep the heat on."[81]

JIG-PLUS 5 AND 6—29 AND 30 JULY 1944

With slightly over half of Tinian captured in only five days' fighting and with the landing force intelligence officer expressing the belief that "the 50thInfRegt will be encountered in force in the southeastern part of the island,"[82] General Schmidt's operation order for 29 July was sufficiently fluid to allow the two Marine divisions to push forward as fast as they chose. Both would attack at 0700, seize the "O–6 line then . . . advance and seize the O–7 line." (See Map 10.) Here, then, in a single sentence, the divisions were given leeway to move an average distance of 5,000 yards. With each step forward, the Marines would narrow their front and further bottle up the Japanese in the southern end of the island. As the situation developed, however, Objective O–7 proved out of

reach on 29 July, so that, on 30 July, General Schmidt merely directed the divisions to "continue operations to complete mission assigned [yesterday]."

In contrast to orders issued for the first five days of the operation, Schmidt specified neither a main effort nor a concentration of fire support for the 29 and 30 July advances. The general authorized his two division commanders "at their own discretion to conduct local attacks, within their zones of action, to straighten lines and occupy favorable positions in preparation for further offensive operations."[83]

To and through Tinian Town

The 4th Marine Division moved into its attack on 29 July without preparatory fires. Evidence indicated that the bulk of the defenders had pulled back to the island's extreme southern end and, since there were no suspicious appearing areas to the division's front, it seemed unwise to expend ammunition.

Against only "light resistance," from small groups of Japanese who lurked in the dense cane growth, the two assault regiments (24th on the right along the coast, 25th on the left) moved forward at a steady pace. As had been the case on previous days, tanks proved extremely valuable in leading the assault. The only stubborn enemy positions encountered during the day—a series of well-camouflaged cave positions along the western coast—fell under the combined assault of infantrymen from the 1st Battalion, 24th Marines, and tanks from Company B, 4th Tank Battalion. By 1545 the division reached favorable terrain about 600 to 1,000 yards forward of Objective O–6 (see Map 10). From this area, the Marines had an unimpaired view of Tinian Town and the entire valley that cuts the island from east to west at this point. Since such commanding terrain provided an ideal defense position, General Cates requested and received General Schmidt's permission to halt for the night.

The 4th Division's action report summarized the activities after six days of combat as follows: "Morale and combat efficiency were very

[79] NTLF G–3 Report, 10.

[80] Spruance had arrived in the *Indianapolis* early on Jig-Day. Smith had arrived with Admiral Turner in the *Rocky Mount* on Jig-plus 1.

[81] NTLF G–3 Operational Dispatches 27–29Jul44.

[82] NTLF G–2 Periodic Report 44, 1800, 27 July, to 1800, 28 July.

[83] NTLF Opn Orders 35 and 36, 28–29Jul44.

THIRSTY JAPANESE CHILD reaches for a cup of water. Too young to understand what the war was all about, this little girl wandered alone into the 3d Battalion, 6th Marines, lines on 29 July. Like the other 13,000-odd civilians who eventually entered Marine lines, she was cared for at an internment camp established by the Island Command.

satisfactory. The troops were 'heading for the barn.' " [84]

It rained and rained and rained on the night of 29–30 July. The bad weather offered an advantage to would-be counterattackers: excellent concealment. But the same bad weather forced a rather back-handed advantage on the Marine defenders: all were wide awake. When enemy mortar shells began falling within the 25th Regiment's positions and when front-line Marines heard activity to their front, it appeared that the Japanese were forming for an assault. Immediately, Marine mortars began thumping the spongy ground forward of the lines and artillery began searching areas farther

to the front. The drenched Marines readied their weapons for the expected attack. None came. Morning and a cessation of the downpour revealed a battlefield strewn with 41 dead Japanese and seven machine guns. Most of these were victims of the 25th Marines' mortars.[85]

In preparation for its 30 July attack the 4th Division called upon its artillery regiment (14th Marines) to lay down 10-minutes' fire against areas close to the lines that appeared potentially dangerous. When, at 0745, the Marines with their supporting tanks jumped off

[84] 4th Mar Div Report, Sect IV, 29.

[85] 3d Bn, 25th Mar Report, 6. 1st Bn, 25th Mar Report, 34.

MOVEMENT THROUGH TINIAN TOWN was much easier than Marines had expected. The 24th Regiment combed the ruins on the afternoon of 30 July, carefully avoiding the heavily mined Tinian Town beaches.

for O–7, the artillery increased range 400 yards again, and fired five more minutes.

Principal feature in the division's zone for 30 July was Tinian Town, a locality that the Japanese had planned to defend from amphibious attack. So much had the enemy concentrated on the seaborne approach to the town that all other directions—including the one used by the Marines—had been ignored. Most of the prepared positions in the area prohibited, by their construction, enemy gunners from shifting weapons to fire at Marines to the north. By this late date, of course, U. S. ships, aircraft and artillery had destroyed nearly all af the Japanese coast defense weapons anyway.

The only difficulty experienced by the 4th Division in its move from the commanding ground down to the Tinian Town flats came on the right, where Marines of the 1st Battalion, 24th Regiment, encountered several Japanese machine gunners and riflemen holed up in caves near the coast. The tactics employed against these were consistent both in application and effectiveness: medium tanks and armored amphibians blasted the positions while light (flame-thrower) tanks moved in close enough to pour streams of fire into the openings. Then followed assault by combat engineers (carrying

flame-throwers, demolitions, and bazookas) covered by surrounding Marine riflemen and machine gunners.

While operating against caves north of Tinian Town's outskirts, tanks of Company B, 4th Tank Battalion, became the targets of several Japanese field pieces that remained active despite the odds. Firing from the cliff line overlooking the Tinian Town flats on the south, the enemy gunners hit and knocked out one of the U. S. machines. Marine tanks immediately directed retaliatory fire against the suspected Japanese positions but achieved no observed results other than temporary cessation of the enemy shelling.

Meanwhile, as Marines of the 24th Regiment routed Japanese from coastal hideouts, the left assault regiment, the 25th, met only "slight resistance" and surged ahead. This situation developed a minor contact problem and demanded that the 24th Marines' left battalion, the 3d, be echeloned forward to hang on to the 25th Marines' flank. At one point during the day the contact battalion stretched itself to the breaking point, creating an internal gap. This was patched later in the day, however, when the 24th Marines caught up with the 25th.

The 24th Marines entered Tinian Town at 1420. In most instances the town's streets could not be distinguished from its buildings; the entire area was a mass of rubble. Naval gunfire, air and artillery had done a thorough job. Only one Japanese was found among the debris, and he was alive. Just what this outnumbered individual hoped to accomplish by resisting was not revealed. The advancing Marines spent slightly less time with him than did the 4th Division D-2 who reported: "He was killed." [86]

Enemy weapons—thought to be tanks—firing from somewhere to the south contested movement into and through the town indirectly and impotently. All shells fell harmlessly. Vehicles and men stayed clear of the Tinian Town beaches, where hundreds of mines poked through the sand. By 1700 the ruins had been

[86] 4th Mar Div D-2 Periodic Report 77.

thoroughly combed, and the 24th Marines occupied the O-7 line just south of the town (see Map 10).

The 25th Regiment pushed without difficulty across Airfield No. 4 to Objective O-7. There, after a shift in the boundary between divisions (discussed later), the unit was relieved from the front lines. The 23d Marines assumed the right half of the 25th's sector, the 8th Marines the left half. After relief, the 25th Marines, less 3d Battalion, became NTLF reserve; the 3d Battalion went into 4th Division reserve. The 25th Marines would remain in reserve for the rest of the operation.

While the 24th and 25th Marines pushed from O-5 to O-7, the 23d Regiment remained in reserve. On 29 July the 2d Battalion had been held in NTLF reserve, the remainder of the regiment in division reserve; 30 July was similar, except that the 3d and 2d Battalions exchanged assignments. After moving into the

MACHINE-GUN POSITION in the center of Tinian Town was well-constructed, well-sited, and, fortunately for the Marines, unoccupied. No dead and only one live Japanese remained in the town on 30 July.

PRIVATE JOSEPH W. OZBOURN, 1st Battalion, 23d Marines, posthumously awarded the Medal of Honor for intentionally smothering a grenade's explosion with his own body on 30 July 1944 and thereby protecting several comrades nearby.

front lines and relieving the 25th Regiment, all subordinate units of the 23d Marines reverted to parent control.

The 14th Marines, in the first five days of the Tinian operation (24–28 July), fired slightly less than 23,000 rounds. For 29 and 30 July the total exceeded 29,000 rounds and the average daily output multiplied by over three times. This increase reflected more than anything else the plenitude of ammunition, which allowed artillery units to fire upon every suspicious area without fear that stocks would become depleted. The 14th Marines furnished support during the 29–30 July attack as follows: 1st Battalion in direct support of the 25th Marines; 2d and 3d Battalions in general support; 4th 105mm Howitzer Battalion, V Amphibious Corps, in direct support of the 24th Marines.[87]

---

[87] 4th Mar Div Report, Sect IV, 29; 14th Mar Report, 6–8; 23d Mar Report, 23; 24th Mar Report, 10–12; 25th Mar Report, 4.

The 2d Division's Push to O-7

The 2d Division, its formation unchanged (2d and 6th Marines abreast), attacked at 0700, 29 July. Since Objective O–7 was nearly 5,000 yards forward of the line of departure, General Watson, the division commander, specified an intermediate objective where assault regiments could reorganize before the push to O–7. Designated O–7A, the 2d Division's phase line embraced dominating terrain about 3,000 yards to the front. (See Map 10.)

Initially, the two leading regiments encountered no enemy; but, as they crossed O–6 and headed toward O–7A, the opposition got progressively stiffer. The right regiment, the 6th, advancing with its 1st and 3d Battalions abreast, met machine-gun and mortar fire all along its front but particularly on the left in the 3d Battalion's zone. The Japanese resistance never localized, however; as soon as the Marines deployed to assault a particular source of trouble, it would suddenly become vacant of defenders. Against this hesitating defense pattern, the 6th Marines maintained a jerking advance. Never did the enemy hold up more than a portion of the front; never was the delay more than momentary. By 1500, 29 July, the 6th Marines reached commanding ground just short of Objective O–7A. There the regiment dug in for the night.

The left regiment (the 2d) experienced similar, but more stubborn resistance, particularly on the extreme left in the 1st Battalion's zone. The latter unit faced a 340-foot hill mass on Masalog Point that, although only lightly defended, proved an obstacle to rapid movement. The other two assault battalions—2d in the center and the attached 2d Battalion, 8th Marines, on the right—moved with less difficulty. By 1500 these two units were several hundred yards ahead of the 1st Battalion, and Colonel Stuart, the regimental commander, decided to exploit their success.

Upon his order, two companies of the reserve 3d Battalion moved through the zone already cleared by the two right battalions and struck the Masalog Point hill mass from the right flank. Thus, the tactical locality received pressure from two directions, north and west. By

1715 the western slopes and a portion of the peak were in the 2d Marines' hands, but the rest of the feature remained to be captured. In this position, roughly midway between O–6 and O–7A, the regiment dug in for the night.

The night of 29–30 July was disturbed only once in the 2d Division's sector. A 20-man Japanese patrol attempted to enter the 6th Marines' lines. All intruders were killed.

The 2d Division's 30 July attack was in all respects a continuation of that begun the day before. Late afternoon of 29 July had found two companies of the 3d Battalion, 2d Marines, striking the Masalog hill mass from the west. Since it was immediately apparent that this approach offered better chances for success than one from the north, Colonel Stuart ordered the entire 3d Battalion to take over this mission on 30 July. As soon as the Marines moved out in the attack at 0745, the hill's defenders could see their predicament: pressure from north and east, assault from the west. Most of the Japanese took the one favorable alternative: They pulled off the hill and headed south.

As soon as the 3d Battalion, 2d Marines, captured the dominating ground, the 1st Battalion moved rapidly along the coast of Masalog Point. The 3d Battalion then swung its direction of attack to the south and moved abreast of the 1st Battalion toward the day's objective. By about noon these two units had assumed the entire regimental front, pinching out the 2d Battalion and the attached 2d Battalion, 8th Marines.

From shortly after noon until nearly dark, the 3d Battalion, 2d Marines, engaged in its busiest period of the entire Tinian operation. As narrated by the unit's commanding officer, Lieutenant Colonel Walter F. Layer:

On or about 1230, 30 July 1944, [we] were temporarily halted by machine gun and 70mm gun fire coming from the right front of the battalion's zone of action. Captain Robert F. O'Brien, commanding officer of Love Company . . . dispatched a patrol which destroyed the enemy guns and crews. I believe this 70mm gun was the one that Lieutenant Colonel Easley, commanding officer, 3d Battalion, 6th Marines, could not locate [see below].

After Captain O'Brien's patrol had destroyed the guns that held up the battalion, the attack was continued across an open field approximately two hundred yards wide where on the far side approximately ten well constructed machine gun positions were captured complete with the guns. The enemy had abandoned these positions and had retreated approximately one hundred yards south. They moved down a steep cliff, approximately eighty feet high, via a dirt road into a large cave running back north under the cliff.

Marines of Love Company pursued the enemy, chasing them into the afore-mentioned cave. The enemy were contained in the cave until the entire 3d Battalion advanced down the cliff and had taken positions ready to continue the attack. [I] requested and received from the commanding officer, 2d Marines the assistance of a flame-throwing tank which along with Marines from the 3d Battalion destroyed approximately eighty enemy and approximately four machine guns [in] the afore-mentioned cave.

As the cave was being attacked, enemy forces approximately five hundred yards to our front (south) deployed in rocky terrain took the 3d Battalion, 2d Marines, under fire with mortars.

It is beyond my memory as to the number of casualties the 3d Battalion suffered at that time. I personally rendered first aid to two wounded Marines and remember seeing six or seven Marines who were either wounded or killed by that enemy mortar fire.

Tanks and half-tracks that were attached to the 3d Battalion, 2d Marines, took the enemy under fire, destroying the enemy mortars. . . .[88]

Despite the resistance met by the 3d Battalion, the 2d Marines maintained the momentum of its attack, and as early as 1345 Colonel Stuart reported his regiment on Objective O–7. There it prepared defenses for the night. (See Map 10.)

The 6th Marines' 30 July advances were made against "sporadic small arms and machine gun fire . . . along with light mortar and artillery fire." The right battalion, the 1st, moved fast and reached O–7 at 1245. On the left, however, the 3d Battalion encountered direct fire from an enemy field piece that threatened to inflict heavy casualties if the advance continued. Since the piece could not be located, no target existed for mortars or artillery. In this situation, Lieutenant Colonel Easley, commanding the 3d Battalion, sent a combat patrol to locate and destroy the Japanese gun. This effort was unsuccessful in that the position was not found, but successful in that no more was heard of the enemy weapon. It was surmised that the gunner had abandoned his hidden piece in the

_____

[88] Ltr from LtCol W. F. Layer to CMC, 16Nov50.

face of the patrol activity.[89] Thereafter the Marines pressed forward rapidly, and by 1604 the 3d Battalion joined the 1st Battalion at O–7.

The 8th Regiment was split into three parts on 29 July: 2d Battalion attached to the 2d Marines, 3d Battalion in NTLF reserve, the remainder in division reserve. By 1400, 30 July, for the first time in four days, all battalions of the 8th Marines were under parent control. This came about as a direct result of an impending change in the boundary between divisions, a change that would broaden the 2d Division front and require commitment of additional 2d Division troops. Colonel Wallace received a warning in the early afternoon that his 8th Regiment would be committed on the extreme right of the division front. Wallace accordingly started his battalions on the march long before he received the actual order to move into the lines. By 1830 the regiment had assumed its assigned sector, relieving leftmost elements of the 4th Division and rightmost elements of the 6th Marines in the process. To fill vacancies created by this commitment, the 2d Battalion, 6th Marines, became reserve for the 2d Division and the 2d Battalion, 2d Marines, for NTLF.[90]

---

[89] As pointed out by Lieutenant Colonel Walter F. Layer, this may have been the same weapon destroyed by Marines of the 3d Battalion, 2d Marines.

[90] 2d Mar Div Report, 3; 2d Mar Report, 3–4; 6th Mar Report, 2–3; 8th Mar Report, 4–5.

TRAMPING THE CANE was tiring work, especially when the direction of advance did not parallel the rows of the fields. Each stalk was strong enough to trip a man careless about where he stepped. Despite the Marines' systematic search, many Japanese lay hidden in the cane and escaped detection for months.

And so, the two divisions, in a week, captured about four-fifths of the island. Now, with all of the Japanese congested in the other one-fifth, the Marines wondered when and where the showdown fight would develop. Although there could be no serious question regarding the outcome of any enemy effort at this late date, everyone realized that the fighting in a given sector could be vicious and bloody. The Marines knew that the Japanese were capable of the same type of frenzied reaction characteristic of a cornered animal. No one took the enemy capabilities lightly.

The terrain south of the Marine lines on the evening of 30 July was flat for about 2,000 yards; then it rose in an abrupt, wooded escarpment to a plateau. Along the east coast the rise was so sheer as virtually to prevent scaling, and even in the center it was steep enough that a road up it followed a double hairpin pattern. Only near the west coast did the cliff become gentler and easier to climb.

A prisoner, Warrant Officer Akiyama of the 56th Naval Guard Force, indicated that, at the time of his capture (29 July), the bulk of the enemy was disposed either in the cliff area or in the terrain forward of it. His estimate of remaining Japanese in the principal Army and Navy organizations—50th Infantry, 1700 to 1800; 56th Naval Guard Force, 500—if accurate, meant that these units had averaged about 50 percent casualties by 29 July. The NTLF G–2's estimated enemy casualties, based upon daily reports from the divisions, showed about 3,000 Japanese soldiers and sailors killed or captured by 29 July, about 33 percent of the total known pre-Jig-Day strength. Even accepting the prisoner's estimate of remaining Japanese, Marines could expect to pay dearly for the last fifth of the island.

CHAPTER **IV**

Up the Cliff

JIG-PLUS 7—31 JULY 1944

The Japanese faced an unenviable situation on the last day of July 1944. Compressed in the southern end of Tinian, they could withdraw no farther. Anticipating the usual bitterend resistance from these cornered troops, General Schmidt issued the most detailed operation order since the Jig-Day landings and disseminated a special naval gunfire annex for this single day's move. The annex provided that, in addition to those fire support ships working directly with shore fire control parties,[1] the battleships *Tennessee* and *California*, the heavy cruiser *Louisville*, and the light cruisers *Montpelier* and *Birmingham* would combine their efforts and fire power against the wooded cliff line facing the two Marine divisions.

During the period 0600–0715 and 0755–0830, these warships threw approximately 615 tons of shells into their targets. During this entire period, front-line Marines were directed to remain in their foxholes as protection against errant rounds. There were none, however; the cliff was easy for the ships to spot and hit.[2]

The naval gunfire by no means rounded out the preliminary bombardment picture for 31 July; aircraft of the Northern Attack Force (including a majority of U. S. Army Air Force planes flying from Aslito Airfield on Saipan) struck the cliff line during a 40-minute break— 0715–0755—in the ships' shelling. Every available bomb-carrying plane in the area, a total of 126,[3] took part in dropping a total of 69 tons of explosives. All bombs landed in or very near to the target area.[4] Even horizontal bombers were used, 16 B-25's hitting the cliff from an altitude of about 800 to 1,000 feet.

Artillery also threw its weight into the preparatory effort; but, unlike air and naval gunfire, it was not ordered by NTLF to fire at any specified time. The artillery regiments of the

---

[1] For 31 July ships (all destroyers) were assigned for direct support as follows: *Saufley* and *Cony*—1st and 2d Battalions, 2d Marines; *Pringle* and *Twining*—1st and 2d Battalions, 6th Marines; *Monssen*—2d Battalion, 8th Marines; *Halsey Powell, Yarnall, Mugford* and *Bryant*—1st Battalion, 23d Marines; *Waller* and *McGowan*—2d Battalion, 23d Marines; *Sigourney*—2d Battalion, 25th Marines.

[2] NTLF Opn Order 37–44, Annex B. TF 52 Report, 79–80.

[3] These planes were divided as follows: 86 P-47's (from the Army Air Force's 318th Air Group), 16 B-25's (from the Army Air Force's 48th Bomber Squadron), and 24 torpedo bombers (from the escort carrier *Kitkun Bay*).

[4] TF 52 Report, 132.

two divisions as well as the XXIV Corps Artillery fired throughout the night on the cliff, and as dawn broke, they picked up the tempo. Records are incomplete as to the numbers of rounds fired by the various units during the preparations,[5] but front-line Marines recall that the whine of "outgoing mail" was almost continuous from midnight until jump-off time.

Following this noisy prelude, the Marines attacked at 0830. The 4th Division moved with the 23d and 24th Regiments abreast, the latter on the right along the west coast. (See Map 11, facing page 103.)

The 24th Marines' zone included a vast coastal plain, thickly covered with clutching undergrowth that greatly hampered tank operations. Here again, the trusty armored amphibians (LVT(A)'s) rendered valuable fire support by moving along in the water abreast of the right flank. Most of the difficulty was encountered along the coast in the 1st Battalion's zone, where the terrain afforded numerous hideouts for the enemy. Resistance became more stubborn at 0945 as the 1st Battalion closed upon an isolated enemy position near the beach. At 1000 the desperate Japanese defenders—about a platoon—lashed out in a vicious counterattack. Lead flew wildly for a time, but in the end the Japanese were annihilated. When the Marines resumed their advance after the flurry, one company remained behind to mop up stragglers. The attached platoon of flame-thrower tanks from Company D, 4th Tank Battalion, proved valuable in burning selected stretches of undergrowth where Japanese riflemen were hidden.

As already noted, the bulk of the 24th Marines' difficulties occurred on the extreme right in the 1st Battalion's zone. The regiment's left assault battalion, the 3d, moved against only sporadic rifle and machine-gun fire until about 1600 when, from the cliff to its left front, the unit received a hail of small-arms fire that

nearly stopped forward movement. Tanks from Company B, 4th Tank Battalion, and half-tracks from the 24th Marines' Regimental Weapons Company immediately moved against the trouble spot but soon found themselves amidst an enemy mine field that, because of its location along a restricted section of road, could not be by-passed. Engineers from Company B, 20th Marines, subsequently cleared 45 mines from this area.

The lateness of the afternoon forced the regiment to halt its advance for the night. The Marines then prepared defenses (in the words of the division's action report) "on the least unfavorable ground" in the area. (See Map 11.)

The 23d Marines, attacking on the left of the 24th, experienced similar difficulties. Soon after the regiment moved out, a gap developed between it and the 2d Division, a gap that would assume greater importance as the day wore on.[6] From the cliff to the left front and from a tiny village at its base came galling small-arms fire that slowed the regiment's movements. Nor was this the only trouble; from the front came direct fires of a larger caliber weapon—first believed to be a 5-inch naval gun—that threatened to impose severe casualties if the frontal approach were continued.

What about an envelopment? Impractical—there was no room for maneuver, since flanking units were generally abreast. What about supporting arms? Practical—but the enemy weapon could not be located. Without a definite target, artillery, air and naval gunfire were usually ineffective. Tanks attempted to do some good by blasting suspicious fissures in the cliff, but approaches to better firing positions were blocked by an enemy mine field.

What happened in the next few minutes was difficult to describe, not only here but wherever it occurred. Nothing changed, no new stratagem was employed, no new order issued, no fresh troops committed; the Marines simply started stealing forward. This move was not marked by the bravado of a single individual or

---

[5] The 10th Marines operations officer later estimated that the regiment had fired about 5,000 rounds during the night. Ltr from LtCol W. H. Hitt to CMC, 22Dec50. Between midnight 30 July and 0830 31 July, the 14th Marines fired 2,419 rounds in preparation for the attack. 14th Mar Report, 8.

[6] The NTLF Operation Order for 31 July had prescribed that contact would be maintained from right to left.

ESCARPMENT near the island's southern end was scene of principal action on 31 July. Offering caves for cover and undergrowth for concealment, the cliff line provided excellent natural defensive positions. Because they expected the enemy to exploit fully the cliff's defensive possibilities, U. S. commanders ordered a preparatory bombardment more intense than any Tarawa and Saipan veteran had ever witnessed.

even the urging of a leader. Rather it represented that extraordinary discipline and spirit that caused men to close with the enemy. Attempt it the easy way, try to knock out the resistance with supporting arms; but if that failed (as it often did), move out anyway. First, one Marine dashed forward about 10 yards, flopped quickly to the ground before the enemy gunner could train his piece, and opened fire himself. Now a second and a third lurched forward in a running zig-zag motion and dived behind a small fold in the terrain. In a matter of moments a squad had gained 10 yards, and the leap-frog advance resumed—another 10 yards, and another. This type of aggressiveness, multiplied over a battalion or regimental front, paid dividends.

Meanwhile, medium tanks of Company C, 4th Tank Battalion, kept their cannon barking

against any point in the cliff that appeared to be occupied by the enemy. The "large-caliber" weapon that had uttered so many challenges had still not been located. Suddenly, the left flank tank received six hits in rapid succession. The vehicle, though penetrated, remained operative and backed away from the swathe of fire. Here was evidence that the enemy weapon was close at hand; the improvement in marksmanship indicated that. The commander of the wounded tank thought he spotted the position and immediately fired two smoke rounds to mark the target. Rockets, naval gunfire and tanks plastered the designated area; and, when the dust and smoke cleared, all was quiet.

The advance was resumed, this time with another tank on the left flank. When it reached the point where the first tank had been hit, the same Japanese gun opened again, delivering six

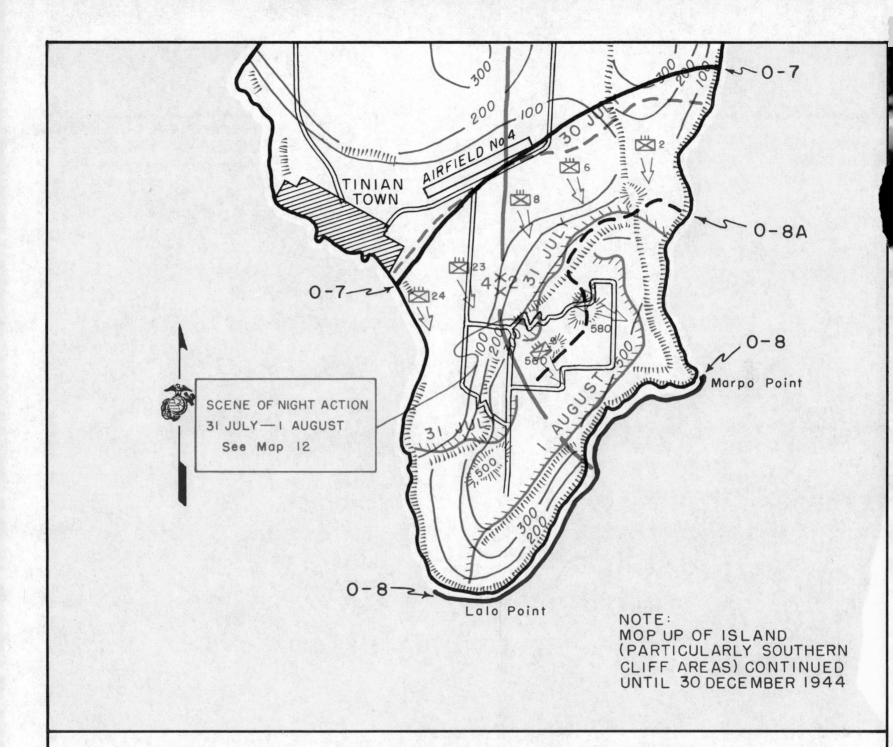

AIRFIELD No 4

TINIAN TOWN

⊠ 2

⊠ 6

⊠ 8

O-7

30 JUL

O-8A

⊠ 23

⊠ 24

4 × 2   31 JULY

X 2

O-7

580

O-8

580

Marpo Point

SCENE OF NIGHT ACTION
31 JULY—1 AUGUST
See Map 12

31 JULY

1 AUGUST

500

300
200

O-8

Lalo Point

NOTE:
MOP UP OF ISLAND
(PARTICULARLY SOUTHERN
CLIFF AREAS) CONTINUED
UNTIL 30 DECEMBER 1944

PROGRESS LINES FOR 31 JULY AND 1 AUGUST, 1944

0   2000   4000

YARDS

MAP 11

RD 7418

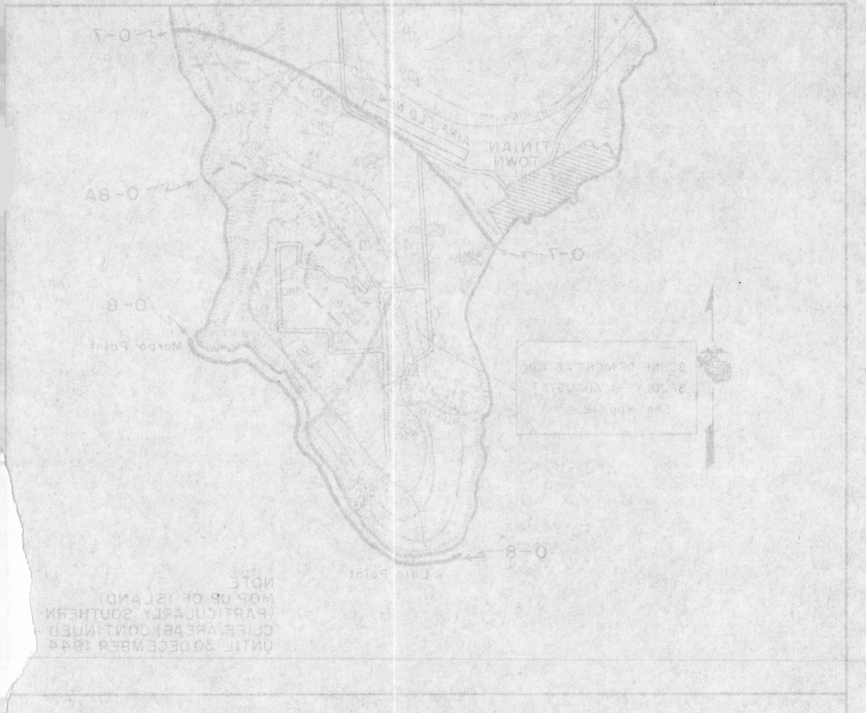

more shells, three of which penetrated the armor. Again, however, the machine remained operative, and this time there was no mistaking where the fire had come from. Both tanks that had suffered blows saw the enemy weapon at the same moment—only 30 yards away. Without a pause to coordinate their scheme of attack, the two tanks achieved quick revenge. One threw a smoke shell in front of the enemy position, while the other maneuvered around behind it, destroyed the gun, and machine-gunned the 20 Japanese who streamed out. During the move the attacking tank received a seventh hit from the enemy gun, but the shell bounced off without doing any damage.

Later examination of the emplacement revealed that it was enclosed with concrete on three sides and roof. A tiny aperture allowed the emplaced 47mm antitank gun to cover only about a 10-yard-wide fire lane into which both tanks had moved. This type of defense was characteristic of the Japanese, who, consistently out-gunned, chose concealment in preference to field of fire.

This tank activity had occurred entirely within the zone of the 1st Battalion, 23d Marines. Tanks operating with the right (2d) battalion also spent an eventful day. After they encountered a mine field on the lower approaches of a road leading up the escarpment, and just as engineers of Company C, 20th Marines, began clearance activities, Japanese riflemen and machine gunners suddenly opened up from an open trench only about 20 yards away. Immediately the tanks roared back an answer, and one machine started proceeding cautiously through the mines to a position from which it could fire down the trench's longer axis. When only five yards from the end of the trench, the tank struck a mine, which shattered the suspension system and wounded the driver, assistant driver and tank commander.

Thus encouraged, the Japanese became increasingly active, darted about more, and presented U. S. tanks even better targets. While most of the mediums poured shells into the trench, one machine moved up behind the disabled one, picked up the beseiged crew and pulled back. The Japanese then put the disabled tank to a use that the U. S. tank manufac-

turer never intended: they set up machine guns in its protection and sprayed fire against the Marines. This situation demanded prompt action: the enemy-occupied machine was blown apart by other U. S. tanks.[7]

The coming of darkness forced the abandonment of further attempts to reduce the enemy position, and the 2d Battalion, 23d Marines, dug in to contain the strongpoint for the night. One company, which had passed to the left of the trouble spot, scaled the cliff and remained on top for the night.

By 1745 the left battalion (the 1st) of the 23d Marines had gained the high ground, while the 2d Battalion had reached positions at the base. One company of the latter unit moved through the 1st Battalion's zone and attained positions on top of the cliff. The 3d Battalion, which had followed the advance in regimental reserve during the day, also followed the 1st Battalion to the top of the cliff and there tied in defenses. The two battalions on the high ground established a perimeter defense with both flanks anchored on the cliff line. Mines on the only road to the top prevented supporting tanks from joining these units until the next day.[8] In the late afternoon, the 3d Battalion, 25th Marines, was attached to the 23d Regiment and ordered to assume positions at the base of the cliff for the night. There it would protect the 23d's left flank, exposed because of the gap between divisions. (See Map 11.)

In addition to the tank casualties in the 23d Marines' zone, Japanese fire from the cliff caused the temporary loss of two 37mm guns and a one-ton truck.[9] The commander of the

---

[7] Destroyed at the same time as the tank were a periscope-mounted camera and considerable footage of combat film photographed at Tinian by Corporal John C. Shutt, who conceived the idea of using a camera in this manner. Because the division did not have a suitable camera for this purpose, Schutt used his own personal one, for the loss of which the Marine Corps later reimbursed him. Ltr from LtCol R. K. Schmidt to CMC, 16Nov50. Ltr from LtCol R. K. Schmidt to author, 7Dec50. Ltr from Cpl J. C. Schutt to CMC 28Dec45.

[8] *L. R. Jones.*

[9] The 23d Marines' report said that the weapons and truck were "knocked out."

TO THE HEIGHTS move Marines of the 4th Division on 31 July as they penetrate the enemy's last desirable defense locality. Underbrush, though battered by U. S. supporting arms, furnished good concealment for Japanese defenders.

regiment's 75mm half-track platoon, Captain Russell M. Paquette, described the incident, in part, as follows:

Ordinarily the 37's would travel slightly in rear of the front lines, coming up during the day for specific targets . . . and taking their place on the front lines at night to cover possible tank approaches. However, because of the mobility of the attack [on 31 July], the 37's were moving with the assault companies, since we were engaging the enemy only sporadically. Actually, I do not believe that the [37's were] forward of the front line, although it would be entirely possible in view of the situation. I was travelling in my radio jeep in the near vicinity of the cliff line when the enemy opened fire from our left flank. The 37's were between my jeep and the cliff, probably 200 yards from the cliff itself. I was never sure, but thought the weapon used by the Japs was a machine gun or automatic weapon of some type.

After withdrawing from the area [because of the enemy fire], I was advised by Sgt. John Benkovich [commander of the 1st 37mm Platoon] that the 37's were left with a one-ton truck. I dispatched one half-track under command of my Platoon Sergeant, Louis Miller, accompanied by Sgt. Benkovich. I maintained radio communication with them until their return with one 37mm. They did not receive heavy fire from the cliff and Sgt. Benkovich was slightly wounded. . . . They had removed the breech block from the remaining 37 and brought back the 50 cal. machine gun mounted on the truck.[10]

---

[10] Ltr from Capt R. M. Paquette to author, 16Nov50. Silver Star Medal citation of Platoon Sergeant John G. Benkovich, 18Aug45.

During the night the Japanese booby-trapped the abandoned truck and gun, but Marines spotted and disarmed the devices the following morning before they could cause trouble.

The 25th Marines continued its assignment received the previous day: 3d Battalion (until its late afternoon attachment to the 23d Marines) in division reserve, the remainder of the regiment in NTLF reserve.

The 4th Marine Division had made an important gain on 31 July. The last desirable defense locality on the island had been penetrated. Troops were now upon the southern plateau, which continued generally flat and open to the coastal cliffs at the island's southern end. The positions for the night defense were poor, with some Marines up on the high ground and others at the base. More serious than this split, however, was the large gap between the 4th Division's left and the 2d Division's right. Patrols sent by the 23d Marines ranged over this expanse but failed to achieve contact.[11]

The Struggle for a Toe Hold

General Watson, foreseeing the difficulties of moving his 2d Marine Division all the way to Objective O–8 without pausing for reorganization, prescribed an intermediate objective, O–8A (see Map 11). This objective's left half followed along the base of the cliff, while its right half included the cliff face and about 500 yards of the plateau above. The reason for this difference was the escarpment itself, which, on the left, virtually forbade scaling but, on the right, presented somewhat easier slopes for climbing. Consistent with this objective assignment, the left regiment, the 2d, would attack to the base of the cliff where it would halt its move and prevent Japanese escape along the east coast. The 6th Marines, the center regiment, would also meet the cliff at a practically insurmountable point, but this unit would then swing to the west and follow the 8th Marines to the top. The latter regiment, being favored with the only

road (a double hairpin design) to the top within the division's zone, would clamber up and grasp a foothold so that other units could follow.

The 2d Regiment, less its 2d Battalion in NTLF reserve, moved toward the assigned objective impeded only by occasional enemy riflemen and numerous Japanese civilians who advanced waving white cloths signifying their desire to surrender. The latter had to be carefully watched lest one of their number turn into an enemy soldier bent upon destroying as many Americans as possible before meeting death himself. By early afternoon the unit reached its objective at the base of the escarpment. The right battalion, the 3d, stretched its lines to the right in order to assume the frontage of the 3d Battalion, 6th Marines, which unit moved into an assembly area preparatory to following the 8th Marines to the top of the cliff.

The 6th Marines advanced against much the same type of resistance encountered by the 2d Marines: "slight rifle and machine gun fire from the face of the cliffs . . . and light mortar fire from the top. . . ." After reaching Objective O–8A and sending patrols to the base of the escarpment, the regiment pulled back about 400 yards where better defense positions were afforded. A great deal of shifting about and change of status occurred within the regiment during the day. The 2d Battalion began the day in division reserve, but at 1410 it reverted to parent control, and the 1st Battalion, which had been pinched from the lines, became division reserve. At 1700 the 3d Battalion, following relief by elements of the 2d Marines, became division reserve, and the 1st Battalion returned to 6th Marines' control. Thus, all three battalions at one time or another during the day served as 2d Division reserve.[12]

The right regiment of the 2d Division, the 8th, was carrying the ball on 31 July. The entire division scheme of maneuver hinged upon this unit's ability to reach the heights. Once at the top, it could expand its holdings and wait for the 6th Marines to follow and join for the drive to the final objective.

The 8th Marines attacked with the 1st and 3d Battalions abreast, 1st on the right. Aside

[11] 4th Mar Div Report, 30–31. 23d Mar Report, 23–24. 24th Mar Report, 12–13. 25th Mar Report, 4. 4th Tank Bn Report, Company B Report, 3; Company C Report, 5–6. *L. R. Jones. Dillon. Dick.*

[12] 2d Mar Report, 4. 6th Mar Report, 4.

THE CLIFF was a formidible obstacle to movement on 31 July. Cutting practically all the way across the island, it provided problems for both divisions. Here Marines of the 2d Division climb the rocky slopes toward the flat plateau on top. The 1st and 2d Battalions, 8th Marines, spent their busiest night (31 July–1 August) of the operation holding a road that curled up this slope.

from scattered machine-gun fire from small patches of woods and from behind a railroad embankment, the two battalions moved steadily toward the escarpment. The closer they approached, the more intense became the enemy fire. But the Marines pushed on.

At 1210 the 3d Battalion reached the cliff within its zone. To support the ascent, the battalion commander, Lieutenant Colonel Gavin C. Humphrey, requested permission to send the tanks (from Company A, 2d Tank Battalion, working with his unit) along the road in the 1st Battalion's zone. This request had

to be denied, because the 1st Battalion had not secured that road as yet. Humphrey then volunteered an estimate to the regimental commander that it would take his battalion about 45 minutes to scale the cliff; but, when the unit started climbing, his over-optimism became evident. The cliff face was gashed with numerous erosion channels, fissures, crannies, and deep caves. All of these were blanketed with scrub undergrowth that concealed their location. From these ideal hideouts, Japanese riflemen and machine gunners directed galling fire toward the Marines below, effectively stopping ascent efforts. Later in the day, when it was clear that his men were stalled at the bottom, Humphrey requested permission to withdraw his unit about 400 yards so that artillery fire could be safely called into the area. Colonel Wallace denied permission, because such a move would have jeopardized the 1st Battalion's left flank.

The 3d Battalion remained at the base of the cliff for the rest of the day and the following night. Medium tanks, which at last located a suitable route into positions, fired hundreds of exploratory rounds into the cliff face in an attempt to find the enemy hideouts, but for the most part these efforts appeared ineffective. Attempts to burn away the vegetation with flame-thrower tanks achieved only fair results.

The 1st Battalion had slightly farther to go to reach the cliff base than did the 3d Battalion (see Map 11), but about 1500, Marines of that unit reached the approaches and began casting anxious eyes up the steep slopes. A mere glance at this natural barrier was enough to convince everyone that a few strategically placed weapons could make the climb very costly. Only up the double-hairpin road could the ascent be made with any degree of facility, and it was soon learned that the Japanese understood this too. All initial attempts to use that route met a blistering hail of enemy small-arms fire. By 1630 it appeared that the trip to the top would await another day.

But clawing its way through the underbrush, one platoon of Company A reached the top at 1650. Five minutes later a platoon from Company C joined the trail-blazers. Nothing for it then but to reinforce the shallow foothold.

It was soon apparent that, to man the salient on the cliff properly, all three rifle companies of the 1st Battalion would have to be committed to the lines. Colonel Wallace was well aware that, if he failed to capitalize on this breakthrough, the entire battle for the cliff might begin anew on the following day. Wallace therefore requested and received General Watson's permission to commit the reserve 2d Battalion, so that it could be rushed up to exploit the success of the 1st, so that the shallow "beachhead" could be expanded. The 2d Battalion was on the move by 1705, about an hour and a half before sunset. Its orders were to join the 1st Battalion, extend the lines to the left and thence down the cliff to attain physical contact with the 3d Battalion at the base.[13]

The Night on the Cliff

By the time the leading company (E) of the 2d Battalion, 8th Marines, arrived at the base of the cliff, all three rifle companies of the 1st Battalion were committed into the lines at the top. Tracer rounds skittered through the gathering dusk as the Japanese realized that the Americans had a toe hold on their plateau. About the time Company E completed the climb, the Japanese launched a vicious local counterattack against it and the 1st Battalion's left. The situation was touch and go for a short time, one section of the Marines' front even being forced back a few yards, but the attackers were too few for the task they had assumed, and the Marines checked and chased them. (Fold-out Map 12, facing page 112.)

The savage hail of grazing rifle and machine-gun fire that swept the broad, level plateau made it immediately apparent that assumption of positions on the flat would be suicidal during daylight. Major William C. Chamberlin, 2d Battalion executive officer, who was reconnoitering the battalion's assigned defense area, therefore ordered Company E to remain just under the lip of the cliff until later.

By 1900 it was sufficiently dark for Company E to move into position in the open. Patrols were immediately dispatched to provide security during the digging-in period. The earlier

enemy counterattack had given an indication that others were to come, and, if the enemy operated true to form, he would likely strike again at the same point. Into this precise area Major Chamberlin moved two 37mm guns from the 8th Marines' Regimental Weapons Company. From these positions they could fire canister across the open ground Chamberlin considered the most probable avenue of enemy approach. Machine guns were emplaced and sited so that their final protective fires would cross in front of the 37's. All the while the enemy remained active; knee-mortar shells fell sporadically, and short bursts of automatic-weapons fire zipped menacingly through the area every few moments.

Company G, the second company in the 2d Battalion's long, reinforcing column, arrived at the cliff base at about 1845, just as the sun set. Since it would be dark before Company G could reach the top of the cliff, Chamberlin directed that it should wait until guides from Company E had arrived to lead the way. When, about 10 minutes later, the officer commanding Company G saw two hazy forms approaching from the cliffside shadows, he assumed them to be the guides from Company E. Through his SCR-300 radio he conveyed the news to the Company E commander: "The two guides that you sent are approaching me." But the Company E commander responded: "They couldn't be approaching you. They're both standing right here beside me." With scarcely a "Roger, Out" the Company G commander dropped the transmitter, flopped upon his stomach, and shouted a challenge to the approaching duo. When the latter broke for cover, the truth was revealed: two prowling Japanese soldiers accidentally arrived when two Marines were expected. Since the pair was between Companies G and E, Marines could not safely fire, and the intruders escaped. Soon after this episode the two guides did, in fact, arrive, and Company G began the trudge up the slope.

At the top, Company G tied its right to Company E, then stretched its lines down the cliff itself. Adjacent foxholes varied in altitude by 10 to 12 feet in most cases. At the bottom, Company G's left flank tied in with headquarters

[13] 8th Mar Report, 5–6.

personnel of the 2d Battalion which had established a command post at the cliff base. A separation of about 350 yards still existed between the 2d and 3d Battalions, but the regimental commander ordered that the 2d Battalion use its reserve (Company F) to provide depth atop the cliff rather than using it to fill this gap. Colonel Wallace made this decision in the belief that the enemy would attempt to push the two battalions off the cliff and that a local reserve at the decisive spot would be more valuable than a tenuous link between the 2d and 3d Battalions.

The 350-yard gap on the left was not the only one to worry about. In forcing the cliff line, the 1st Battalion had shifted to the east in its zone of action, while 4th Division elements had moved slightly west. Now a 600-yard gap existed there.[14] Although the 23d Marines and the 8th Marines both sent patrols to rove the hiatus, contact was not regained. At 2200 even these efforts were abandoned. So, the two battalions of the 8th Marines were in all respects alone on the cliff. This situation, plus the fact that all three rifle companies of the 1st Battalion had already been committed to the lines, made it imperative that the 2d Battalion retain as large a reserve as possible. Therefore, in addition to the 2d Battalion reserve (Company F), Companies E and G each held one of their platoons in support. (See Map 12.)

The 350-yard gap on the left was not especially serious: the terrain there was reasonably flat and a section of machine guns emplaced at the cliff base was sited to cover the area. The double-hairpin road up the cliff was busy with activity; jeeps carrying up ammunition and barbed wire and taking down casualties maintained a steady, creeping stream of traffic. Operating without headlights, the vehicles proceeded very cautiously up and down the sharp grade. The white coral surfacing provided some guide in maintaining direction; but, after 0140 when the moon set, even this could hardly be seen.

Added fire power became available on the cliff shortly after dark when two half-tracks

from the regimental weapons company struggled up the road to the top. These weapons were retained slightly to the rear with plans to employ them in case of tank attack. Against the Japanese automatic-weapons position to the left front, which was complicating the 2d Battalion's efforts to prepare defenses, the half-tracks were of little use. Every time they appeared upon the open plateau, a rain of Japanese knee-mortar shells chased them to cover. The open top of these vehicles ill-suited them to weather mortar fire.

At about 1900, in an attempt to knock out the source of the Japanese automatic-weapons fire, Major Chamberlin ordered the attached medium tank platoon from Company A to move up the road to the plateau. Once up, the tanks would be employed against the enemy position.

Soon after the tank platoon got underway, its leader sent Chamberlin a message stating that the road was mined and that one of his tanks had already been disabled. He suggested that the heavier weight of his tanks had set off mines while the lighter vehicles did not. Because of darkness and the tense situation, Chamberlin had to accept this report at its face value. But it was entirely erroneous. The disabled tank had run over the mine while moving off the road near the cliff base. There were no mines on the road itself. Owing to this inaccurate report, the 2d Battalion was deprived of weapons so desperately needed.

The two battalions, meanwhile, had not relaxed for a moment since arriving on top the cliff. Marines could feel a counterattack in the very air. They needed no encouragement to prepare good defense positions. One problem defied solution: Company E's wire-stringing efforts had all failed because of vicious grazing fire that swept the flat. To stand up and commence work was to invite death. Three Marine combat patrols moved out to relieve pressure; but, though they killed enemy groups within 20 yards of the front-line foxholes, wire-stringing details continued to suffer casualties. Sometime after midnight, Marines found a satisfactory solution: they passed concertina wire from foxhole to foxhole until it stretched completely across the desired frontage; then they merely pushed and rolled the long, barbed

[14] This was one of those rare situations in which a gap existed between two units and yet neither blamed the other for over half of the difficulty.

cylinder about 10 yards in front of their positions.

At 2300, while Company E was in the midst of its wire difficulties, the enemy employed a familiar tactic: a *banzai* charge. Accompanied with wild screaming, the Japanese struck near the boundary between the two battalions—in the same spot as the earlier effort. The thrust faltered, then withered, under the Marines' machine-gun and rifle fire. No one could be sure just how many Japanese were committed to this attack, but one thing was sure: they would need considerably more if they hoped to push the Marines off the cliff. The enemy commander, Colonel Ogata, was no doubt impressed with the defense at that point in the lines, inasmuch as he attempted no further attacks there.

Periods of silence were very infrequent during the night; probing patrols jabbed systematically at Company G—feeling for an opening or a weak spot in the cliff-side defense. They found none.

The double-hairpin road had been extensively used by ambulance and cargo jeeps during the early part of the night. At 0100, however, a force of approximately 150 Japanese suddenly appeared on the road, set up a road block, and burned two ambulance jeeps that happened along. Whether this enemy force had moved around the open right flank or whether it was a by-passed group was not clear. The fact that the enemy was so strong and well-organized seemed to point to the first possibility. If this were true and the Japanese commander continued to pour troops through this chute, the Marine positions on the cliff were indeed in peril.

At 0200 about a platoon of Japanese moved up the road, captured several Marine vehicles parked near the top, and continued into the 2d Battalion's rear. The intruders were very close to Company F's foxholes before they announced themselves. A vicious, bloody, hand-to-hand struggle began.

The situation was critical. The defense area was now in danger of being broken by assaults from the right rear, but, at the same time, attention could not be shifted from the front where sizeable enemy groups still lurked. Nature took this opportunity to make the scene even more sinister—the moon set, the night became pitch black.

Major Chamberlin, who had remained atop the cliff to coordinate the battalion's defense, spotted the threat to the right rear and quickly organized a counterattack force—two platoons of Company F and elements of Company A of the 1st Battalion. There was no time to evolve details of formation and control. Success depended upon speed and vigor of execution. Chamberlin issued an oral operation order (*en toto* version: "Let's go") and struck. The Marines, employing a combination of aggressive movement and blistering fire power, drove back the enemy group; the vehicles were retaken. To prevent a recurrence of enemy action from this direction, Chamberlin established a road block about half-way down the cliff, employing two platoons of Company F on the left of the road and the support platoon of Company G on the right of it.

The counterattack and subsequent establishment of the road block isolated a number of Japanese between the front lines and the road block. Company E's support platoon immediately swept through the area in an effort to mop them up. This effort was generally unfruitful, however; darkness made detection of the enemy very difficult. Early the next morning the 20 trapped Japanese obligingly located themselves by placing grenades against their abdomens and pulling the pins.

Company F had suffered numerous casualties during the close-in assault from the rear. Most of these were hit either by grenade or knee-mortar fragments, others were cut by bayonets. But the bulk were walking wounded who moved under their own power down the precipitous cliff to the battalion aid station.

Communications had remained good throughout the night, and Colonel Wallace was informed at all times of the situation confronting the two battalions. In respect for the enemy capability of moving large forces through the gap between divisions, Wallace requested additional troops from division. General Watson immediately attached the division reserve, the 3d Battalion, 6th Marines, to the 8th Regiment and started it moving toward the cliff. This was at 0330. At about the same time, the division staff alerted the 2d and 6th Regiments to the possibility that the Japanese might move in strength through the gap and strike almost anywhere.

By 0400 the situation to the right rear had clarified somewhat, and anxiety about a strong attack from that direction was reduced. But there was no time for relaxation. Now the left flank platoon of Company E reported mounting pressure and activity to its front. Tension grew as the enemy launched a series of minor probing attacks. Violent action was impending, and not a Marine on the cliff felt that there was any doubt about it.

Twice when it appeared that the enemy had worked up enough steam to explode into a *banzai* attack, the two 75mm half-tracks moved forward onto the plateau. Both times they were greeted with such a rain of enemy mortar fire that Chamberlin ordered them to retire. Marine mortars (60mm and 81mm) retaliated with a booming barrage just in front of the lines in an effort to keep the enemy disorganized. Artillery also entered the picture at this point. From approximately 0330 to 0430, the 10th Marines delivered massed concentrations every 15 minutes; from 0430 to 0500 every five minutes, and after 0500 every two minutes. The artillery fire had as its principal purpose the prevention of enemy reserves moving into attack position.

The support platoon of Company G, no longer required at the rear road block, moved up behind Company E. This economy of force made available an additional platoon for counterattacks should the enemy penetrate the lines.

At 0515 came the final, all-out *banzai* attack. It struck against the left of Company E in a violent, frontal surge. Immediately the entire area was bathed in a bright light as mortars and ships fired illuminating shells over the area. The Marines' battle cry—"flares"—equalled in volume the screams—"*banzai*"—of the Japanese. As long as they could see their foes, Marines felt certain that they could stop them.

The most effective Marine weapons during the onslaught were the two canister-coughing 37mm guns. The crews of these weapons performed magnificently; gunners became casualties and were quickly replaced; replacement gunners were hit and others took over. The turnover was tragic and monotonous. The gunshields' thin upper portions were easily pierced by point-blank small-arms fire, and no gunner remained at his post for over four or five minutes before getting hit. Still the guns were constantly and efficiently manned—never a moment's hesitation, never a lost opportunity. By daybreak only two of ten original crew members were left.

Machine guns and rifles performed well too, cutting down attackers that weathered the 37mm guns' shotgun-like canister sprays.

The attack maintained its frenzied peak for about 30 minutes, during which time the enemy failed to penetrate U. S. lines at any point. The fighting had been close, sometimes intimate. Many Japanese bodies lay within five yards of the Marines' foxholes. The slaughter in this limited area was considerable: over 100 enemy bodies in an area 70 yards square.

At dawn the enemy began to quit the area. He knew that with the coming of daylight U. S. weapons would become more accurate. Friendly planes appeared at daylight, speeding his retreat. Tanks moved up the cliff road onto the plateau to join the pursuit.

Interrogation of enemy prisoners established the number of troops committed to the major enemy efforts of the night: the force that struck from the right rear numbered between 100 and 200, while the attackers who hit the left front totalled between 500 and 600.[15]

Both Colonel Wallace and the enemy commander (probably still Colonel Ogata) had realized the tactical implications of the cliffline penetration. Both knew that it provided a route over which thousands of Marines could move into the Japanese rear. The two commanders' reactions were classic. As soon as one of his battalions grasped a toe hold, Wallace exploited the success by committing his reserve there. The enemy commander, as soon as he received word of the penetration, ordered a counterattack to throw the Marines off the cliff and restore the position. Each selected a tactically sound course of action. Only one could be successful.

[15] 8th Mar Report, 5–8.

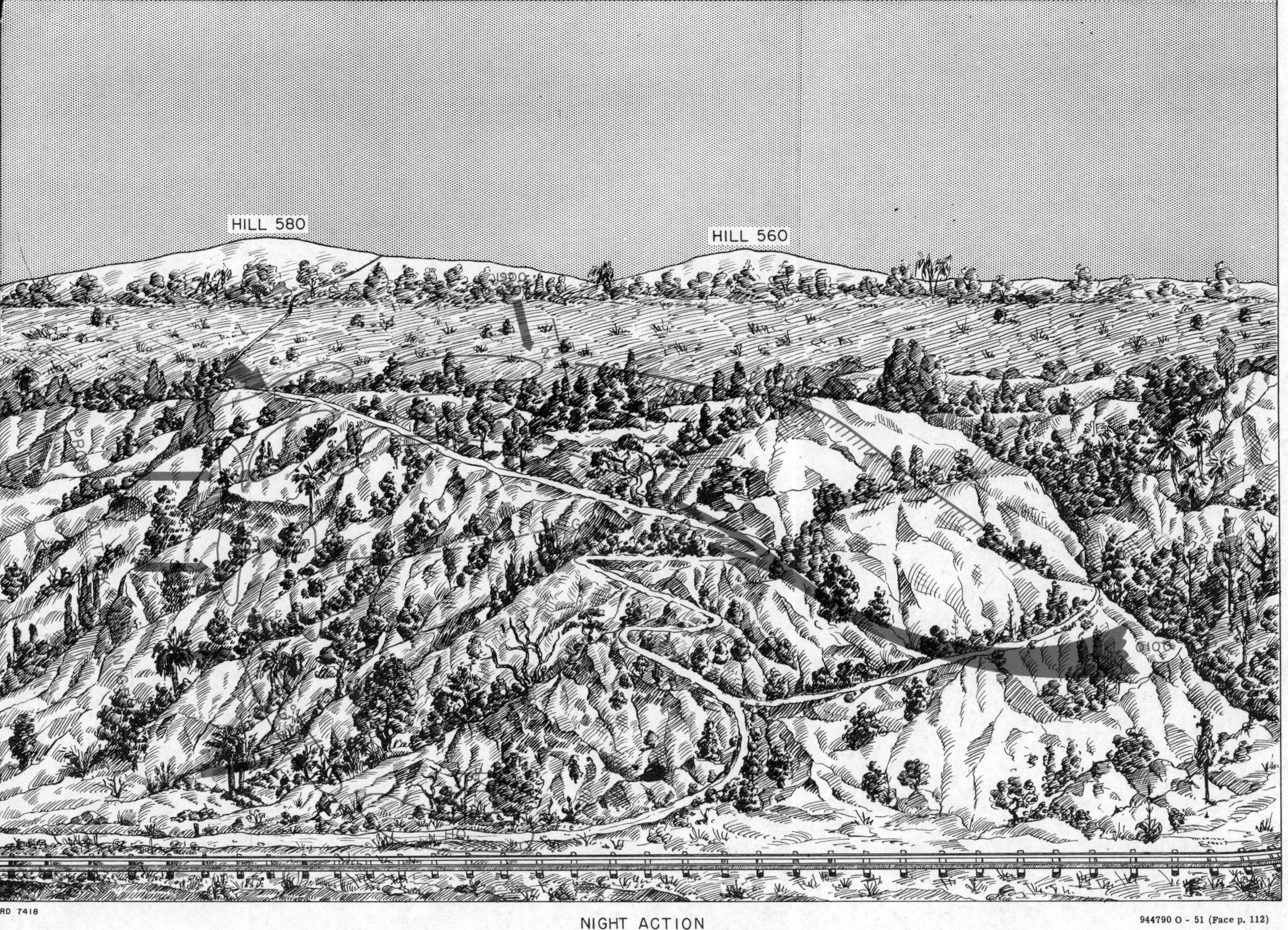

HILL 580

HILL 560

RD 7418

944790 O - 51 (Face p. 112)

NIGHT ACTION
31 JULY — I AUGUST

(PANORAMIC SKETCH LOOKING SOUTHEAST)

MAP 12

JIG-PLUS 8—1 AUGUST 1944

Objective O–8 remained to be seized. This objective, the final one on the island (coinciding with the southern coastline), had been assigned the two divisions in the **NTLF** operation for 31 July. Since neither had moved that far on the 31st, General Schmidt directed that on 1 August they should "continue operations to complete mission assigned. . . ."[16]

The 4th Marine Division, with no change in formation (23d and 24th Marines abreast), commenced its attack at 0800.[17] Preceding the jump-off, the 14th Marines fired a five-minute preparation 600 yards forward of the front lines. Following this at 0805 and 0813, the artillery regiment delivered a two- and a three-minute concentration, the first 900 yards and the second 1,200 yards forward of the line of departure.

The attack followed the model of the previous day. Tanks led the move, and the principal deterrent to rapid movement was rocky terrain and dense undergrowth. Few good artillery targets were presented, the bulk of the fire support being performed by tanks, half-tracks and 37mm guns. Resistance was limited to isolated enemy groups fighting stubbornly from caves, crevasses, and any other cover in the choppy ground.

The palisade formation of the terrain in the 24th Marines' zone demanded by mid-afternoon an alteration of the regiment's formation. Three distinct levels existed—three heavily-carpeted stairsteps down to the sea. To negotiate this, the regimental commander, Colonel Hart, ordered all three of his battalions into the assault, each to assume one of the three levels. From left to right and from high to low, the battalions moved 3, 2, 1. The Japanese, hidden in caves along the route, tossed an occasional grenade or fired a few rounds at the Marines, but these measures were generally ineffective.

---

[16] NTLF Opn Order 38–44.

[17] This account of the 4th Division's 1 August attack is derived from the following sources, unless otherwise indicated: 4th Mar Div Report, 31–32; 23d Mar Report, 24–25; 24th Mar Report, 13–14; *L. R. Jones*.

The regiment reached O–8 at about 1800. (See Map 11, facing page 103.)

The 23d Regiment required adjustment of its frontage before commencing the day's attack, scheduled to begin at 0800. The previous evening had found the 1st and 3rd Battalions atop the escarpment, but darkness prevented them from completely expanding over their assigned zones. The 1st Battalion, therefore, would spread out and shift to the left, while the 3d Battalion would stretch its lines to the right.

The 2d Battalion, meanwhile, remained at the cliff base where it hammered at the pocket of resistance developed late on the preceding day. By 1045 the unit reduced the strong-point, and engineers cleared all mines from the road leading up to the high ground. Now tanks and other vehicles could make the ascent. One rifle company of the 2d Battalion remained along a

CORAL ERUPTIONS in rugged portions of Tinian's southern end slowed progress. Although organized resistance had virtually ceased, this ground lent itself admirably to defense and delay by small determined groups.

THE END IN SIGHT, Marines of the 24th Regiment and medium tanks of the 4th Tank Battalion comb across the coastal plateau at the island's extreme southern end. The 23d Marines, whose zone ended at the top of the steep cliff shown in picture, had to retrace steps in order to reach the lowlands. Aguijan Island (five nautical miles southwest of Tinian) may be seen dimly in the background.

restricted part of the road to prevent enemy groups from setting up an ambush there.

While the 2d Battalion worked at its task, the other two battalions of the 23d Marines encountered unexpected difficulties. Enemy machine-gun and rifle fire contested all efforts to deploy for the attack. One tightly packed group of about 50 Japanese established a firing line close to the 1st Battalion and opened up with a deluge of fire. Accepting the challenge to a duel, Marine machine guns converged upon the enemy from two directions and achieved good effect. The battalion operations officer described the incident as one in which "small-arms fire, at close quarters, and with a target lucrative enough for 'book' employment of machine guns, was able to dispose of the entire group." [18]

Finally, after being delayed for over two hours in their frontage adjustments, the 1st and 3d Battalions moved out in the attack to the south. By 1715 they had reached the point of farthest possible coordinated advance, a cliff line cutting perpendicularly across the regiment's zone of action and dipping sharply to a coastal plateau (see Map 11). To reach the latter area, it would be necessary to retrace steps and follow through the 24th Marines' zone along the west coast. Patrols from the regiment immediately began scouting the cliff to determine how much mopping up would be necessary. They all came back with the same answer: the

_____

[18] *Dick.* During the mop-up that followed, one Marine from the 1st Battalion prodded a prostrate Japanese body to ascertain whether it was dead or alive. The body's reaction was startling: grabbing the Marine's carbine with a quick twisting motion, a very-much-alive

Japanese leaped to his feet and levelled the weapon at a dumfounded Marine. Fortunately, the safety was on, and the Japanese could not pull the trigger. Seeing that the piece would not fire, the Japanese took off on a dead run through the stubble of a cane field. The Marine, recovering from his shock, gave chase, caught his man in a diving football tackle, wrested away the carbine, released the safety, shot the Japanese. It is assumed that one individual maintained a tighter grip on his carbine thereafter.

COASTAL CLIFFS near southeastern end of Tinian provided hideouts for Japanese soldiers and civilians who were reluctant to believe that the Americans would treat them well if they surrendered.

cliff was a honeycomb of occupied caves and deep recesses. It was obvious that clearing all of these would not be accomplished in a day or week. Or, as it developed, even in a month.

To the Cliffs of Marpo Point

The 2d Marine Division had only two battalions up the cliff on the morning of 1 August. The task remained of moving the remainder up the few routes that existed, adjusting the frontages, and continuing on to Marpo Point. This climbing and shifting about would take time, so General Watson ordered an hour's delay in the attack—new time: 0800. The push as far as Objective O–8A would be controlled by the 8th Marines; but at that point the division

zone would be split into two parts, 6th Marines taking the left half, 8th Marines the right half. Then, on division order, the attack to the final objective (O–8) would commence.[19]

The 1st and 2d Battalions, 8th Marines, had spent a frantic night atop the cliff. Both were in need of reorganization and rest. But since the 2d Battalion had borne the brunt of the night's most powerful enemy effort, the regimental commander, Colonel Wallace, decided to relieve it with the attached 3d Battalion, 6th Marines, which would then continue the attack to the coast. The 1st Battalion, 8th Marines, as soon as daylight and the cessation of enemy pressure permitted, began shifting its

---

[19] 2d Mar Div Opn Order 53.

frontage to the southwest in order to contact the 4th Marine Division. The 3d Battalion, 8th Marines, meanwhile, began the difficult ascent of the steep cliff within its assigned zone of action. After a suitable route was located, the Marines filed to the top and joined on the left of the 3d Battalion, 6th Marines.

At about 0800 the 8th Regiment began its move, and a half hour later the three assault battalions (left to right: 3/8, 3/6, 1/8) reported themselves on or near intermediate Objective O–8A. It was necessary to push the front lines about 200 yards beyond this objective, however, in order to reach a point on the plateau sufficiently broad for the deployment of all three battalions. These frontage adjustments took more time than had been anticipated and delayed the scheduled assumption of the left half of the division zone by the 6th Marines.

Finally, at 1125, operational control of the two left battalions (3/8 and 3/6) shifted to Colonel Riseley, commanding the 6th Marines. The latter regiment had begun the day with only one battalion (2d), since its 3d Battalion had been attached to the 8th Marines and its 1st Battalion designated division reserve. When it took over its new zone, the 6th Marines' strength was trebled. At the same moment, the 8th Marines' strength was halved.

At 1150 the final push began. The 8th Marines manned its front with the 1st Battalion and retained the 2d Battalion in reserve. Encountering no organized resistance, the 8th Regiment reached the cliffs overlooking the water at 1455. Patrols immediately began searching the precipitous, rocky slopes in an attempt to locate the Japanese known to be there. Little hunting was necessary; from the deep shadows of the natural caves that abounded in the area enemy soldiers announced themselves with telling bursts of fire. It was apparent that a lengthy mop-up task lay ahead. Though the 1st Battalion, 8th Marines, did not realize it at the time, it would shoulder the lion's share of the job.

The 6th Marines met practically no enemy opposition, but, as the unit neared the coast,

civilians began emerging from hideouts waving white cloths. By 1510 the stream of civilians reached flood proportions and the 6th Marines received orders to hold up for the night (see Map 11). At this time, though the regiment had not reached the cliffs above Marpo Point, its view to the rim of the cliff was unobstructed, and no enemy troops were in evidence. To tighten the lines for the night, Colonel Riseley committed his 2d Battalion on the right of the regiment's lines. So that the 6th Marines would not be caught at a critical moment without a reserve with which to deliver a needed punch, Riseley ordered each of his three battalions to retain at least one rifle company in reserve.

At 1730 the 1st Battalion, 6th Marines, which as division reserve had spent the day mopping up the cliff line near Objective O–7, reverted to parent control. One company (A) of the battalion was ordered to remain at the cliffs so that it would be handy to quell any uprising there; a second company (B) was attached to the 3d Battalion, 6th Marines; and the remainder was held in regimental reserve.[20]

While the 6th and 8th Marines struggled to the heights, juggled frontages, and pushed the last mile, the 2d Regiment held to its assigned task of preventing enemy escape along the east coast. To improve its positions and its zone of observation, the regiment was ordered to "seize high ground about 300 yards to its front."[21] This move was accomplished without difficulty, and the regiment dug in to protect its new holdings. The 2d Battalion, 2d Marines, remained in NTLF reserve, an assignment received on 30 July.[22]

All organized resistance on Tinian having crumpled, General Harry Schmidt, commanding the Northern Troops and Landing Force, declared the island secured at 1855, 1 August 1944.[23]

---

[20] 8th Mar Report, 8–9. 6th Mar Report, 4–5. 2d Mar Div Report, 4.

[21] 2d Mar Div Opn Order 53.

[22] 2d Mar Report, 4.

[23] NTLF Report, 15.

Tinian Mop-Up

As so many Marines, in so many operations, have pointed out, the Japanese never got the word about the island being "secured." They invariably fought on just as if they were unaware that the decision had gone against them—that they had lost. The Japanese were poor losers and good fighters.

Some date had to be selected as the final day of the Tinian operation. The first day of August was chosen because then, for the first time, U. S. forces could roam over all of the island that was worth roaming. This did not include the coastal caves, where hundreds of Japanese still held forth. Merely delaying the "secure" date until 2 August, or 5 August, would have left unchanged the fact that many Marines would be killed and wounded after it was officially all over. As usual, the announcement was ironical to the men still fighting, and the irony escaped no one.

Although the landing force G–2 listed only two enemy capabilities at this time ("To make small infiltrations. . . ." and "To defend from caves. . . ."),[24] everyone was aware that the Japanese could creep from their lairs at night, organize into raiding bands, and strike at any point. The Marines were well familiar with the Japanese fixation for killing as many Americans as possible before falling themselves.

Organized resistance had ceased. But on the early morning of 2 August, an enemy force—estimated variously from 100 to 250—struck headlong into the command post of the 3d Battalion, 6th Marines.[25] Headquarters personnel,

PRIVATE FIRST CLASS ROBERT L. WILSON, 2d Battalion, 6th Marines, posthumously awarded the Medal of Honor for purposely absorbing with his own body the blast of an enemy grenade on 3 August 1944 so that others around him might live and fulfill their mission.

armed for the most part with carbines and pistols (although two automatic rifles were also used), considered the enemy group very well "organized."

Initially, personnel of the aid station bore the brunt, but soon everyone in the headquarters group—clerks, communicators, corpsmen, assault engineers, mortarmen, and staff personnel—rallied behind their commanding officer, Lieutenant Colonel Easley, to defend themselves. The Japanese, carrying rifles, grenades, and machine guns, hurled themselves at the Marines with characteristic violence. As soon as one fell, another took his place. In search of substantial assistance, Captain John R. Steinstra, Headquarters Company commander, dashed to the nearby Company F of the 2d Battalion, 6th Marines, acquired a medium tank and a rifle platoon, and led them back to the fight. Here was welcome reinforcement to the 3d Battalion Headquarters Group, which had fought

---

[24] NTLF G–2 Periodic Report, 1800, 31 July, to 1800, 1 August. The 4th Division G–2 Periodic Report for the same period expressed an enemy capability that events of the next few nights revealed to be the enemy's chosen course of action: "To sally forth from the caves in group banzai charges."

[25] A hint that this installation would be the scene of violent action came at 0330 when a saber-wielding Japanese sneaked through the command post's perimeter defense and blundered upon a corpsman sleeping in the Aid Station. Another corpsman spotted the intruder and dropped him with a well-aimed bullet before he could land a fatal blow. Immediately, the Aid Station doubled its security watch. The main Japanese assault came 45 minutes later. Annual Sanitary Report, 2d Mar Div Fleet Marine Force, 1944, from Div Surgeon to Chief, Bureau of Medicine and Surgery, 88.

LOUD SPEAKER SYSTEM mounted on jeep is used to promise good treatment for Japanese who emerge peacefully from their cave hideouts. Similar invitations were broadcast from ships and craft lying off the coastal cliffs. These efforts, though worthwhile, failed to encourage any mass exodus to U. S. lines.

the enemy at close quarters for over two hours. The machine barged into the battle with guns blazing, and the tide turned. The battalion executive officer later stated that he considered the tank's appearance "vitally important" to the outcome. Those enemy soldiers who remained on their feet hastily departed the area.[26]

Daylight made results of the enemy effort visible: 119 Japanese bodies lay almost side by side in and around the 3d Battalion command post. But the Marines had also taken casualties, one of the dead being Colonel Easley.

Nor was this the only enemy activity in the 6th Regiment's area during the night of 1–2 August. Shortly before Easley's group found itself in the vortex of the Japanese assault, the 2d Battalion command post came under attack, probably by the same enemy force. As described by the battalion commander:

Some one hour before dawn . . . the CP was attacked in the rear by a large Japanese force. This

force illuminated the area with flares and swept the ground with rifle and machine gun fire. Several attempts were made to penetrate the perimeter of the CP, one being partially successful; however, a machine gun [Japanese] was successfully brought to bear on . . . the CP.

This attack continued until first light, at which time three [Marine] tanks that had bivouacked during the night at the CP opened fire on the Japanese, causing their withdrawal toward the 3d Bn 6th CP. It is believed . . . that the entire force . . . which later attacked the 3d Bn 6th CP initially attacked the 2d Bn 6th CP. Particularly noteworthy was the splendid heroic defense of the Mortar Platoon Hq Co, 2d Bn 6th which carried the brunt of the attack.[27]

Of incidental interest in this particular skirmish was the use, by the Japanese, of explosive-filled *sake* bottles as improvised hand grenades.

---

[26] Ltr from LtCol J. E. Rentsch to author, 27Dec50. Ltr from Maj T. H. Fisher to CMC, 27Dec50.

---

[27] Ltr from Col E. B. Games to CMC, 30Nov50. According to the 6th Marines Report, 30 Japanese were killed in attacks on the 2d Battalion command post. The 3d Battalion executive officer (who took over the unit after Easley's death) agrees that the enemy force that struck the 3d Battalion command post had already hit the 2d Battalion and had prodded at the 1st Battalion. Interview with LtCol J. E. Rentsch, 4Dec50.

One witness stated that "they made a big noise but did little damage."[28] Whether the Japanese got their inspiration for this use of *sake* bottles before or after drinking the contents is not known.

Another smaller effort that preceded the thrust into Easley's command post came against the 3d Battalion, 8th Marines. There a small Japanese force punched with full vigor, suffered 14 casualties, rebounded like a rubber ball from the stone wall of resistance.[29]

Again the next night (2–3 August), the 6th Marines received a local counterattack by a mixed Army-Navy group numbering about 150. The enemy effort was poorly planned and coordinated, having as its only redeeming feature the vigor of its execution. Personal bravery was an important adjunct to, but never a substitute for, intelligent employment of available forces. Marines of 3/8 (still attached to the 6th Regiment) and 3/6 repelled the hostile thrust without special difficulty. Forward of the lines lay 124 more Japanese[30] who no doubt shared with their fallen comrades of other battles the conviction that death was preferable to surrender.

The 6th Marines had a monopoly on the post-operation *banzai* attacks, having experienced two on as many nights following "securing" of the island. These dying-gasp efforts represented the last times that reasonably strong attacks were mounted against the Marines. On many another night, individuals, pairs, or small groups would make the final decision to expend themselves against the Americans. Then would follow the inevitable screaming, a grenade or two, the blistering hail of U. S. lead, finally, silence. Killing the enemy in this manner was an altogether easier proposition than rooting him out of his hideouts. Far too many of the Japanese realized this and waited in the deep shadows of caves for a Marine to silhouette himself at the entrance. In this manner each Japanese could be almost certain of claiming at least one American before falling himself.

In an attempt to save as many lives as possible, amplifying equipment, installed ashore and afloat, was used to announce to persons still hiding in caves that they could expect good treatment if they would emerge during daylight hours carrying white cloths. When prominent citizens of Tinian lent their voices to this enterprise, the results were good. Thousands of civilians, many clad in colorful Japanese silk, responded to the promises—though it was plain from the expressions on their faces that they expected the worst.

Others did not get the word and blundered into the lines at night. The Marines had no alternative; they opened fire. Situations in which civilians lost their lives naturally saddened the Marines, but under the circumstances no one would have suggested that fire be held until a positive identification could be made.

As the Marines set about their mopping-up activities, they witnessed a number of incidents made all too familiar at Saipan: mass hysteria leading to a veritable orgy of self-destruction. Of activities on 3 August the 23d Marines' action report noted:

Several freak incidents occurred during the day: (1) Jap children thrown [by their parents] over cliff into ocean; (2) Military grouped civilians in numbers of 15 to 20 and attached explosive charges to them, blowing them to bits; (3) Both military and civilians lined up on the cliff line and hurled themselves into the ocean; (4) Many civilians pushed over cliff by [Japanese] soldiers.[31]

In an effort to save as many lives and as much time as possible, the Marines issued an ultimatum on the afternoon of 3 August: "Come out by 0830, 4 August, or caves will be blown up." This message, conveyed by amplifying equipment to the cave hide-outs, stimulated large numbers of civilians and a few

---

[28] Interview with Maj T. H. Fisher, 8Feb51.

[29] 6th Mar Report, 5.

[30] One of these dead, according to the testimony of five Japanese prisoners, was Colonel Ogata, Tinian Island Commander. Marines did not identify his body, but one Japanese lance corporal stated that he saw the colonel's body draped dead on the barbed wire, a victim of machine-gun fire. 2d Mar Div Periodic Report 84, 1800, 3 August, to 1800 4 August. 4th Mar Div Representative Translations Made on Tinian, IX, Reconstruction of Enemy Movements from Interrogations of POW's.

[31] 23d Mar Report, 25. *L. R. Jones.*

MAIL CALL, most popular of all calls.   Attitudes, as usual, ranged from studied nonchalance to dreamy expectancy.

soldiers into emerging. But many more remained where they were.[32] The Marines' threat, in most instances, was an empty one. The huge grottos virtually defied demolition, and were so numerous that only a minute portion could be destroyed with the resources available.

On 6 August the 8th Marines assumed responsibility for the entire 2d Division sector and continued mopping-up activities. The next day the regiment also took over the 4th Division area, relieving the 23d Marines, which had patrolled that sector since 4 August.[33]

With the relief, General Cates commenced embarkation of his 4th Division for transportation to Maui, Territory of Hawaii, where the 4th Division would rehabilitate in preparation for other tests.[34] General Watson, likewise, began the shuttle of 2d Marine Division elements back to Saipan, where the unit would establish its camp.

Thus, the whole mop-up burden suddenly lay on the 8th Marines, and a weighty one it would be for a long time to come.

At noon, 10 August, the 8th Marines became part of the Tinian Island Command (Major

---

[32] *Lanigan.*

[33] Actually, the "23d Marines" designation is somewhat misleading here. The mop-up organization, commanded by Colonel L. R. Jones, was composed of two composite battalions—one under Major Robert N. Fricke from the 24th Marines, the other under Lieu-

tenant Colonel Ralph Haas from the 23d Marines. Ltr from LtCol R. N. Fricke to CMC, 2Jan51.

[34] The embarkation provided inspiration for the worst pun of the operation, written as the final entry in the 4th Division Surgeon's Log: "Here today and gone to Maui."

General James L. Underhill), under which the mop-up progressed.

It is not the purpose of this narrative to recount the numerous patrols, ambushes and ruses employed by Marines of the 8th Regiment in carrying out their mission. Neither is it pertinent to dwell upon the feeling-of-being forgotten that settled about men of the 1st Battalion, 8th Marines, when they learned on 25 October that other elements of their regiment were returning to Saipan, that the mop-up task was now theirs alone.[35] This unit continued at its unglamorous, costly business until 1 January 1945, when it too moved to Saipan.

Japanese killed after the Island Command took over totalled 542. With their 542 lives the Japanese tied up portions of one Marine regiment for five months and inflicted 163 casualties (38 killed, 125 wounded). The Tinian situation during this period bore a capsule resemblance of the entire Pacific situation in the last half of 1944: Japan was striving for a delayed decision in the hope that the United States would tire of the effort. The final outcome— defeat for Japan—was predictable; but the longer it took the United States to realize this end, the better Japan's chance for surrendering conditionally. Or so reasoned the Japanese.

---

[35] One Marine was moved to comment with some accuracy: "Those Japs down there have us outnumbered if they only knew it."

CHAPTER V

Conclusions

The battle for Tinian ended officially in nine days, with more than 5,000 Japanese killed, counted and buried; more than 9,000 civilians interned; and with 252 military prisoners. U. S. losses, meanwhile (including personnel lost aboard the *Colorado* and the *Norman Scott* on Jig-Day), totalled 389 killed and 1,816 wounded.[1]

The Expeditionary Troops Commander at Tinian, General Holland M. Smith, evaluated the operation as follows:

In war as in every other phase of activity, there are enterprises so skillfully conceived and successfully executed, that they become models of their kind. Our capture of Tinian, southern sister island of Saipan, belongs in this category. If such a tactical superlative can be used to describe a military maneuver, where the result brilliantly consummated the planning and performance, Tinian was the perfect amphibious operation in the Pacific war.[2]

At Tinian, sound planning and skillful determined execution again paid off. Capitalizing on an unparalleled (in the Central Pacific) opportunity for achieving tactical surprise, Marines of the 2d and 4th Divisions carried out a remarkably efficient landing. But Tinian cannot be compared with Saipan as an amphibious operation. At Saipan, U. S. forces were projected 1,000 nautical miles from their nearest base; at Tinian, three nautical miles. Measured on a Saipan yardstick, then, the Tinian operation must stand as an overgrown river crossing. In regard to General Smith's evaluation ("the perfect amphibious operation"), it is only proper to point out that, at Tinian, the proportion of attackers to defenders was greater and the period of preparatory bombardment more protracted than in other island conquests. This does not detract from the skill of the planning or the vigor of the execution but rather qualifies the success and places it in the correct perspective.

U. S. TACTICS

Certain tactical and logistical factors of a special nature presented themselves at Tinian, as indeed they do in like shore-to-shore operations: There was a greater opportunity for gathering accurate intelligence; planning required less time than did that for overseas operations of like magnitude; tactical surprise was easier of attainment; landings could be supported effectively by artillery emplaced on the

---

[1] Though the total Tinian casualties were moderate in comparison with those of many other operations, the toll of Navy chaplains was greater than for any other operation in World War II. One was hit aboard the *Colorado* during the Jig-Day demonstration, three more were hit ashore. Captain Clifford M. Drury, USNR, *The History of the Chaplain Corps, United States Navy,* Volume II, 1939–1949 (Washington: U. S. Government Printing Office, 1950), 159.

[2] General H. M. Smith, *Coral and Brass* (New York: Charles Scribner's Sons, 1949), 201.

near shore (Saipan); operations could be conducted with less regard to the strategic air and naval situation than was the case in an overseas operation; tactical plans were more flexible; and troops involved were not subjected to a lengthy, crowded, enervating voyage.

In addition to the foregoing tactical considerations, several special logistical factors also existed: The total shipping required to transport and supply like-sized landing forces was less; logistical plans were more flexible; overwater supply lines were secure against disruption by hostile naval forces; and air transportation contributed more important and effective supply and evacuation support than is possible in an overseas operation.

U. S. commanders, examining every decision in the light of these special tactical and logistical factors, arrived at a plan in all respects classic. Of the plan's features, those exploiting the possibilities for *surprise*, *mass*, and *economy of force* emerge most well-defined. The advantages accruing to an attacker using the Japanese-neglected northwestern beaches had been at once recognized and appreciated by U. S. planners. All admitted from the outset that landings there should achieve tactical surprise. But, one top commander opposed use of the beaches and others hesitated because of the extremely limited size of these areas. The studies and discussions on this subject led to the inevitable imponderable: Would the advantages outweigh the disadvantages in the use of the small northwestern beaches? Only after physical reconnaissance revealed the areas in question satisfactory for landings was the final decision made to use them. The wisdom of this decision was demonstrated by the decisive results achieved.

An important consideration in reaching the White Beach decision was that a landing there could be supported by artillery emplaced on Saipan. In order that this support might strike the landing areas with maximum power, General Schmidt concentrated under one command all artillery of the landing force except four light battalions. With fire support massed, he further concentrated his available power by transferring to the assault division all

available armor and all light (75mm pack) artillery. These allocations were designed to insure the greatest punch at the decisive point. The landing force organization for combat at Tinian fully exploited organic flexibility and adaptability to fit the unusual circumstances.

The Tinian plan was executed with a resolve and determination that would have made even a less brilliant plan successful. While it is apparent that the landing force failed to realize how decisive had been the first night's victory and that it therefore proceeded very methodically and carefully, there is no indication that a faster advance would have cost less men or that the Japanese would have chosen any place other than the cliff line to make their last stand. The enemy prepared his cliff-line defenses long before Jig-Day, so that, regardless of how fast the Marines moved, they could hardly have caught the Japanese in the open.

The situation at Tinian permitted General Schmidt to spend ammunition lavishly, men economically. He exploited that situation throughout the operation.

Against the only Japanese defense line encountered on Tinian (the southern cliff), the 2d Marine Division performed a classic maneuver. Attacking on a broad front, the division made a small penetration, which it quickly exploited and then held against the bitter Japanese counterattack. That penetration, then expanded in division strength, proved to be the key that quickly and economically unlocked the Japanese final defense line.

U. S. INTELLIGENCE

As summarized by the landing force G–2:

It is apparent . . . that the enemy had not given serious consideration to the possibility of our landing on the northwest coast (White Beaches) of the island, and it is clear that our landings there were achieved with complete tactical surprise.[3]

The great opportunity for gathering accurate, detailed, and timely intelligence before the landing was fully recognized and exploited. Efforts of intelligence personnel in the Tinian operation understandably surpassed in demonstrable results those achieved in any other Pacific battle.

[3] G–2 Report, 7.

Much credit for the economical and expeditious execution of the operation must be attributed to those efforts.

Aided by the terrain, which permitted easy movement in most localities and afforded long fields of observation, reconnaissance patrols functioned both day and night during the operation. Generally these patrols were very small (four to six men) so that, if spotted by enemy observers, they would present unremunerative targets. These detachments, in most cases, did not proceed far enough to achieve definite contacts and usually returned with negative (no enemy located) results. Strong combat-reconnaissance patrols, with missions of pushing forward until they encountered the enemy, were seldom employed.

Photographic coverage of Tinian was good, pictures taken between 15 June (Saipan's D-Day) and 24 July (Tinian's Jig-Day) being particularly excellent. Cloudless conditions made it possible to produce aerial mosaics greatly superior to those developed for Saipan.

Preliminary night reconnaissance of the landing beaches, made on 10–11 July and 11–12 July by the Corps Reconnaissance Battalion and naval Underwater Demolition Teams, was notable both for smoothness of operation and excellence of information gained.

Prisoner of war interrogation was generally better planned on Tinian than on Saipan. Information thus gained, however, was limited somewhat in its utility because of the speed of the U. S. advance. By the time POW's were interrogated, the enemy situation had often changed radically.[4]

JAPANESE TACTICS AND TECHNIQUES

The Japanese compounded their disadvantages of inferior strength and relative immobility by accepting an extremely unsatisfactory command relations set-up and by leaving their back door (the White Beaches) unlocked if not open. The former condition threw them into a tottering unbalance in their defense preparations, the latter staggered them on Jig-Day.

Of the three top officers on the island (Admiral Kakuda, Captain Oya, Colonel Ogata),

the first was an airman who neither had, nor cared to assume, tactical responsibility, the second was a naval officer who refused to submit to Army authority, the third was an Army officer who, though designated as island commander, failed to demand integration of the Tinian forces. The individuality and independence of this trio served U. S. purposes well.

After resisting the landing with local defense forces, the Japanese launched strong counterattacks against each flank of the beachhead during Jig-night. Thereafter, the defenders broke contact with U. S. forces early in each successive engagement, withdrawing without becoming heavily engaged, until their defense stiffened at the island's southern end.[5] Their withdrawals were skillfully executed in all cases.

The weight of the U. S. combined naval gunfire, aerial bombardment, artillery and infantry attack did not permit the enemy to employ any major tactical moves except the first night's counterattack. He tried to follow his plan: to defeat us at the beach; to defeat us by counterattack on our beachhead if we succeeded in landing; to harass us by infiltration and by occasional artillery fire from concealed positions; to use his artillery at times when our artillery fired, hoping to create the impression that our own artillery was firing shorts; and to deliver final *banzai* attacks at the end.

Though strong in total numbers, Japanese counterattacks did not concentrate effective power against a single point. Instead, several independent, isolated assaults attempted to penetrate well-prepared U. S. positions. The *banzai* attack, so effective against irresolute defenders, appeared illogical and unsound to the Marine command. The Japanese *banzai* thrusts all obtained the same result: failure,

---

[4] 4th Mar Div D–2 Report, 4.

[5] Estimated daily enemy casualties (from the NTLF G–2 Periodic Reports) indirectly reveal where and when the enemy resisted most determinedly: on the first two days of the operation (24–25 July), including the first night's counterattack, over 2,000 Japanese were killed; during the next five days (26–30 July), enemy killed totalled only 876; on last two days of the operation (31 July–1 August), 1,862 Japanese were killed. For the two days following the "secure" date, the Japanese lost 876.

quick and decisive. Their fanatic efforts usually occurred at night and generally were directed frontally against U. S. lines.

Fighting during the later phases at Tinian reverted to cave warfare. Here the enemy's use of terrain and his tenacious nature combined to exact a higher price from the Marines. His cave positions were often invulnerable to the Marines' supporting weapons and had to be assaulted without effective preparatory fires. Once the Marines had captured a cave, they either had to guard or demolish its entrance to prevent reoccupation by Japanese infiltrators.

In his fight-to-the-death spirit, the enemy's morale was excellent. But his military efficiency decreased under the continuous U. S. pressure, until at the last he resisted with only disorganized, poorly supplied groups.

Japanese of the 50th Infantry were particularly well trained. Their excellence in marksmanship, camouflage and security consciousness was especially notable. In their withdrawal to the south, Japanese soldiers carefully removed or destroyed all unit identifications, so that, during the final days of the operation, U. S. forces lacked conclusive evidence as to which enemy units opposed them.

Thought of the battle's ultimate outcome was apparently not the concern of the individual Japanese soldier or sailor. His duty was simply to fight until death. Some prisoners from the 56th Naval Guard Force said that their commander, Captain Oya, had received word from Japan during the last days of the operation that the Japanese Fleet was coming to their rescue. This message may have been invented by Captain Oya to bolster morale.

One defensive measure extensively used by Japanese at Tinian was the scattering of mines over probable invasion routes. In general, this employment was haphazard in plan, promiscuous in execution. Of several types used, including two antiboat specimens and the long-familiar tape-measure variety, the most effective was the magnetic antitank mine. The latter could be thrown or placed against a U. S. tank where it would stick and explode.

In addition to those mines designed to destroy tanks, boats and vehicles, the Japanese

JAPANESE TAPE-MEASURE MINE planted flush with the ground. Though the enemy used a great number of mines and booby traps, he achieved negligible results. In most cases, Marines discovered and removed them before they could cause serious trouble.

improvised a number of ineffective antipersonnel mines and placed them in cane fields, along roads and paths, and in pieces of abandoned equipment. These home-made mines were particularly numerous in Tinian Town and along the waterfront there. Only one known accident occurred as a result of a booby trap, illustrating that the Japanese were unskillful in preparation of these devices and that the individual Marines were wary of all suspicious-appearing objects.

One Japanese mine innovation employed at Tinian was nothing more than a one-inch steel rod approximately 20 feet in length fastened to the horns of antiboat mines. If pressure were applied to any part of the rod, two or three of the mines would detonate simultaneously. U. S. engineers found and disarmed the mines without determining their effectiveness.

Between the edge of the reef and the White Beaches, the Japanese buried antiboat mines at depths as great as four feet. But many of these—unaccountably—were unarmed.[6] The

---

[6] One plausible explanation is that the Japanese, not wishing to hamper their defensive preparations, had deliberately postponed arming the mines. Plans to pull the pins when U. S. landings seemed imminent were probably frustrated by the U. S. bombardment.

Tinian Town beaches were a maze of horned mines, yardstick mines, and plate mines.

The Japanese constructed a number of tank obstacles to impede the movement of U. S. machines. The most common types were ditches, blown bridges, timber cribs filled with stones, and piles of logs at restricted sections of road. Tactically, the blocks were well located and in most cases protected by small-arms positions on high ground overlooking them. As soon as these protecting positions were destroyed, however, it was a relatively simple matter for U. S. bulldozers and individuals working with hand tools to destroy the obstacles.

FIRE SUPPORT

The most significant, influencing factor of fire support in the Tinian operation was the proximity of recently captured Saipan, three nautical miles to the north. During operations on the latter island, U. S. intelligence agencies maintained current records of Japanese positions on Tinian, records that allowed representatives of the three supporting arms (air, naval gunfire, artillery) to plan their fires with careful precision. In addition, the chosen invasion beaches were within effective range of artillery located on Saipan's southern shores. Lessons in fire coordination, so recently learned at Saipan, were fresh in the minds of all operation officers concerned, and every effort was made to take advantage of the experience.

Preparatory bombardment of Tinian had begun on 11 June, when Task Force 58 moved into the Marianas to prepare Saipan for the 15 June landings. From that date until Jig-Day, Tinian's preliminary bombardment continued on an hour-by-hour, round-the-clock, basis.

On 26 June, with the Saipan operation 12 days old, Admiral Turner had ordered an increase in the intensity of the Tinian bombardment, dividing the island into a north and a south half with air and naval gunfire alternating daily between the two halves. Artillery then undertook destruction of any targets escaping the attention of the other arms. A combined target map was maintained upon which new targets were posted and all destroyed targets erased. Planes for this plan were furnished by Carrier Support Groups One and

Two, naval gunfire by the cruisers *Birmingham, Montpelier* and *Indianapolis*, artillery fires under XXIV Corps Artillery control.

Admiral Turner's 26 June plan remained effective and generally unchanged until Saipan's secure date (9 July), at which time the Tinian bombardment tempo was accelerated. Then the three supporting arms began to specialize on missions for which they were best suited, with more regard to specific targets than to a strict assignment of sectors. Never in the Pacific War did U. S. forces subject a single island to such prolonged intensive bombardment.[7]

Naval Gunfire wasn't worth shit

Relieved of much of the fire support burden it had shouldered in previous operations, naval gunfire achieved a zenith of efficiency at Tinian. Lieutenant Colonel Ellsworth G. Van Orman, Expeditionary Troops Naval Gunfire Officer, summarized the fire before Jig-Day as follows:

The painstaking reduction of enemy defenses on Tinian . . . left the enemy with almost no heavy instruments of defense and considerably reduced quantity of personnel.

Relative to naval gunfire subsequent to the Jig-Day landings, Colonel Van Orman continued:

In the occupation of Tinian call fire procedure was carried out *much more satisfactorily than at either Saipan or Guam* [author's italics] because of experience gained by all hands at Saipan and exchanged and clarified in meetings of all personnel both afloat and ashore prior to J-Day. Ships and SFCP's [Shore Fire Control Parties] worked in far greater mutual understanding than on any prior operation.[8]

Continuous day and night naval bombardment for a 43-day period might have demoralized a less persistent foe. The Japanese, however, retained the will to fight even though their communications were shattered and troop movements made exceedingly hazardous. Systematic efforts by the other two U. S. supporting arms (air and artillery) joined with naval gunfire in tripling the enemy's problems.

The marked improvement of naval gunfire support at Tinian over that of Saipan derived

---

[7] TF 51, Report, Encl F, 22.
[8] TF 56 NGF Report, 136 and 138.

from several factors: First, the number of divisions to be supported was reduced from three to two; second, artillery relieved naval gunfire of some of the preparatory burden; third, there was better indoctrination in the proper use of naval gunfire; and fourth, the terrain was more favorable for the location of targets.

Air Support *facked up*

Air support for the Tinian operation came from two sources: Navy planes from the escort carriers and Army planes from Aslito Airfield on Saipan. Because the latter planes had such a short run from Saipan bases, practically their entire airborne time was spent over the target. This helped maintain a generally high caliber of air support. Beachhead areas, Tinian Town, and other located enemy installations were thoroughly saturated with explosives and shells.

Where coordination between air and artillery was required, however, results left something to be desired. Difficulty occasionally arose, and a great number of close-support missions were cancelled, because field artillery was firing into the same area assigned to the planes. Interesting, if sometimes sarcastic, testimony in this regard:

Mission #18, 25 July
The strike, strafing of enemy troops above northwest beach, was cancelled due to the refusal of artillery to lift fire. They suggested that the planes fly up to the area from the sea, strafe and then turn away. Suggest flying lessons for artillery personnel.
Mission #9, 27 July
Cancelled because of artillery fire.
Mission #7, 29 July
Cancelled, artillery could not be cleared.
Mission #14, 30 July
Cancelled. Usual reason, artillery would not stop.[9]

Not content with merely stating the problem, the Task Force 52 Report advanced a logical solution, not only to the air-artillery problem, but to the air-naval gunfire problem as well:

In amphibious operations involving large land masses, the volume of fire of naval gunfire is not so great as is the volume of shore-based artillery.
Naval gunfire can be controlled in the earlier stages at least, by contact with one central agency i. e., the

gunnery officer on the flagship. The maximum ordinate of naval gunfire is normally much lower than that of shore-based artillery. Thus the interference with air strikes is far less. An arbitrary maximum ordinate . . . can be imposed on naval gunfire, with the provision that no ship will exceed this ordinate unless previous notification is given to Commander Support Aircraft. Commander Support Aircraft can likewise impose a minimum altitude [on aircraft]. . . . This would then allow air strikes and naval gunfire to work simultaneously on the same target. . . .

However, movement of CSA [commander support aircraft] control ashore as soon as adequate radio facilities could be provided, would infinitely reduce the more difficult problem of coordination with shore-based artillery and would allow a direct contact with the shore-based aircraft squadrons which provide close support of troops. In this manner of operation, the particular desires of troops for certain types of air strikes could be satisfied much more quickly and more exactly than by trying to accomplish the same thing by voice radio. . . .

The air-artillery coordination difficulty, while serious, did not in itself prevent both arms from performing a great number of important missions. Several of these have been mentioned at pertinent points throughout the narrative.

One weakness in the close-air-support technique at Tinian (which also had been noted at Saipan) was the lengthy time lapse between request for and execution of a mission. The air liaison officer with the 23d Marines commented that ". . . a *minimum* of one half hour was needed to schedule an air attack at a designated time [even] when aircraft was available and on station."[10] While this represents the experience of one officer with one regiment, similar delays were also common in other units. The 2d Marine Division Air Liaison Officer, Captain Hunter Moss, was "in agreement with the Air Liaison Officer of the 23d Marines . . ." but noted that in one exceptional case an air strike was completed "within 15 minutes from the time it was called in."[11] Rear Admiral R. F. Whitehead, USN, who as a Captain in 1944 served as Commander Support Aircraft, Pacific, noted that, "Some missions were executed immediately, others were delayed because of numerous urgent air support missions. . . . the

[9] TF 52, Air Support Operations, Summary of Daily Air Strikes.

[10] 23d Mar Report, Air Liaison, 50.

[11] Ltr from Capt Hunter Moss to CMC, 27Dec50, hereinafter cited as *Moss*.

small size of the objective area, the irregular front lines, and other reasons. . . ." [12]

The primary cause of delay, however, may be traced directly to time spent coordinating with artillery and naval gunfire and in making certain that neither of these arms fired missions that would endanger planes. Captain Moss commented in this connection: ". . . it was difficult to coordinate with Corps artillery which was firing from the southern tip of Saipan. When the Tinian advance carried beyond the range of Corps artillery, the elapsed time from request to completion of air attacks was shortened." [13] All air officers arrived at a similar solution to cut down the time lag: locate representatives of all three arms together to simplify integration. [14]

The Northern Attack Force's Commander Support Aircraft, Commander Lloyd B. Osborne, considered that delay would be reduced if a senior officer presided over the three representatives and rendered immediate decisions as to which arm should have priority on a given target. Furthermore, Osborne suggested that, when the senior officer specified an air strike, it would be wise to:

Take greater chances by sending aircraft onto the target immediately . . . and without waiting for confirmation that artillery and naval gunfire have *actually* been stopped. This does not involve as much risk as it first seems. Unless a concentrated barrage is in effect, the chance of actually hitting an aircraft with artillery or naval gunfire is extremely small, and the chance would probably be worth taking if an emergency air strike on five minutes' notice is required. [15]

Another feature—if not a weakness—of Tinian close-support missions: very few strikes were directly handled by air liaison parties with the forward battalions. Thus, persons in the best position to coach planes onto targets were not, in most cases, permitted to do so directly. This despite the fact that air liaison parties were equipped with radios intended for contact-

ing planes. Reluctance to turn over aircraft to battalion observers stemmed, in some cases, from a lack of confidence in the observers' ability, in others, from communication difficulties, and in still others, from a firm belief that close-support planes should function, practically without exception, directly under Commander Support Aircraft. Admiral Whitehead advanced another reason why air liaison parties were not permitted to take over strikes:

[It] was not so much the lack of confidence in the observers' ability as it was in the danger of planes operating in such large numbers over a small objective area under control of numerous air liaison parties. On a narrow front with irregular front lines it was not practical (except in rare instances) in such a congested area as Tinian to turn control over to the air liaison parties of the unit (Battalion) being supported without endangering the troops operating on the flanks.

In regard to the communication situation, Admiral Whitehead commented:

The limited number of aircraft frequencies . . . involved required [that we exercise] careful coordination to avoid a liaison party from utilizing one frequency over a protracted period to the exclusion of other missions by planes operating on the same frequency. The lack of aircraft multichannel VHF [very high frequency] also hindered flexibility. [16]

Admiral Harold B. Sallada, who commanded a task group of five escort carriers at Tinian, felt that there were three causes for reluctance in turning over planes to battalion observers for close-in missions at Tinian: "Uncertain air-ground communications, inadequately trained Air Liaison Parties and, frequently, pilots entirely inexperienced . . . in close air support. . . ." [17]

The necessity for adequate communications and thorough training in close-air-support work is underlined by Captain Moss:

. . . our Air Liaison Section did not have satisfactory VHF radio equipment and, therefore, we were not able to maintain contact with all of the planes on station. Furthermore, the Air Liaison Officers of the Second and Fourth Marine Divisions had not had sufficient practice in direct controlling of aircraft, and I feel this lack of training would have made it impossible

---

[12] Ltr from RAdm R. F. Whitehead to CMC, 30Dec50, hereinafter cited as *Whitehead*.

[13] *Moss.*

[14] *Whitehead. Moss.* Ltr from Capt H. P. Cooper, USN, to CMC, 2Jan51. Ltr from Cdr L. B. Osborne, USNR, to CMC, 26Jan51, hereinafter cited as *Osborne*.

[15] *Osborne.*

---

[16] *Whitehead.*

[17] Ltr from Adm H. B. Sallada to CMC, 20Dec50, hereinafter cited as *Sallada*.

to obtain satisfactory results even if the radio equipment had been in working order.[18]

The technique of close air support had been a continuing study in the Marine Corps for years, and the subject of how planes could be controlled most effectively during the execution of close-support missions was not a new one. On 19 December 1943 (seven months before Tinian) the Commanding General, V Amphibious Corps (Lieutenant General Holland M. Smith), had written the Commander, V Amphibious Force (Vice Admiral Richmond K. Turner), on the subject. At least one paragraph of the letter treated a situation germane to Tinian close-support difficulties:

Air Liaison Parties attached to the unit being supported should control direct support aircraft after it has been assigned the mission by the Air Support Commander.[19]

To this recommendation Admiral Turner responded:

Agree in principle; practical considerations such as lack of adequate training of Air Ground Liaison parties and communications may interfere.[20]

Admiral Sallada, an officer well-familiar with the abilities of Navy pilots in 1944, later commented pertinently in connection with General Smith's recommendation:

The procedure . . . was undoubtedly sound when applied, for example, to Marine Corps [pilots] properly trained in their primary mission of close air support. Such work by carrier pilots available during the period in question [at Tinian], who initially had inadequate opportunity for training with ground troops, was a somewhat different problem.[21]

And so, the problems of executing close air support in the manner desired by the Marine Corps came into sharp focus at Tinian. It is significant to note that, during the same period, less than 100 miles away, an apparent solution had been reached. Or, stated differently, the same close-air-support technique that received infrequent trials at Saipan and Tinian passed extensive, thorough and unremitting combat tests at Guam. For, there, battalion air liaison parties held a much freer rein than at the other Marianas objectives; in the words of the Commander Support Aircraft, Pacific (Whitehead), "almost all" of the missions "were handled directly by the Air Liaison Parties." By comparison with Saipan-Tinian close air support, Guam results taught an important lesson, which Captain Whitehead stated as follows: "It is expected that in future operations, aircraft on close support will continue to be coached onto targets directly by the Air Liaison Parties."[22]

Two aircraft weapons employed at Tinian are worthy of special mention: rockets and napalm bombs. The former, having had their first extensive Central Pacific employment at Saipan, proved again that their rifle-like accuracy had a wide variety of uses. Continued employment and development of aerial rockets was significant in looking to the future.

Napalm or "fire" bombs made an auspicious debut at Tinian. Of the 120 jettisonable tanks dropped during the operation, 25 contained the napalm mixture, and the remainder an oil-gasoline mixture. Of the entire number only 14 were duds, and eight of these were set afire by subsequent strafing runs. Carried by Thunderbolts (P–47's), the "fire bombs" burned away foliage concealing enemy installations. Although there was a diversity of opinion regarding the bomb's effectiveness at Tinian, the important fact was that a new offensive weapon had received its first combat trials. In the months that followed, the U. S. experimented with, and finally produced, napalm bombs of far-reaching strategic consequences. Carried from the island of their weaning and growing pains, napalm bombs devastated by fire large portions of Japan's "paper" cities.

---

[18] Moss. Commander Osborne considered that air-ground communications at Tinian ". . . lacked reliability from electronic, mechanical, atmospheric and human . . ." standpoints. Osborne.

[19] Ltr from CG, VAC to ComFifthAmphFor, 19Dec43, Ser 00732, para j.

[20] Ltr from ComFifthAmphFor to CG, VAC, 28Dec43, Ser 00393, para j.

[21] Sallada.

---

[22] Reports of Support Aircraft Operation, Marianas, with comments by Commander Support Aircraft, Pacific, 11Sep44, 27. Much of the background information regarding early close-air-support thinking in the Marine Corps was obtained in an interview with Colonel Frank C. Croft on 6Dec50.

In addition to its fire-support contribution at Tinian, air's reconnaissance and aerial photography services were also invaluable. Through air observers' searching eyes, the landing force knew about all significant developments before and during the operation. Represented on this "bird's eye view" mission were planes of the Army Air Force and Navy, as well as Marine artillery spotting planes (OY's).[23]

In recognition of the excellent support provided by the 7th Air Force's planes in the Marianas, General Holland Smith and Admiral Turner issued a joint message of commendation:

> We send a hearty "well done" to the men in the Seventh Air Force who have provided our overhead cover and effectively slashed the enemy on Saipan, Guam and Tinian. All of us have been greatly impressed with your eagerness to do what we asked you to do.
>
> When we walk down the Ginza in Tokyo en route to Hirohito's palace, we hope that you will supply the overhead guard for us.[24]

Against the overpowering array of U. S. air overhead, the Japanese could employ only passive defense measures. One device, which achieved some success, was the burying of 500-pound bombs beneath the anticipated flight path of low-flying U. S. aircraft. When the planes swept in at treetop level, the enemy electrically detonated the bombs from a remote vantage point, hurling fragments of debris high into the air. After Lieutenant Wayne F. Kobler, USAAF, lost his life because of one of these devices, other pilots were wary lest they meet a similar fate.[25]

Most of the Japanese air personnel had left the Marianas during May and early June to provide air support for the reinforcement of Biak Island. Operational losses and disease claimed a large percentage of these, so that,

when the survivors were ordered back to the Palaus and Marianas early in June, few reached even the Palaus on the return trip. Apparently none reached the Marianas.

Artillery

At Tinian, for the first time since Eniwetok, artillery was employed from an adjacent island to prepare the objective area and support the landings. Represented in the array were eight battalions of 105mm howitzers, three of 155mm howitzers, and three of 155mm guns. Nor did this number exhaust U. S. artillery resources; four battalions of 75mm pack howitzers landed with the leading division and were in action by evening of Jig-Day.[26]

Japanese artillery resources, though proportionate with infantry strength, were rather limited. Stretching the possibilities to the breaking point, the Japanese might have had 20 operable pieces (mobile and fixed) of 70mm or greater ready to fire on the U. S. beachhead. Across the channel on Saipan 156 pieces of U. S. artillery (105mm or greater) waited to hit any targets that presented themselves. During the period from H-minus 30 to H-Hour, General Harper massed all 13 battalions on the White Beach area in preparation for the landings. If Colonel Ogata had similarly massed fires of his artillery (however limited) in that same area after H-Hour, he could have created a serious, if temporary, tactical problem for the congested U. S. forces.

But the Japanese fired by single pieces, depending in their choice of targets upon individual spotters or gunners. This led to the unanimous conclusion in Marine action reports that the defenders' artillery fires were "uncoordinated." A number of factors explained the enemy artillery situation: First, he had too many static positions; second, he had poor communications; third, he lacked unity between Army and Navy; and fourth, he had faulty doctrine.

U. S. artillery was expertly coordinated and extremely effective throughout the operation. A Japanese prisoner testified pertinently in this connection: "You couldn't drop a stick without

---

[23] Planes from VMO-2, with observers from the 4th Marine Division, flew a total of 123½ hours on artillery observation missions during the operation.

[24] Quoted from *One Damned Island After Another*, 236. Following this quotation, the 7th Army Air Force source noted that "The Marianas, the Marines and the Navy were ours!"

[25] *The AAF Against Japan*, 191. A B-24 field at Saipan was later named for Kobler.

[26] V Phib Corps Report on Marianas Phase III, 11.

PACK HOWITZER, lashed on a precarious perch at the brink of a sheer cliff at Marpo Point, blasts an otherwise inaccessible Japanese cave. To get it to this position, the 75 was disassembled and carried in separate parts over a rugged trail. This veteran howitzer served the 10th Marines at Guadalcanal, Tarawa and Saipan before its Tinian appearance.

bringing down [U. S.] artillery." [27] Further, there were few instances of friendly artillery falling within Marine lines, circumstances that had occurred all-too-frequently at Saipan. U. S. artillery, from positions on Tinian, fired 188,565 rounds.[28]

TANKS

The terrain on the island with its extensive flat fields and well-planned road communications system was far more suitable for tank operations than were the rugged hills and wooded valleys of Saipan. A close approximation of a tanker's Shangri-La, Tinian had almost perfect tank terrain.

The procedure of operating one tank company with each infantry regiment worked well at Tinian: a regiment in reserve automatically gave the supporting tank company an opportunity for repair and maintenance. In addition, the tactical situation at Tinian aided the

rotation system. U. S. tank losses were few; the enemy's antitank fire achieved very little, and his most effective antitank weapon—the magnetic mine—failed to create any serious problem. As protection against magnetic mines, Marines covered the flat surfaces of most of their tanks with oak planking, a protective technique first used at Roi-Namur, improved in the Marianas, and nearly perfected at Iwo Jima and Okinawa.[29]

Infantry-tank cooperation was for the most part excellent. Indeed, much of the operation took on the proportions of a tank-infantry sweep. Flame-thrower tanks, which had made their combat debut at Saipan a month before, proved reasonably effective—considering their short stream of fire—for roasting areas honeycombed with caves.[30]

Tank communications and supply were good to excellent and, with respect to supply, tank officers felt that infantry officers at last understood the tankers' problems. On the negative side, tank officers complained that little or no advantage could be gained from using tanks in the front lines at night. With their limited visibility, the machines became "sitting ducks" for enemy infiltrators. Many infantrymen took an opposite view: let the tankers dig in around their vehicles and protect them from infiltrators. Then, if a counterattack developed, the tanks would be handy to lend their firepower to the defense.

Some use was made of these vehicles to crush foliage forward of the infantry's night positions, so that better fields of fire would be provided. While effective, this activity proved extremely hard on tank clutches. Officers recommended that clearing-fields-of-fire missions be accomplished by flame-throwers.[31]

---

[27] 4th Mar Div Representative Translations Made on Tinian.

[28] NTLF G–4 Report, Encl D.

---

[29] Ltr from LtCol R. K. Schmidt to CMC, 5Dec49.

[30] At the conclusion of the Saipan operation, the 4th Tank Battalion had requested napalm for the use of its flame-throwers, in the hope that the range of these weapons could be increased. Because napalm was in extremely short supply and because the limited amounts available were being used for the bomb, higher headquarters refused the request. Ltr from LtCol R. K. Schmidt to CMC, 16Nov50.

[31] 2d Tank Bn Report, Co B Report, 6.

MEDIUM TANK awaits a mission on the last day of the operation. Generally favored by open rolling countryside, tanks operated with great effectiveness at Tinian. A 75mm half-track and two more tanks stand by farther down the hill.

Most effectively employed when exploiting success, tanks were in their glory at Tinian, where the entire operation (after the first day and night) was an exploitation of success.

All Japanese tanks encountered at Tinian were the light models mounting 37mm guns and a 7.7cm machine gun.[32] These vehicles, powered

by six-cylinder, air-cooled diesel engines, had undergone no apparent changes in design from models encountered in previous operations. The sergeant at Saipan who scornfully called one of these "the kitchen sink" still had an apt description.

The 12 tanks included in the Japanese Tinian forces actually did little to hinder the Marines' advance; and only once (the night of 24–25 July) did they venture forth in strength and actively assist their infantry. This sally proved exceedingly costly: five tanks met only Marine fire and destruction without accomplishing

[32] Ltr from CG, 2d Mar Div to CINCPOA, 15Aug44, subj: Japanese tanks and armored vehicles encountered during Tinian Operation, report on. Another Japanese armored vehicle found at Tinian, but which did not play an important role in the operation, was the half-track, probably designed after its German counterpart. A powerful, rugged vehicle, it could be used as a prime mover for artillery and as a personnel carrier. It was powered by a large six-cylinder diesel engine, and its construction permitted it to travel over

almost any type of terrain. Two extra braking pedals that stopped each track individually allowed the vehicle to make sharper turns than could U. S. half-tracks.

132

much real damage. The remainder of the Japanese tank force was accounted for one-by-one in subsequent days of the operation and never again offered effective resistance. The 2d Division encountered and destroyed four of these machines in its sector, while the 4th Division knocked out eight, including those hit during the first night's counterattack.[33]

LOGISTICS

The selected landing beaches keyed the entire logistical situation. Their narrowness demanded the mobile loading of matériel coming ashore, so that supplies could be transported across the beaches to combat units or inland dumps without handling.

Movement of supplies from LST's to dumps on Tinian was a closely-knit process. All items were neatly packaged in cargo nets so that, once a DUKW or LVT pulled alongside an LST, it was a simple matter for small cranes to lift the nets and lower them into the vehicles for the trip to (and through) the beach. With a few exceptions, initial unloading was completed by Jig-plus 2. Included in this early supply were two-day reserves of water, rations and ammunition.

At Tinian, divisions did not deliver small-arms and mortar ammunition to regiments. Instead, regiments drew from division dumps and delivered by truck directly to battalions. This system, designed to avoid movement of large regimental dumps, worked well in this fast-moving operation.

Concerning this system, one of the regimental logistics officers wrote:

The Second Marines in the course of the fighting on Tinian moved their supply dump only twice as opposed to some five or six such moves on Saipan. . . .

A representative amount of food, water and ammunition was kept on hand in the regimental dump for emergency purposes. However, that was never permitted to exceed what could be carried at one time in the trucks assigned to the regimental quartermaster. . . .

. . . on several occasions when battalions had halted for the day and following the emplacement of forward security, trucks were driven along the trace of the front line positions and the rolls of concertina wire dropped off at spaced intervals. . . .[34]

Initially, vehicles ashore used the fuel they carried, such small replacements as had been landed, and Japanese aviation gasoline when it could be located. But on Jig-plus 4, when these sources dwindled, the landing force became critically short—particularly of 80-octane gasoline and lubrication oils. Saviors in this situation were the DUKW's, which, by repeated trips through the angry surf to the fuel barges, carried in sufficient quantities to relieve the shortage somewhat.

Fresh water posed a minor problem: with the exception of a pond about 1,000 yards inland from the White Beaches, natural sources did not come within friendly lines until shortly before the island was secured. Consequently, throughout the operation the landing force depended for water upon its initial supply and the output of its distillation units (operated by engineer personnel—see page 139).

Two items of logistical support equipment in use at Tinian were especially noteworthy: the special portable LVT ramp and the pontoon causeway. The first of these, the portable ramp, was an innovation (see page 28 for description). It was designed to provide a means for access over the three- to ten-foot coral ledges flanking the White Beaches. The 4th Marine Division's action report summarized the ramp's use as follows:

Ten special ramps mounted on LVT's were brought over from Saipan in the second trip of the LSD's. Two were launched about 1700 on Jig-day and sent in with a view of utilizing them in the area south of White 1. One was lost when the LVT struck a coral head on the edge of the reef and turned over. The other was landed successfully and used by LVT's landing supplies. The remaining 8 ramps were launched on the afternoon of Jig-Plus-1. Two were swamped and sank on the way in to the beach but the crews were saved.[35] The remaining 6 were landed and placed in operation. The ramps were used to land vehicles until the pontoon causeways were established.

---

[34] *Throneson.*

[35] The accident occurred as a result of an overpowering wake set up by an LCM which crossed the bows of the two nose-heavy LVT's. Ltr from Maj F. A. Durand to CMC, 28Nov50.

---

[33] 2d Mar Div, Japanese Tank Report, 2. 4th Mar Div Report, B, 13.

Their use in this operation to the limited extent available, was reasonably successful.[36]

Another especially noteworthy logistical item, the pontoon causeway, which had already proved its worth at Saipan, came into use again at Tinian. Two were used, one on each of the White Beaches; and , until broached by the six- to eight-foot swells that arose on 29 July,[37] they contributed materially to logistical support. Here was proved the fact that use of pontoon causeways was limited to fair weather or to sheltered sea conditions.

The plan of resupply—shuttle service in LST's, LCI's and LCM's from Saipan depots, plus traffic from three loaded cargo ships on call off Tinian—worked satisfactorily until rough weather precluded further ship-to-shore unloading. Thereafter, the landing force was not able to maintain prescribed levels of supply. Though some shortages developed during the operation,[38] equitable distribution and weak enemy resistance combined to prevent the logistical situation from becoming critical.

The soldiers, sailors, Marines, seabees, airmen and engineers who shouldered the logistical task deserve much credit. The stockpile put ashore during the battle's early stages and the carefully conceived and well-executed emergency air-supply plan saved the situation after bad weather reared its ugly head. That the logistical plan had sufficient flexibility to meet difficult conditions was illustrated by results achieved.

[36] 4th Mar Div Report, Sec 3, 21.
[37] Salvaged sections were later used to extend the existing south pier at Tinian Town.

[38] Particularly in 60mm illuminating, 81mm light and 75mm howitzer shells (plus the already-mentioned fuel and oil difficulties).

CURTISS "COMMANDO" (R5C–1) of Marine Transport Squadron 252 takes aboard a load of casualties at Ushi Point Airfield. Approximately 1,500 wounded Marines were evacuated by air from Tinian to Saipan. Battered Japanese plane parked under skeleton hanger was caught on the ground during early naval attacks on the Marianas.

DUKW UNLOADS JEEP by means of "A" frame, which lifts vehicle from the truck and places it on the ground. The 140 DUKW's available to the landing force fulfilled an urgent need at Tinian, especially after 1800, Jig-plus 4, when rough weather precluded all unloading by means other than DUKW's.

Although the Japanese had an excellent network of roads and adequate amounts of food and matériel, supply became one of their most acute problems after troops and civilians crowded into the island's southern tip. Japanese supply dumps in caves and other hiding places were rendered inaccessible in many cases by the U. S. bombardment and the rapid advance.

As to individual equipment the Tinian defenders were generally well-outfitted, most carrying new rifles, gas masks and hand grenades.[39]

Japanese vehicles, when compared with the Marines', were generally inferior, being mostly light commercial types. Marines captured and used several of these military-type vehicles including gasoline trucks, water sprinklers and half-track command cars. At the Ushi Point Airfield trucks and power cranes to handle aero torpedoes and bombs were found in substantial numbers.[40]

Experiences of past operations, past maneuvers, and past schooling stood U. S. planners in good stead at Tinian. For example, Tarawa had demonstrated that the amphibian tractor

---

[39] NTLF G–2 Report, Sec B, 19, **37.**

[40] NTLF G–4 Report, Sec B, 2, 3.

was the answer to the reef problem and that these vehicles must be in sufficient numbers to do the job. Only 125 were available to one division at Tarawa in November 1943;[41] 533 were available to one division at Tinian in July 1944. In all functions, the LVT's performed well.

Even more valuable than the LVT's as supply vehicles at Tinian were the DUKW's. That this was true may be attributed primarily to two factors: the reef posed only a minor obstacle, and a good road network existed. Had either or both of these conditions not obtained, the LVT's might have been the more valuable for supply. The DUKW's operated more successfully under varied sea conditions and, once ashore, preserved the roads better and moved faster than the clawing LVT's. In addition, DUKW's gave drivers better all-around vision than did LVT's. Both vehicles had one important characteristic in common: they could carry supplies directly from ships to inland dumps, making supply one process rather than two or three. Had it not been for the rapidity with which dumps of ammunition, food, water, fuel and other supplies were built up during the early stages, plus the work of the DUKW's during the rough weather, the Tinian operation might well have been delayed by the "near-miss" typhoon.

Use of DUKW's as artillery carriers was an adaptation first used in the Marianas. Artillery pieces, embarked in DUKW's, could be moved from LST's afloat directly to their firing positions ashore.[42] Such convenience naturally gladdened the hearts of artillery crews.

DUKW's (totalling 140) remained directly under the landing force throughout the operation, while the LVT's experienced three shifts: first the 4th Division, then the 2d Division, then NTLF controlled them. Landing craft control was satisfactory at Tinian, because commanders had good communications with all subordinate echelons and, more important, because enemy fire against landing craft was negligible.[43]

JAPANESE AMPHIBIAN TRUCK, one of several captured at Tinian. It operated as a conventional 4x4 truck on land and could function afloat by disengaging the front-wheel drive and engaging a propeller on the vehicle's stern.

Crude by comparison to the U. S. amphibian truck was the Japanese-developed model, a bizarre contraption that contributed nothing to the island's defense. It operated as a conventional 4 x 4 truck on land and could function on water by disengaging the front-wheel drive and engaging the propeller. Since it had no rudder the front wheels probably did the steering while it was in the water.[44]

Medical arrangements for Tinian were extremely satisfactory. Admittedly, shortage of medical personnel (particularly affecting care of civilian casualties), and a paucity of hospital equipment ashore, occasionally cropped forth to complicate the situation. But, since casualties were fewer than at Saipan, personnel and matériel shortages did not adversely affect the conduct of the operation. Certain casualty-evacuation techniques—some already familiar, others developed for Tinian—are worthy of special mention.

Until disrupted by bad weather, the casualty-evacuation plan proved satisfactory. A special medical control vessel, immediately following the assault waves, anchored close inshore. Wounded Marines were transported in LVT's

---

[41] See Marine Corps Historical Monograph *The Battle for Tarawa*, Capt J. R. Stockman.

[42] DUKW's mounting "A" frames lifted the pieces out of other vehicles and placed them on the ground.

[43] Ltr from Maj H. G. Lawrence, Jr., to author, 16Jun 50. Ltr from Maj F. A. Durand to CMC, 28Nov50.

[44] TF 52 Pictorial History of Capture and Occupation of Tinian.

to this vessel, where a medical officer supervised their transfer to LCVP's, which in turn carried them to designated APA's. Casualty evacuation by July 1944 had developed into a systematic and efficient procedure.

The plan of evacuating casualties from pontoon causeways located on the White Beaches directly to two specially equipped and staffed hospital LST's (for transportation to Saipan) was used only once.[45] Further use of the piers for this purpose was prohibited by poor sea conditions. But this one example demonstrated that such a plan would have been feasible if the weather had been favorable.

When heavy westerly swells made use of Tinian causeways and beaches virtually impossible, air evacuation from Ushi Point Airfield became the primary means of removing serious casualties, approximately 1,500 wounded Marines being airborne to Saipan.[46]

The enthusiasm and determination of the crews who flew the planes in and out despite hazardous weather conditions is worthy of note. The report of the Corps Surgeon, Captain John

[45] For the fate of the ship that participated in this evacuation, see page 92.

[46] NTLF Medical Report, 3. Ltr from Dr. George W. Mast to author, 22Aug50.

STRETCHER CASE receives plasma as he is loaded in an LVT which carried him to a special control vessel anchored close inshore. There a Navy doctor supervised his transfer from the LVT to an LCVP for a fast trip to a designated transport (APA). This system of casualty evacuation was terminated by bad weather on Jig-plus 4, and was replaced by air evacuation.

B. O'Neill (MC), USN, summed up the situation:

> Evacuation from Tinian to Saipan was unique in that in spite of only a three mile channel separating the two islands, it became necessary to depend almost entirely upon air evacuation across the channel as the result of an unpredicted swell resulting from a nearby typhoon.[47]

The Navy Medical Corps conclusively demonstrated at Tinian its flexibility in the face of a fast-changing situation [48] and again proved the usefulness of air evacuation in the island war.

Japanese Army forces at Tinian received medical care from a medical company with a staff of 130 and a detachment from the 29th Division field hospital with a staff of 150. This developed a ratio of medical personnel to total Japanese Army personnel of about 1 to 18. For U. S. Marine units at Tinian the ratio of doctors and corpsmen to total personnel was about 1 to 17. From this it appears that the Japanese at Tinian valued medical care as highly as did the Marines.

Japanese Army medical installations were located east and southeast of Mount Lasso. Dressing stations were located at accessible points in the various units' areas. In addition to one field hospital located in a schoolhouse northeast of Airfield Number 2, a second was to be set up wherever the battle developed.[49] No information is available on how these field hospitals actually functioned.

Japanese naval units, being generally more security conscious than their Army brothers, revealed little information regarding their medical activities, aside from the fact that the 523d Naval Air Group Hospital had about 60 men.[50]

No treatment was given to wounded civilians by Japanese military doctors after the beginning of the operation; but U. S. medical units treated thousands of civilians during and after the battle.[51]

The multifarious engineer functions were dispatched with the expediency that characterized their efforts in previous operations. Where their activities directly affected the tactical situation (as in mine clearance), engineer functions have been described in appropriate passages of this narrative. Many another endeavor, however, not directly related to the day by day progress of the attack, rendered vital service and played a significant role in the eventual success.

The engineers were divided into two categories; the assault engineers (1st Battalions of the 18th and 20th Marines) and the NTLF construction forces (18th and 121st Naval Construction Battalions). An important job of both of these was the widening and maintenance of existing roads and trails and construction of additional ones. The assault engineers bent their full attention upon forward areas and the NTLF construction forces to rear areas in this road work.[52]

Both (in cooperation with Shore Parties) also improved the beaches and routes inland from them. This task was begun by the assault engineers and finished by the construction forces. The development of additional landing points likewise received a full measure of attention from, first, the assault engineers and subsequently the construction forces. Work was continuous in each case, with no break in the continuity of effort when one took over from the other.

---

[47] NTLF Medical Report, 6.

[48] The speed of the advance was, on at least one occasion, matched by the speed of medical attention. The commanding officer of the 4th Medical Battalion cited the following in this connection: "We were watching some tanks move out, and one of the crew fell off a tank, hit the ground, and dislocated his elbow. . . . I reduced the dislocation, and he hopped back on his tank before it lost any speed. I never saw him again." Ltr from Capt Stewart W. Shimonek, (MC) USNR, to author, 3Aug50.

[49] NTLF G–2 Report, Sec B, 8–9.

[50] See Appendix V, Japanese Order of Battle.

[51] NTLF G–2 Report, Sec B, 43–44.

[52] One road-preservation technique successfully employed at Tinian: engineers constructed a tracked-vehicle road network that allowed tanks and other tracked vehicles to move parallel to, but not on, normal routes. Ltr from LtCol M. D. Henderson to CMC, 21Dec50.

Relative to water supply, the assault engineers, using their distillation and purification systems, more than met the landing force's requirement "to provide a minimum of two gallons per man per day."[53] The construction forces, meanwhile, developed a more or less permanent water-supply system using not only distillation units but natural sources as well. Here again, close integration between the two engineer echelons was the rule.

There the relationship of functions ended. While the assault engineers constructed prisoner of war and civilian internment enclosures, the construction forces repaired Ushi Point Airfield and operated a Japanese narrow-gauge railroad.[54]

SIGNAL COMMUNICATIONS

The terrain and the rapidity of advance had an important bearing on U. S. communications at Tinian. The speedy sweep across the island's flats made it difficult for Marine wiremen to keep up. This, coupled with a shortage of field wire (occasioned by unloading difficulties), plus damage to wire caused by the heavy traffic along routes of approach, made it impossible to keep wire communications operating at optimum efficiency. On the other hand, an advantage was realized in that few hiding places were offered by-passed or infiltrating Japanese, and Marine wiremen could operate behind their own lines with more safety than usual in the Pacific War.

Using the 23d Marines as a typical example, wire communications were 90 per cent effective from division to regiment, 70 per cent from regiment to battalions.[55] The better record of the former was attributed to the fact that signal supply from division to regiments was regular and satisfactory while regiments encountered difficulties in getting signal gear to battalions

because of a lack of transportation. Poor beach conditions and a heavy surf further complicated the signal-supply problem.

It was sometimes necessary, therefore, to maintain contact by radio alone. The proficiency and discipline of radio operators appeared to have improved over Saipan. Although plain language was used almost entirely for tactical traffic, security violations, as compared with D-Day on Saipan, were greatly reduced. Generally speaking, there was no serious breakdown or delay in operational traffic because of interference, jamming or faulty equipment. Traffic was more evenly distributed on available circuits than at Saipan.

The plan for radio communications on Tinian differed from that on Saipan in at least two interesting respects: infantry battalion commanders carried their radio jeeps ashore in LVT (4)'s;[56] and tank commanders were given SCR–300 radios with which to communicate in infantry command nets.

The tiny, temperamental SCR–536 radio, carried by platoon leaders and company commanders, worked with reasonable success as long as it did not rain, as long as the stations were close together, and as long as other stations on the net did not blanket the transmission. All too often, however, one of these restrictive conditions obtained.

One of the infantry's most dependable sets, the SCR–300, provoked slightly varied comments. The 4th Division considered it "excellent," while the 2d Division reported that its performance was not so good as on Saipan. The latter unit failed to explain this reduction in the set's efficiency.[57]

Captured diagrams and field phones indicated that the Japanese had the entire island wired for telephonic communication. Other than general statements by prisoners of war, however, very little is known about how this system worked. Several prisoners stated that some of their units were equipped with portable

---

[53] The officer commanding the 18th Marines later pointed out that "water supply was controlled at engineer regimental level. . . ." Ltr from Col E. S. Laue to CMC, 27Dec50.

[54] NTLF Opn Plan 30–44, Annex M.

[55] 23d Mar Report, 43.

---

[56] The LVT (4) had a ramp at its stern that allowed convenient discharge of vehicles.

[57] Ltr from Signal Officer to Commanding General, (TF 56), 20Aug44, 16.

radios, and that, using these, they were able to carry on communications after the U. S. bombardment destroyed telephone lines. The enemy's ability to effect an orderly withdrawal to the south indicated that fair interior communications must have been present.[58]

TREATMENT OF CIVILIANS

Civilians on Tinian were for the most part Japanese subjects who had been living on the island for an average of 15 years. Usually they were share croppers, working in the hot cane fields for the South Seas Development Company.

Of 17,900 civilians shown in a Japanese census report of 1 January 1944, only 2,468

had been accounted for on 1 August 1944 when all Tinian civil affairs shifted to the island commander (General Underhill). Three days later the number had grown to 8,491, and 13,000 were counted on 10 August. Between 3,000 and 5,000 had been evacuated to Japan after U. S. invasion of the Marshalls.[59]

Japanese military personnel had little respect for civilians, even their own. That Japanese military doctors refused to minister to them after the U. S. landings would seem to emphasize this fact. Eyewitness accounts indicate that Japanese soldiers massacred many civilians; and, although it is not known whether civilians submitted voluntarily, the presence of

---

[58] NTLF G–2 Report, Sec B, 41, 50, and 51.

[59] S/Sgt Bill Miller, *Marine Corps Gazette*, Nov44, "Beachhead Government."

TOP COMMANDERS gather for flag-raising at conclusion of Tinian operation. From left to right: Admiral Hill (Commander Northern Attack Force), General Schmidt (Commander Northern Troops and Landing Force), Admiral Spruance (Commander Fifth Fleet), General Smith (Commander Expeditionary Troops), Admiral Turner (Commander Expeditionary Force), General Watson (Commander 2d Marine Division) and General Cates (Commander 4th Marine Division).

BEARDED MARINE gives candy to a child in an internment camp, Japanese propaganda notwithstanding.   Tinian civilians had been warned that Americans would inflict vile tortures upon them.

small children—who must be presumed to have been mentally incapable of consenting to be killed—gave the actions at least the aspect of atrocities.[60]

But Japanese civilians had been saturated with propaganda to the effect that the Americans would subject them to the cruelest, vilest of tortures. This indoctrination had its consequences. A captured Japanese warrant officer from the 56th Naval Guard Force stated that about 1,000 "loyal citizens" allowed the military to blow them up in caves.[61]

U. S. propaganda texts,[62] encouraging civilians to dissociate themselves from the military and come over to American lines, were prepared and distributed early in the operation. All texts promised good treatment once American lines were reached.

[60] Signed statements of 2d Lt T. C. Smith and 2d Lt D. L. Anderson. NTLF G–2 Report, Sec B, 51–53.

[61] NTLF G–2 Report, Sec B, 54.

[62] See Appendix VII for sample texts.

Although it is impossible to evaluate the effectiveness of the leaflets with full accuracy, indications support the belief that they were of some help. Large numbers of civilians (and even some military personnel) reported having seen and read the leaflets. Most of the civilians expressed themselves as being surprised to learn that they would receive good treatment from the Americans.

The majority of the civilians who came over, particularly at the end of the operation, were suffering from lack of food, water, and medicine.[63] These indispensable items, when they could be spared, were administered by U. S. forces to help relieve suffering.

THE ASSESSMENT

And so, the techniques and tools of amphibious warfare again passed the unremitting tests of combat. Tinian produced a number of *firsts* in Pacific amphibious warfare: It was the *first* Corps-sized Marine shore-to-shore operation; it was the *first* time that large Marine forces had landed on beaches the size of, and therefore with the limited capacity of, the Tinian landing areas; thorough aerial reconnaissance by unit commanders prior to an amphibious operation was possible for the *first* time; it was the *first* occasion upon which combat troops were employed so shortly after another major operation; the operation saw the *first* combat use of the napalm bomb, a weapon that later spread havoc among Japanese cities.

The Tinian operation was an expansion and consolidation of the Saipan gain rather than a distinctive amphibious step in itself. For to have seized Saipan and not Tinian (or vice versa) would have been to invite the Japanese on the unconquered island to conduct extensive harassing activities and to observe U. S. operations and report them regularly to Tokyo. Capture of Tinian was important for another reason: the island's vast plains, on which the

Japanese had built or were building four airfields, offered space for construction of almost as many additional strips as desired.

Writing about a trip he took several years before the war, traveller-author Willard Price described Tinian as "one in a series of anchored aircraft carriers," [64] but this apt description should now be enlarged: Tinian was developed into the greatest of the B–29 bases in the war against Japan. At its zenith of development, Tinian provided fields for two Army Air Force B–29 wings (313th and 58th) as well as for considerable Navy and Marine aircraft.

Tinian was one of the three essential parts of the Marianas strategic objective, an objective from which the U. S. could control sea areas farther west in the Pacific and, more important, strike telling blows at the home islands of the Japanese Empire. From coral runways in the Marianas, day in day out, the B–29's flew northward to the very heart of Japan, devastating cities and mining coastal waters. Total war achieved a real meaning to the Japanese. To a people already somewhat disheartened by a long series of reverses, massive air raids launched from the Marianas helped put the capstone on their disillusionment.

From the time the B–29's started operating in the Marianas until the end of the war in August 1945, they flew a total of 29,000 missions against Japan and dropped 157,000 tons of bombs of which 52,000 tons were high explosives, 96,000 tons were incendiaries and 9,000 tons were mines. The Japanese have stated that air attacks killed 260,000 people, left 9,200,000 homeless, and demolished or burned down 2,210,000 homes.[65]

Tinian had a strategic significance not fully apparent to the Marines who captured it during that humid period in July 1944: slightly over a year later, 6 August 1945, the island provided the Army Air Force a site from which the B–29 *Enola Gay* carried the first atomic bomb to Hiroshima. From the same field three days later another B–29 carried a second bomb, which

---

[63] Mothers are the same the world over. Some parched-lipped women, offered a precious drink of water from Marines' canteens, accepted with a polite bow, then dampened a scarf or small cloth and washed their babies' faces.

[64] Price, *op. cit.*, 45.

[65] *Mission Accomplished*, prepared by Assistant Chief of Air Staff, Intelligence Headquarters, Army Air Forces (U. S. Government Printing Office, 1946).

was dropped on Nagasaki. These two bombs accounted for between 105,000 and 120,000 persons killed or missing, another 110,000 injured.[66]

---

[66] United States Strategic Bombing Survey, *The Effects of Atomic Bombs on Hiroshima and Nagasaki* (U. S. Government Printing Office, 1946), 15. P. M. S. Blackett, *Fear, War, and the Bomb* (New York: Whittlesey House, 1949), 40.

On 10 August, the day following the Nagasaki disaster, the Empire of Japan, which three months earlier had unsuccessfully sought peace negotiations, finally surrendered unconditionally.[67]

---

[67] United States Strategic Bombing Survey, *Summary Report Pacific War* (U. S. Government Printing Office, 1946), "Japan's Struggle to End the War."

APPENDIX I

Bibliography

Approximately 350 sources, both official and unofficial, have been used in writing the narrative of the Tinian operation. In specific actions or phases of the operation, the reports of the units most intimately concerned with the particular actions or phases have been consulted. Likewise, individuals in the best positions to observe given periods were asked to comment on the author's interpretation of the information contained in the action reports and to elaborate upon that interpretation. This step corrected several errors and uncovered a wealth of additional information. The lowest echelon reporting on a specific incident was generally considered the most dependable source for details, whereas a report of a higher unit, more familiar with the over-all situation, was generally more dependable for the evaluation and results of a particular action. In rare instances where two sources disagreed upon a basic detail, additional sources were consulted until one version emerged correct, the other incorrect. Where it was impossible to resolve a discrepancy by this means, the alternative that appeared correct to the Marine Corps Historical Division was used in the text and the other alternative mentioned in a footnote.

Unless otherwise indicated, the below-listed bibliographical material is filed in the Marine Corps Historical Division.

DOCUMENTS

Proceedings of Joint Chiefs of Staff and Combined Chiefs of Staff meetings and the papers and studies considered at those meetings. Filed at the Naval Records and Library.

CINCPAC-CINCPOA Campaign Plan GRANITE (13Jan44) and GRANITE II (3Jun44). Filed at the Naval Records and Library.

JICPOA Information Bulletins 7–44 and 29–44. The former, entitled "Marianas," gives detailed facts concerning the islands' appearance, history, geography, climate and people. The latter, entitled "Weather Survey for Carolines and Marianas," gives weather statistics for the islands.

CINCPAC-CINCPOA Operation Plan 3–44, 23Apr44. Assigns southern Marianas as a specific objective. Filed at Naval Records and Library.

COMINCH P–007, 30Dec44, "Invasion of the Marianas, June to August 1944." Prepared at the Headquarters of the Commander in Chief, United States Fleet. This document is a valuable synthesis of action reports received from major subordinate units participating in the Saipan, Tinian and Guam operations.

ComFIFTHFleet Final Report on the Operation to Capture the Marianas Islands, 30Aug44. Draws general conclusions (chiefly strategic) regarding the entire Marianas campaign.

Task Force 51 Report (Saipan, Tinian and Guam).

Task Force 52 Report (Tinian).

Task Force 52 Pictorial History of Capture and Occupation of Tinian.

USS *Calvert* Action Report (Tinian).

USS *Cleveland* Action Report (Tinian).

USS *Colorado* Action Report (Guam and Tinian).

Task Force 56 Report on FORAGER, 2Oct44. Basic report of Commanding General Expeditionary Troops, seven enclosures in separate volumes, covering planning, operations, intelligence, logistics, personnel and special staff officers' reports (Saipan, Tinian and Guam).

Northern Troops and Landing Force Report (Tinian).

Northern Troops and Landing Force Operation Orders 30–44 through 39–44 (Tinian).

Northern Troops and Landing Force G–1 Report (Tinian).

Northern Troops and Landing Force G–2 Report (Tinian).

Northern Troops and Landing Force G–2 Periodic Reports 40 through 49 (Tinian).

Northern Troops and Landing Force G–3 Operational Dispatches (Tinian).

Northern Troops and Landing Force G–4 Report (Tinian).

Northern Troops and Landing Force LVT Report (Tinian).

Northern Troops and Landing Force Medical Report (Tinian).

Northern Troops and Landing Force Naval Gun Fire Report (Tinian).

V Amphibious Corps Amphibious Reconnaissance Battalion Report (Tinian).

VAC G–2 Study of the Theater of Operations, Southern Marianas. Contains descriptions of Saipan, Tinian, Aguijan, and Rota, together with information on terrain, climate, and meteorology.

V Amphibious Corps Report on Marianas, Phase III, Tinian.

XXIV Corps Artillery Report (Saipan and Tinian).

2d Marine Division Report (Tinian).

2d Marine Division Operation Orders 45 through 55 (Tinian).

2d Marine Division D–2 Periodic Reports 74 through 82 (Tinian).

2d Marine Division D–3 Journal (Tinian).

Annual Sanitary Report, Second Marine Division Fleet Marine Force, 1944, from Division Surgeon to Chief, Bureau of Medicine and Surgery.

2d Marines Report (Saipan and Tinian).

6th Marines Report (Saipan and Tinian).

8th Marines Report (Saipan and Tinian).

10th Marines Report (Saipan and Tinian).

1st Battalion, 8th Marines Report (Saipan and Tinian).

2d Battalion, 18th Marines Report (Saipan and Tinian).

2d Tank Battalion Report, including reports from Companies A, B, C, and D (Tinian).

4th Marine Division Report (Tinian).

4th Marine Division Operation Orders 33–34 through 44–44 (Tinian).

4th Marine Division D–2 Periodic Reports 71 through 80 (Tinian).

4th Marine Division Representative Translations Made on Tinian. Prepared by 4th Marine Division Language Section, document contains Japanese orders, battle plans, and miscellaneous material.

14th Marines Report (Tinian).

20th Marines Report (Tinian).

23d Marines Report (Tinian).

24th Marines Report (Tinian).

25th Marines Report (Tinian).

24th Marines, Special Action Report of Battalions (Saipan and Tinian).

1st Battalion, 25th Marines Report (Saipan and Tinian).

3d Battalion, 25th Marines Report (Saipan and Tinian).

3d Battalion, 23d Marines Report (Tinian).

4th Tank Battalion Report, including reports from Companies A, B, C and D (Tinian).

27th Infantry Division Artillery Report (Saipan and Tinian).

PRIMARY SOURCES

Joint Army Navy Assessment Committee. "Japanese Naval and Merchant Shipping Losses During World War II by All Causes." February 1947.

King, Fleet Admiral Ernest J. Second Report to the Secretary of the Navy, 27 March 1945. *U. S. Navy at War.* Washington: Government Printing Office, 1945.

Military Reports. Military Intelligence Division, War Department. Report No. 23.

Mission Accomplished. Prepared by Assistant Chief of Air Staff, Intelligence Headquarters, Army Air Forces, Washington: Government Printing Office, 1946. (Interrogations of Japanese Industrial, Military and Civil Leaders of World War II.)

United States Strategic Bombing Survey. *The Campaigns of the Pacific War.* Washington: Government Printing Office, 1946.

United States Strategic Bombing Survey. *The Effects of Atomic Bombs on Hiroshima and Nagasaki.* Washington: Government Printing Office, 1946.

United States Strategic Bombing Survey. *Interrogations of Japanese Officials.* 2 Volumes, Washington: Government Printing Office, 1946.

The War Reports of General George C. Marshall, General Henry H. Arnold and Admiral Ernest J. King. New York and Philadelphia: J. B. Lippincott Company, 1947.

SECONDARY SOURCES

Arnold, Henry H. *Global Mission.* New York: Harper and Brothers, 1949.

Blackett, P. M. S. *Fear, War, and the Bomb.* New York: Whittlesey House, 1949.

Buchanan, A. R., editor. *The Navy's Air War, A Mission Completed.* New York: Harper and Brothers for Aviation History Unit OP–519B, DCNO (Air), 1946.

Daniel, Hawthorne. *Islands of the Pacific.* New York: G. P. Putnam's Sons, 1943.

Drury, Captain Clifford M., USNR. *The History of the Chaplain Corps, United States Navy,* Volume II,

1939–1949. Washington: Government Printing Office, 1950.

Haugland, Vern. *The AAF Against Japan.* New York and London: Harper and Brothers, 1948.

Hough, Frank O. *The Island War: The United States Marine Corps in the Pacific.* Philadelphia and New York: J. B. Lippincott Company, 1947.

Howard, Clive, *et al. One Damned Island After Another.* Chapel Hill: University of North Carolina Press, 1946.

Johnston, Richard W. *Follow Me!* New York: Random House, 1948.

Josephy, Alvin M., *et al. Uncommon Valor: Marine Division in Action.* Washington: Infantry Journal Press, 1946.

Karig, Captain Walter, USNR. *Battle Report, End of an Empire.* New York: Rinehart & Co., Inc., 1948.

Kenney, George C. *General Kenney Reports.* New York: Duell, Sloan and Pearce, 1949.

Knox, Dudley W. *A History of the United States Navy.* New York: G. P. Putnam's Sons, 1948.

Krieger, Herbert W. *Smithsonian War Background Studies Number Sixteen, People of the Western Pacific, Micronesia and Melanesia.* Baltimore: Lord Baltimore Press, 1943.

Miller, Francis Trevelyan. *History of World War II.* Philadelphia and Toronto: The John C. Winston Company, 1945.

Pratt, Fletcher. *The Marines' War.* New York: William Sloane Associates, 1948.

Price, Willard. *Japan's Islands of Mystery.* New York: John Day Company, 1944.

Proehl, Carl W. *The Fourth Marine Division in World War II.* Washington: Infantry Journal Press, 1946.

Robson, R. W. *The Pacific Islands Handbook, 1944.* New York: The MacMillan Company, 1945.

Schmidt, R. K. "The Tinian Operation, A Study in Planning for an Amphibious Operation." Marine Corps Schools, Quantico, Virginia, 1948–1949.

Smith, Holland M. *Coral and Brass.* New York: Charles Scribner's Sons, 1949.

Stockman, Captain James R., USMC. *The Battle for Tarawa.* Washington: Government Printing Office, 1947.

Stockman, Captain James R., *et al. Campaign for the Marianas.* Philadelphia: Marine Corps Publicity Bureau for Historical Division, U. S. Marine Corps, 1946.

Yanaihara, Tadao. *Pacific Islands Under Japanese Mandate.* New York: Oxford University Press, 1940.

PERIODICALS

All Hands. Bureau of Naval Personnel Information Bulletin. January 1945.

Chevron. Marine Corps Base, San Diego, California. 29 July 1944.

Miller, S/Sgt. Bill. "Beachhead Government," *Marine Corps Gazette.* November 1944.

Thomason, Captain John W., III. "The Fourth Marine Division at Tinian." *Marine Corps Gazette,* January 1945.

LETTERS AND INTERVIEWS

The many valuable letters and interviews concerning this monograph cannot be cited individually in this bibliography because of space limitations. But all are available in the working files of the Marine Corps Historical Division for the reference of any bona-fide student of this phase of military history. Many letters and interviews have been cited at appropriate places in the book. Others, although not specifically cited, served to corroborate information already available.

APPENDIX II

Chronology*

1944

2 January	U. S. Army troops land at Saidor, beginning drive up New Guinea coast.
30 January–23 February	U. S. Marines and Army troops seize Marshall Islands.
16–17 February	Task Force 58 strikes Truk, revealing weakness of that base. Decision to by-pass comes soon after.
22–23 February	*Task Force 58 strikes Southern Marianas.*
29 February	U. S. Army troops land at Los Negros in the Admiralties.
6 March	1st Marine Division lands near Talasea on New Britain.
12 March	*Joint Chiefs of Staff direct seizure of Southern Marianas, target date 15 June.*
20 March	4th Marines (Reinforced) seize Emirau.
20 March	*Admiral Nimitz issues FORAGER Joint Staff Study setting forth the purpose of the Marianas Operation.*

*Entries relating specifically to the Tinian operation are shown in *italics*.

23 March	*Admiral Nimitz issues operation order for Marianas; Admirals Spruance and Turner follow suit.*
30 March–1 April	Task Force 58 strikes Western Carolines.
22 April	U. S. Army troops land at Hollandia and Aitape.
26 April	*Expeditionary Troops operation order states mission ". . . to capture, occupy and defend Saipan, Tinian and Guam. . . ."*
17–19 May	Northern Troops and Landing Force maneuvers and rehearses at Maui and Kahoolawe, Hawaiian Islands.
21 May	Six LST's, embarking assault elements of the 2d and 4th Divisions, burn at Pearl Harbor.
25 May	LST's, carrying assault elements of the 2d and 4th Marine Divisions, LVT's and artillery, depart Pearl Harbor.
29–30 May	Portions of the Northern Troops and Landing Force not embarked in LST's, depart Pearl Harbor.
6 June	D-Day in Normandy.

11 June	Northern Attack Force departs Eniwetok for Saipan.
11 June	*Task Force 58 begins bombardment of Tinian and Saipan.*
14 June	*Fire support ships of the Northern and Southern Attack Forces commence bombardment of Saipan and Tinian.*
15 June	2d and 4th Marine Divisions land at Saipan.
16 June	27th Infantry Division begins landing at Saipan.
	Guam bombardment by surface ships commences.
19–20 June	Battle of the Philippine Sea. Japanese Navy suffers decisive defeat.
20 June	*Battery B, 531st Field Artillery Battalion, XXIV Corps Artillery, commences fires on Tinian from Saipan positions.*
21 June	Aslito Airfield on Saipan becomes operational for fighter aircraft.
24 June	*Entire 531st Field Artillery Battalion commences firing on Tinian from Saipan positions.*
26 June	*Admiral Turner issues new plan for intensification of Tinian bombardment.*
6–7 July	Japanese launch savage all-out attack along Tanapag Plain, Saipan.
9 July	4th Marine Division reaches Marpi Point; Saipan declared secured; mop-up begins.
10 July	*2d and 4th Marine Divisions get ready for Tinian operation.*
10–11 July	*Amphibious Reconnaissance Battalion, V Amphibious Corps, and Underwater Demolition Team 5 reconnoiter Tinian landing beaches.*
12 July	*Major General Harry Schmidt assumes command of Northern Troops and Landing Force, relieving Lieutenant General Holland M. Smith; Major General Clifton B. Cates assumes command of the 4th Marine Division.*
	Capture and Occupation Phase for Saipan ends; Defense and Development Phase begins under command of Major General Sanderford Jarman, USA.
13 July	*Northern Troops and Landing Force issues Tinian Operation Order.*
15 July	*Rear Admiral Harry W. Hill assumes command of the Northern Attack Force, relieving Vice Admiral Richmond K. Turner.*
18 July	Japanese Premier Hideki Tojo and Cabinet resigns.
20 July	*First troops for Tinian invasion embark aboard ships at Saipan.*
21 July	Southern Troops and Landing Force lands on Guam.
24 July	*4th Marine Division lands on Tinian.*
24–25 July	*Japanese launch powerful night counterattacks against 4th Marine Division beachhead, suffer decisive defeat.*
25 July	*2d Marine Division lands on Tinian.*
27 July	*Ushi Point Airfield, Tinian, becomes operational.*
30 July	*Tinian Town captured.*
31 July	*At 0200, Japanese counterattack strikes 1st and 2d Battalions, 8th Marines, on Tinian.*
1 August	*All organized resistance ceases on Tinian; island declared secured.*
3 August	*At 1500, American flag is officially raised over Tinian.*
9 August	Aslito Airfield, Saipan, becomes operational for Liberator bombers (B–24's).
10 August	Organized resistance ends on Guam; island declared secured.

Northern Troops and Landing Force as a task force designation is dissolved; staff resumes duties as V Amphibious Corps Staff.

10 August	*Capture and Occupation Phase for Tinian ends; Defense and Development Phase begins under island commander, Major General James L. Underwood, USMC.*
12 August	*Commander Forward Area (Vice Admiral John H. Hoover) relieves Commander Joint Expeditionary Force (Vice Admiral Richmond K. Turner) of responsibility for Defense and Development of Saipan and Tinian.*
14 August	Major General Harry Schmidt relieves Lieutenant General Holland M. Smith as Commanding General, Expeditionary Troops.
	Major General Allen H. Turnage relieves Major General Roy S. Geiger as Commanding General, Southern Troops and Landing Force.
15 August	Commander Forward Area (Vice Admiral John H. Hoover) relieves Admiral Turner of responsibility for the Defense and Development of Guam. TF 51 (Joint Expeditionary Force) is dissolved.
	The Capture and Occupation Phase of Guam ends. Major General Henry L. Larsen, USMC., takes over command of the Guam Garrison Force.
15 September	1st Marine Division lands at Peleliu; U. S. Army troops seize Morotai.
17 September	U. S. Army troops land on Angaur.
23 September	U. S. Army troops seize Ulithi as advanced naval base.
15 October	Aslito Airfield, Saipan, becomes operational for B–29's.
20 October	U. S. Army troops land at Leyte and open Philippines Campaign.
25 October	*8th Marines (less 1st Battalion) leaves Tinian and moves to Saipan.*
24 November	Saipan-based B–29's raid Tokyo.
30 December	*B–29's land at Tinian.*

1945

1 January	*1st Battalion, 8th Marines, after five months' garrison duty, leaves Tinian and moves to Saipan.*
4 February	*Tinian-based B–29's raid Kobe area, Japan.*
6 August	*Atomic bomb, carried by Tinian-based B–29, is dropped on Hiroshima.*
9 August	*Second atomic bomb carried from Tinian dropped on Nagasaki.*
10 August	Japan sues for peace.

NTLF Casualties

APPENDIX **III**

	KILLED OR DIED OF WOUNDS		WOUNDED		TOTAL	
	Officers	Enlisted	Officers	Enlisted	Officers	Enlisted
NTLF Troops [1]	0	2	0	8	0	10
XXIV Corps Arty [2]	0	0	1	2	1	2
27th Inf Div Arty [3]	0	0	0	0	0	0
2d Marine Division: [4]						
2d Marines	0	21	8	134	8	155
6th Marines	3	31	2	163	5	194
8th Marines [5]	3	33	8	286	11	319
10th Marines	1	0	2	9	3	9
18th Marines	0	12	3	15	3	27
Division Troops	0	1	5	18	5	19
4th Marine Division:						
14th Marines [6]	4	10	5	24	9	34
20th Marines [7]	0	7	2	31	2	38
23d Marines [8]	2	52	14	173	16	225
24th Marines [9]	6	60	15	299	21	359
25th Marines [10]	4	55	9	260	13	315
Division Troops [11]	1	13	5	38	6	51
Amph. Vehicle Units: [12]						
2d Amph Trac Bn	0	1	0	9	0	10
5th Amph Trac Bn	0	1	0	0	0	1
10th Amph Trac Bn	0	0	0	3	0	3
715th Amph Trac Bn	0	0	0	1	0	1
534th Amph Trac Bn	0	1	0	0	0	1
773d Amph Trac Bn	0	1	0	0	0	1
2d Armd Amph Bn	0	2	1	18	1	20
708th Amph Tank Bn	0	1	0	0	0	1
GRAND TOTAL	24	304	80	1,491	104	1,795

[1] NTLF G–1 Report, 3
[2] *Ibid.*
[3] 27th Div G–1 Periodic Report for 24Jul–1Aug44.
[4] 2d Mar Div G–1 Periodic Report #83, 5Aug44.
[5] These figures do not include 8th Regiment's casualties suffered during mop-up period.
[6] 14th Mar Report, 10.
[7] 4th Mar Div Report, Annex A, 1.
[8] 23d Mar Report, 2.
[9] 24th Mar Report, 40.
[10] 4th Mar Div Report, Annex A, 1.
[11] *Ibid.*
[12] NTLF–LVT Report, 5–6

APPENDIX IV

Command and Staff List of Major Units[1]

Expeditionary Troops

Commanding General	LtGen Holland M. Smith
Chief of Staff	BrigGen Graves B. Erskine
G–1	LtCol Albert F. Metze
G–2	Col St. Julien R. Marshall
G–3	Col John C. McQueen
G–4	Col Raymond E. Knapp
G–5	Col Joseph T. Smith

Northern Troops and Landing Force

Commanding General	MajGen Harry Schmidt
Chief of Staff	BrigGen Graves B. Erskine
G–1	LtCol Albert F. Metze
G–2	LtCol Thomas R. Yancey (USA)
G–3	Col Robert E. Hogaboom
G–4	LtCol Joseph C. Anderson (USA)

2d Marine Division[2]

Commanding General	MajGen Thomas E. Watson
Asst. Div. Commander	BrigGen Merritt A. Edson
Chief of Staff	Col David M. Shoup
D–1	LtCol James T. Wilbur
D–2	LtCol Thomas J. Colley
D–3	LtCol Wallace M. Greene, Jr.
D–4	Col Robert J. Straub

2d Marines

Commanding Officer	Col Walter J. Stuart
Executive Officer	LtCol John H. Griebel
R–1	Capt Leonard G. Hicks
R–2	Capt John L. Schwabe
R–3	Maj Samuel D. Mandeville, Jr.
R–4	Maj Harold K. Throneson

1st Battalion, 2d Marines

Battalion Commander	LtCol Wood B. Kyle
Executive Officer	Maj Wendell W. Andrews
Bn–3	Maj Charles P. Lewis, Jr.

2d Battalion, 2d Marines

Battalion Commander	LtCol Richard C. Nutting
Executive Officer	Maj Michael P. Ryan
Bn–3	1stLt William B. Somerville

[1] Changes in *commanders only* are shown. Officers listed in other staff positions are those who *originally landed* with the unit at Tinian. Casualties other than commanders are not shown.

[2] The 2d Marine Division's Task Organization for Tinian listed the following units under the Support Group: H&S Co 18th Mar; Hq Co 1st Bn 18th Mar; 4th Plat Co B 1st Bn 18th Mar; 2d Bn 18th Mar (4th Plat Co A and 4th Plat Co C 1st Bn 18th Mar); Hq Co Div Hq Bn; Sig Co Div Hq Bn; MP Co Div Hq Bn; Rcn Co Div Hq Bn; Hq Co 2d Serv Bn; Ord Co 2d Serv Bn; Serv & Sup Co 2d Serv Bn (less dets); H&S Co 2d MT Bn; Co B 2d MT Bn; Co C 2d MT Bn; H&S Co 2d Med Bn (less dets); Co D 2d Med Bn (less Coll Sec); Co E 2d Med Bn (less Coll Sec); 2d JASCO (less SFC Sec and Air Ln Sec). No commander for the 2d Division's Support Group was specified for the Tinian operation.

3d Battalion, 2d Marines

Battalion
Commander_____ LtCol Walter F. Layer
Executive Officer____ Maj Frederick R. Smith
Bn–3_____ Capt Richard Phillippi

6th Marines

Commanding Officer_ Col James P. Riseley
Executive Officer____ LtCol Russell Lloyd
R–1_____ Capt Philip J. Costello
R–2_____ Capt Donald V. Nahrgang
R–3_____ Maj Loren E. Haffner
R–4_____ Maj Cyril C. Sheehan

1st Battalion, 6th Marines

Battalion
Commander_____ LtCol William K. Jones
Executive Officer____ Maj James A. Donovan, Jr.
Bn–3_____ Capt Paul S. Hospodar

2d Battalion, 6th Marines

Battalion
Commander_____ LtCol Edmund B. Games
Executive Officer____ Maj LeRoy P. Hunt, Jr.
Bn–3_____ Maj Hulon H. Riche

3d Battalion, 6th Marines

Battalion
Commander_____ LtCol John W. Easley
                   (KIA 2 August)
                   Maj John E. Rentsch
                   (from 2 August)
Executive Officer____ Maj John E. Rentsch
Bn–3_____ Capt Royal E. North

8th Marines

Commanding Officer_ Col Clarence R. Wallace
Executive Officer____ LtCol Jack P. Juhan
R–1_____ Capt Lloyd E. Iverson
R–2_____ 1stLt James H. Kavanagh, Jr.
R–3_____ Maj William H. Souder, Jr.
R–4_____ Maj Alfred E. Holland

1st Battalion, 8th Marines

Battalion
Commander_____ LtCol Lawrence C. Hays, Jr.
Executive Officer____ Maj Robert J. Oddy
Bn–3_____ Maj Daniel V. McWethy, Jr.

2d Battalion, 8th Marines

Battalion
Commander_____ LtCol Lane C. Kendall
Executive Officer____ Maj William C. Chamberlin
Bn–3_____ Maj Harry H. Phillips

3d Battalion, 8th Marines

Battalion
Commander_____ LtCol Gavin C. Humphrey
Executive Officer____ Maj Stanley E. Larsen
Bn–3_____ Capt William H. Pickett

10th Marines

Commanding Officer_ Col Raphael Griffin
Executive Officer____ Col Presley M. Rixey
R–1_____ 1stLt Russell C. White
R–2_____ 1stLt Norman W. Milner
R–3_____ Maj Wade H. Hitt
R–4_____ Capt Cecil H. Yount

1st Battalion, 10th Marines

Battalion
Commander_____ LtCol Donovan D. Sult
Executive Officer____ Maj Wendell H. Best
Bn–3_____ Capt Stephen J. Burich

2d Battalion, 10th Marines

Battalion
Commander_____ Maj David L. Henderson
Executive Officer____ Maj Kenneth C. Houston
Bn–3_____ Capt Richard B. Cavanaugh

3d Battalion, 10th Marines

Battalion
Commander_____ LtCol William C. Capehart
Executive Officer____ Maj James O. Appleyard
Bn–3_____ Capt Alan H. Tully

4th Battalion, 10 Marines

Battalion
Commander_____ LtCol Kenneth A. Jorgensen
Executive Officer____ Capt William P. Oliver, Jr.
Bn–3_____ 1stLt Edwin D. Smith

18 Marines [3]

Commanding Officer_ Col Cyril W. Martyr
Executive Officer____ LtCol Ewart S. Laue
R–1_____ Capt Winfield S. Haltom, Jr.
R–2 and R–3_____ Capt Murdoch J. McLeod
R–4_____ Capt Walter J. Hulsey

---

[3] Command and staff list of 18th Marines is from the unit's muster roles. However, since Colonel Cyril W. Martyr was on temporary duty with Headquarters, V AC functioning as NTLF Shore Party commander, Lieutenant Colonel Ewart S. Laue (executive officer, 18th Marines) acted as regimental commander while Lieutenant Colonel August L. Vogt, commanding 1st Battalion, 18th Marines, performed the additional duties of regimental executive officer.

1st Battalion, 18 Marines

Battalion
    Commander_____ LtCol August L. Vogt
Executive Officer and
    Bn–3_____ Capt Joseph G. Polifka

2d Battalion, 18 Marines

Battalion
    Commander_____ LtCol Chester J. Salazar
Executive Officer and
    Bn–3_____ Capt Jerome R. Walters

2d Tank Battalion

Battalion
    Commander_____ Maj Charles W. McCoy
Executive Officer and
    Bn–3_____ Capt John C. Richards, Jr.

2d Amphibian Tractor Battalion

Battalion
    Commander_____ Maj Fenlon A. Durand
Executive Officer_____ (not shown)
Bn–3_____ Capt William H. Housman, Jr.

5th Amphibian Tractor Battalion

Battalion
    Commander_____ Capt George L. Shead
Executive Officer_____ Capt William C. Stoll, Jr.
Bn–3_____ (not shown)

2d Motor Transport Battalion

Battalion
    Commander_____ Maj Milton J. Green
Executive Officer_____ Maj Robert H. Sanders
Bn–3_____ (not shown)

2d Service Battalion

Battalion
    Commander_____ Maj Edward V. Dozier
Executive Officer_____ Capt Robert V. Perkins
Bn–3_____ (not shown)

2d Medical Battalion

Battalion
    Commander_____ LCdr Claude R. Bruner (USN)
Executive Officer_____ (not shown)
Bn–3_____ (not shown)

4th Marine Division

Division
    Commander_____ MajGen Clifton B. Cates
Asst. Div.
    Commander_____ BrigGen Samuel C. Cumming
Chief of Staff_____ Col William W. Rogers
D–1_____ Col Walter I. Jordan
D–2_____ LtCol Gooderham L. McCormick
D–3_____ Col Walter W. Wensinger
D–4_____ Col William F. Brown

Support Group

Commander [4]_____ Col Orin H. Wheeler

14th Marines

Commanding Officer_ Col Louis G. DeHaven
Executive Officer_____ LtCol Randall M. Victory
R–1_____ Capt Cecil D. Snyder
R–2_____ Capt Harrison L. Rogers
R–3_____ Maj Frederick J. Karch
R–4_____ Maj Richard J. Winsborough

1st Battalion, 14th Marines

Battalion
    Commander_____ LtCol Harry J. Zimmer
                      (KIA 25 July)
                      Maj Clifford B. Drake
                      (from 25 July)
Executive Officer_____ Maj Clifford B. Drake
Bn–3_____ Maj Thomas McE. Fry

2d Battalion, 14th Marines

Battalion
    Commander_____ LtCol George B. Wilson, Jr.
Executive Officer_____ Maj William McReynolds
Bn–3_____ Capt Jack H. Riddle

3d Battalion, 14th Marines

Battalion
    Commander_____ LtCol Robert E. MacFarlane
Executive Officer_____ Maj Harvey A. Feehan
Bn–3_____ Capt Benton H. Elliott

4th Battalion, 14th Marines

Battalion
    Commander_____ LtCol Carl A. Youngdale
Executive Officer_____ Maj John B. Edgar, Jr.
Bn–3_____ 1stLt Russell F. Schoenbeck

4th 105mm Howitzer Battalion, V Amphibious Corps

Battalion
    Commander_____ LtCol Douglas E. Reeve
Executive Officer_____ Maj Marvin R. Burdett
Bn–3_____ Capt Joe H. Daniel

20th Marines

Commanding Officer_ LtCol Nelson K. Brown

---

[4] The 4th Marine Division's Task Organization for Tinian listed the following units under the Support Group: Hq Bn (less dets); 4th MT Bn (less dets); 4th Tk Bn (less Cos A, B and C, and dets Co D); 4th Med Bn (less dets); 4th Serv Bn; VMO–4; 1st JASCO (less dets); 2d Tk Bn; and the Prov LVT Gp, V Phib Corps (less dets), which included the 5th, 715th and 534th AmphTrac Bns (all less dets).

Executive Officer____ Maj Richard G. Ruby (additional duty)
R–1_____ Capt Martin M. Calcaterra
R–2_____ Capt Carl A. Sachs
R–3_____ Maj Melvin D. Henderson
R–4_____ Capt Samuel G. Thompson

1st Battalion, 20th Marines

Battalion
  Commander_____ Maj Richard G. Ruby
Executive Officer____ Maj George F. Williamson
Bn–3_____ Capt Martin H. Glover

2d Battalion, 20th Marines

Battalion
  Commander_____ Maj John H. Partridge
Executive Officer____ Capt Howard M. Dowling
Bn–3_____ Capt George A. Smith

23d Marines

Commanding Officer_ Col Louis R. Jones
Executive Officer____ LtCol John R. Lanigan
R–1_____ Capt Charlie J. Talbert
R–2_____ Capt Richard W. Mirick
R–3_____ Capt William E. Buron
R–4_____ Capt Henry S. Campbell

1st Battalion, 23d Marines

Battalion
  Commander_____ LtCol Ralph Haas
Executive Officer____ Maj James S. Scales
Bn–3_____ Capt William L. Dick

2d Battalion, 23d Marines

Battalion
  Commander_____ LtCol Edward J. Dillon
Executive Officer____ Maj Robert H. Davidson
Bn–3_____ Capt James W. Sperry

3d Battalion, 23d Marines

Battalion
  Commander_____ Maj Paul S. Treitel
Executive Officer____ Capt Philip J. Maloney
Bn–3_____ Capt Donald S. Callaham

24th Marines

Commanding Officer_ Col Franklin A. Hart
Executive Officer____ LtCol Austin R. Brunelli
R–1_____ Capt Kenneth N. Hilton
R–2_____ Capt Arthur B. Hanson
R–3_____ LtCol Charles D. Roberts
R–4_____ Maj Clyde T. Smith

1st Battalion, 24 Marines

Battalion
  Commander_____ LtCol Otto Lessing

Executive Officer____ Maj Robert N. Fricke
Bn–3_____ Capt Gene G. Mundy

2d Battalion, 24th Marines

Battalion
  Commander_____ Maj Frank E. Garretson (until 27 July)[5]
                LtCol Richard Rothwell (from 27 July)
Executive Officer____ Maj George D. Webster
Bn–3_____ Capt Charles C. Berkeley, Jr.

3d Battalion, 24th Marines

Battalion
  Commander_____ LtCol Alexander A. Vandegrift, Jr.
Executive Officer____ Capt Doyle A. Stout
Bn–3_____ Capt Webb D. Sawyer

25th Marines

Commanding Officer_ Col Merton J. Batchelder
Executive Officer____ LtCol Clarence J. O'Donnell
R–1_____ Capt George K. Dunn
R–2_____ Capt Charles D. Gray
R–3_____ LtCol William F. Thyson, Jr.
R–4_____ Maj Arthur E. Buck, Jr.

1st Battalion, 25th Marines

Battalion
  Commander_____ LtCol Hollis U. Mustain
Executive Officer____ Maj Henry D. Strunk
Bn–3_____ Capt Fenton J. Mee

2d Battalion, 25th Marines

Battalion Commander. LtCol Lewis C. Hudson, Jr.
Executive Officer____ Maj William P. Kaempfer
Bn–3_____ Capt Victor J. Barringer

3d Battalion, 25th Marines

Battalion
  Commander_____ LtCol Justice M. Chambers
Executive Officer____ Maj James Taul
Bn–3_____ (not shown)

4th Tank Battalion

Battalion
  Commander_____ Maj Richard K. Schmidt
Executive Officer
  and Bn–3_____ Maj Francis L. Orgain

---

[5] This command shift resulted when Lieutenant Colonel Rothwell, 2/24's regularly assigned commander, returned after having been sick in the hospital.

10th Amphibian Tractor Battalion

Battalion
Commander_____ Maj Victor J. Croizat
Executive Officer____ Maj Harry T. Marshall, **Jr.**
Bn–3_____ (not shown)

4th Motor Transport Battalion

Battalion
Commander_____ LtCol Ralph L. Schiesswohl
Executive Officer____ Maj Vaughan H. Huse
Bn–3_____ 1stLt Walter W. Alford

4th Service Battalion

Battalion
Commander_____ Col Richard H. Schubert[6]
Executive Officer____ (not shown)
Bn–3_____ 2dLt James T. Willis

4th Medical Battalion

Battalion
Commander_____ Cdr Stewart W. Shimonek
(USN)
Executive Officer____ LtCdr George W. Mast (USN)
Bn–3_____ (not shown)

---

[6] Actually, the 4th Service Battalion Commander remained with the rear echelon at Maui, T. H., during the Marianas campaign.

XXIV Corps Artillery

Commanding
General_____ BrigGen Arthur M. Harper
(USA)
Adjutant_____ Capt Wayne B. Young (USA)
S–2_____ Maj Milford W. Wood (USA)
S–3_____ LtCol F. W. Wheless (USA)
S–4_____ Maj E. P. Waggoner, Jr. (USA)

27th Division Artillery[7]

Commanding
General_____ BrigGen Redmond F. Kernan,
Jr. (USA)
Executive Officer____ Col Harold G. Browne (USA)

104th Field Artillery Battalion

Commanding officer__ LtCol George P. VanNostrand
(USA)

105th Field Artillery Battalion

Commanding officer__ LtCol Nicholas D. LaMorte
(USA)

106th Field Artillery Battalion

Commanding officer__ LtCol John J. Fitzgerald (USA)

249th Field Artillery Battalion

Commanding officer__ LtCol Dwight McCallum (USA)

---

[7] Complete staff and command list for 27th Division Artillery units not available.

APPENDIX V

Japanese Order of Battle—Tinian

*Estimated Strength
at Tinian
on 24 July 1944* [1]

Army Units

50th Infantry Regiment—Colonel Kiyochi, Ogata.[2]

Headquarters, 50th Infantry Regiment_____	60
1st Battalion, 50th Infantry Regiment—Captain Matsuda_____	880
2d Battalion, 50th Infantry Regiment—Captain Kamityama_____	880
3d Battalion, 50th Infantry Regiment—Captain Yamamoto_____	880
Artillery Battalion, 50th Infantry Regiment—Major Kahi_____	360
Communication Company, 50th Infantry Regiment—Lieutenant Hayashi_____	141
Engineer Company, 50th Infantry Regiment—Lieutenant Yano_____	169
Supply Company, 50th Infantry Regiment—Lieutenant Nozaki_____	200
Medical Company, 50th Infantry Regiment—Lieutenant Narizawa_____	130
Antitank Platoon, 50th Infantry Regiment—Lieutenant Otani_____	42
Fortification Detachment, 50th Infantry—Captain Hiruma_____	60
Detachment, 29th Field Hospital—Captain Hayashi_____	200
Platoon, 164th Independent Vehicle Company__	60
Tank Company, 18th Infantry Regiment—Lieutenant Shikamura_____	90
1st Battalion, 135th Infantry Regiment[3]—Captain Izumi_____	900
Total Army_____	5,052

Navy Units [4]

56th Naval Guard Force (Keibitai)—Captain Goichi Oya_____	1,400
233d Construction Battalion, 56th Keibitai_____	600
23d Air Group_____	450
Hospital, 523d Air Group_____	60
Construction Battalion, 523d Air Group_____	400
Headquarters, 1st Air Fleet—Vice Admiral Kakuda _____	200
833d Construction Battalion_____	400
116th Construction Battalion_____	400
Naval air stragglers_____	200
Total Navy_____	4,110
Grand Total_____	9,162

[1] No two sources consulted gave exactly the same numbers of Japanese at Tinian. Figures, therefore, are only reconciled approximations.

[2] Colonel Ogata was also Tinian Island Commander, a job he performed under administrative control of the Northern Marianas Group with headquarters on Saipan. After Saipan's fall, Ogata's command came under the 29th Division on Guam.

[3] The other two battalions of the 135th Infantry Regiment participated in the defense of Saipan.

[4] Japanese Navy Units were generally more security conscious than were Army units; therefore, the order of battle for Navy units at Tinian is much less detailed and less accurate than that for Army forces.

156

APPENDIX VI

Task Organization

Northern Troops and Landing Force—Major General Harry Schmidt.

Corps Troops

Headquarters and Service Battalion, V Amphibious Corps (less detachments).

Signal Battalion, V Amphibious Corps (less detachments).

Motor Transport Company, V Amphibious Corps (less detachments).

Provisional Engineer Group, V Amphibious Corps.

  Headquarters, Provisional Engineer Group, V Amphibious Corps.

  18th Naval Construction Battalion.

  121st Naval Construction Battalion.

  34th Engineer Battalion (Army).

7th Field Depot (less detachments) (Reinforced).

Medical Battalion, V Amphibious Corps.

31st Field Hospital (Army).

38th Field Hospital (Army).

96th Portable Surgical Hospital (Army).

97th Portable Surgical Hospital (Army).

98th Portable Surgical Hospital (Army).

477th Amphibian Truck Company (Army) (less detachments).

Amphibious Reconnaissance Battalion, V Amphibious Corps.

1st Battalion, 29th Marines.

Communication Unit 18.

Group Pacific 6.

a. *4th Marine Division (Reinforced)*—Major General Clifton B. Cates.

  4th Marine Division (less 3d and 4th Battalions 14th Marines) with 1st and 2d Battalions, 10th Marines attached.

  Provisional LVT Group, V Amphibious Corps (less detachments).

    2d Armored Amphibian Battalion.

    2d Amphibian Tractor Battalion.

    5th Amphibian Tractor Battalion.

    10th Amphibian Tractor Battalion.

    708th Amphibian Tank Battalion (Army).

    715th Amphibian Tractor Battalion (Army).

    773d Amphibian Tractor Battalion (Army).

    534th Amphibian Tractor Battalion (Army).

  1st Joint Assault Signal Company.

  1341st Engineer Battalion (Army).

  1st Amphibian Truck Company.

  2d Amphibian Truck Company.

  1st Provisional Rocket Detachment.

  2d Tank Battalion.

b. *2d Marine Division (Reinforced)*—Major General Thomas E. Watson.

  2d Marine Division (less 10th Marines and 2d Tank Battalion).

  2d Joint Assault Signal Company.

  2d Provisional Rocket Detachment.

c. *27th Infantry Division (Reinforced)*— Major General George W. Griner, USA.

27th Infantry Division (Reinforced) (less 105th Infantry).

762d Provisional Tank Battalion.

Company D, 766th Tank Battalion.

295th Joint Assault Signal Company.

95th Bomb Disposal Squadron.

Detachment, 604th Quartermaster Graves Registration.

Company C, 88th Chemical Battalion.

152d Engineer Battalion.

d. *Corps Artillery*—Brigadier General Arthur M. Harper, USA.

XXIV Army Corps Artillery.

Headquarters and Headquarters Battery, XXIV Corps Artillery.

420th Field Artillery Group (155mm Gun) (Army).

531st Field Artillery Battalion.

532d Field Artillery Battalion.

419th Field Artillery Group (155mm Howitzer) (Army).

145th Field Artillery Battalion.

225th Field Artillery Battalion.

10th Marines (less 1st and 2d Battalions).

3d and 4th Battalions, 14th Marines.

4th 105mm Artillery Battalion (Howitzer), Corps Artillery, V Amphibious Corps.

27th Infantry Division Artillery.

Provisional Motor Transport Company.

e. *Tinian Garrison Forces*—Major General James L. Underhill.

17th Marine Antiaircraft Battalion.

Other units as assigned.

f. *Saipan Garrison Forces*—Major General Sanderford Jarman, USA.

105th Infantry.

Army Defense Troops.

Army Service Troops.

Other units as assigned.

APPENDIX VII

Propaganda Texts [1]

Propaganda texts were employed by United States forces to avoid needless killing and bloodshed, as well as to encourage Japanese troops, civilians, and natives to enter the American lines for interrogation. Effectiveness of this method may be judged in part by the fact that large numbers of civilians reported having seen and read these leaflets. A small number of the Japanese military personnel captured made similar statements.

Propaganda texts were disseminated by means of aerial drops, artillery (which fired bundles of leaflets), and public address systems. Because of language variations the texts were prepared for three groups: Japanese, Koreans and natives. Samples of each of these follow:

JAPANESE TEXT NO. 1

"Your officers have been lying to you." GUADALCANAL, TULAGI, ATTU, NEW GEORGIA, LAE, BOUGAINVILLE, MAKIN, TARAWA, KWAJALEIN, ENIWETOK, ADMIRALTY GROUP ISLANDS.

Your officers told you that the Japanese Navy and Air Force would come to your aid in all of these places. However, these statements of your officers were all lies. Haven't the Japanese troops who had faith in their officers come to a miserable end?

Why do you go on fighting for officers who lie to you? It is not necessary to fight to the last man or to commit suicide.

---

[1] NTLF G–2 Report, Appendix F.

Your officers are not thinking of your interests. They are lying to you. They tell you it is the duty of the soldier to die along with them. They told you such lies because they were thinking only of their own honor. You do not gain anything by dying. Do not sacrifice your valuable lives in order to protect their honor. "While there is life there is hope." When the American forces attack this island, use the Life-Saving Guarantee without fear.

"Your officers have been lying to you."

JAPANESE SURRENDER TICKET

Life-Saving Guarantee

1. The bearer of this card has the special right to be aided by the American forces.

2. According to international law, we will give you fair treatment and will grant you sufficient clothing, food, and shelter as well as tobacco and medical treatment.

3. American troops will make every effort to preserve the lives of persons who desire aid.

Rules for the use of this card

1. Raise both hands high above your head, and, holding nothing in your hands except this card, advance slowly toward the positions of the American troops.

2. Don't crowd up; advance one by one.

3. Never approach American positions at night unless specifically invited to by radio broadcast. This card can be used by Japanese troops, Japanese civilians, Korean laborers, and islanders. Use this card and save your life.

KOREAN TEXT NO. 1

KOREANS!

The Japanese cannot protect you! Even though the Japanese are unable to protect you, you will still die because of them.

Have the Japanese bayoneted or shot your people?

Kill the Japanese if they threaten to bayonet or shoot you!

Even if they haven't bayoneted or shot you it is of course an actual fact that they don't trust you. If you haven't been bayoneted or shot, look out for yourselves and think of the ways to save your lives. Without hesitation come quickly toward the American lines. Don't worry because the American definitely will not kill you.

Use this opportunity to save your lives!

You are KOREANS!

You are not Japanese!

Why should you die for the Japanese?

Use this opportunity to save yourselves NOW!!

Act immediately!

Even if you are not able to get ahold of this all-important Life-Saving Guarantee, if you raise your hands over your heads and come toward the American lines, you will be in no danger. Why should you die for the Japanese? Save yourselves!!

KOREAN SURRENDER TICKET

Life-Saving Guarantee

All persons coming to the American side bearing this paper will be saved.

This is in accordance with international law.

You will receive sufficient food, clothing, tobacco and medical treatment.

All of you who want to save your lives use this Life-Saving Guarantee and be saved by the American troops.

With both hands over your heads and holding up this paper, go to the American troops.

Come individually, not in a group!

Don't go to the American positions at night.

Even during the daytime, wait until the Americans give the order.

Japanese soldiers, Japanese and Korean laborers, islanders, Japanese civilians all can use this ticket.

Take this paper and save your life.

SURRENDER TICKET

Native Text (in Katakana) No. 2
Islanders!

America is not fighting the inhabitants of this island. When the American troops attack this island, take this opportunity to save your life and do as it says below:

1. If you can, get away from the fighting area and take cover.

2. Don't help the Japanese troops at all.

3. When the fighting subsides a little, come to the American side as quickly as possible.

The American troops will give you food, clothing and tobacco. If you are wounded, they will give you medicine. When the fighting is over you can return home. Don't help the Japanese troops at all. If you can come to the American side without endangering yourself, come.

Origin of the White Beach Plan

APPENDIX VIII

The name of the officer who first conceived the plan for landing on Tinian's northern beaches (a scheme that later proved brilliant) has never been established definitely. Evidence in this connection is interesting, if inconclusive. General Harry Schmidt wrote:

Many high ranking officers have asked who originated the plan for attacking Tinian "through the back door." While the 4th Division was under my command and prior to the Marianas Campaign, my planning officer, Lieutenant Colonel E. F. Carlson, made such a plan and probably such a plan was turned in to the 5th Amphibious Corps.[1]

The 4th Marine Division intelligence officer, Lieutenant Colonel Gooderham L. McCormick, agrees with General Schmidt:

I feel certain Col. Carlson did originate the plan to land over the northern beaches of Tinian. . . . I worked with Col. Carlson, personally doing a series of photo interpretations for him to assist him in his original study to decide the possibilities of the subject landing, and read his original plan when formulated.[2]

Another 4th Division viewpoint is furnished by Lieutenant Victor Maghakian, a member of the division reconnaissance company and a personal friend of Carlson's:

This man who definitely planned that landing was . . . Evans F. Carlson. . . . He told me all about that Tinian plan before he was wounded [22 June] on Saipan.[3]

From this testimony it is apparent that Lieutenant Colonel Evans F. Carlson actually prepared a plan of landing on Tinian's northern beaches. But judging by the statements of several officers who participated prominently in the Tinian planning, the decision to land on the northern beaches was also reached by other officers, without reference to Carlson or his scheme. Major General Graves B. Erskine, who as a Brigadier General served as Chief of Staff of the V Amphibious Corps wrote:

Lieutenant Colonel Carlson was at one time attached to the Fifth Amphibious Corps. . . . I assigned Lieutenant Colonel Carlson various staff duties from time to time, but at no time [did he] actively participate in any operational planning.

All of the plans utilized by the Landing Force for the seizure of Tinian were the results of a combined effort by the Fifth Amphibious Corps Staff and General Holland Smith.[4]

Colonel Robert E. Hogaboom, NTLF operations officer for Saipan and Tinian, commented along the same lines:

I would say that no concept prepared by Colonel Carlson had any influence whatever on either the development of the plan or on the final acceptance of such a plan.

The advantages of landing on the northern beaches were so great that all of us who worked on the plan

---

[1] Ltr from Gen H. Schmidt to CMC, 17Apr47.

[2] Ltr from LtCol G. L. McCormick to CMC, 16Jan51.

[3] Ltr from 1stLt V. Maghakian to CMC, 14Nov50.

[4] Ltr from MajGen G. B. Erskine to CMC, 22Dec50. General Holland Smith, after reading General Erskine's statement, wrote: "I concur fully. . . ." Ltr from Gen. H. Smith to CMC, 23Dec50.

immediately searched for a possible solution based on landing in that area. The Corps Artillery Commander was embarked with the NTLF staff and the advantages of placing artillery on the southern beaches of Saipan to support a landing on northern Tinian were obvious, and a powerful argument for such a concept.[5]

Admiral Harry W. Hill, who commanded the Northern Attack Force at Tinian, stated the naval point of view, as follows:

If there were plans, and I presume that there were some tentative ones, none of them were available to me or my staff. We started from the beginning on our plans and after our study of all possible landing places came to a completely independent conclusion that the two small northwest beaches were the best places to land from the naval point of view provided the approaches to them were not too bad.[6]

[5] Ltr from Col R. E. Hogaboom to CMC, 22Jan51.
[6] Ltr from VAdm H. W. Hill to CMC, 16Jan51.

Thus, it appears that more than one officer, from more than one organization, arrived at the decision to land on Tinian's northern beaches. In this connection it is interesting to note that, long before staffs in the Pacific initiated Tinian planning, students at the Marine Corps Schools, Quantico, Virginia, solved tactical map problems with the Saipan-Tinian locale. More than one student submitted the northern-beaches solution to the then-theoretical Tinian situation. As a matter of fact, one of the few officers who studied Tinian thoroughly and did not recognize the advantages accruing to an attacker using the White Beaches was Colonel Kiyochi Ogata, Japanese commander at Tinian.

APPENDIX IX   Index

TABLE OF DISTANCES FROM TINIAN

In Nautical Miles

Cape Gloucester	1241
Eniwetok	995
Guadalcanal	1698
Guam	110
Iwo Jima	636
Kwajalein	1354
Manila	1429
Marcus	730
Midway	2205
Pagan	188
Palau	821
Ponape	886
Saipan	3
Rabaul	1217
Tarawa	1815
Truk	588
Yap	548
Yokohama	1268